Clays and Glazes

The Ceramic Review Book of Clay Bodies and Glaze Recipes
Over 900 recipes from professional potters

Edited by Emmanuel Cooper

Third Edition
A Ceramic Review Publication

Ceramic Review Book of Glaze Recipes
First published in 1977
Enlarged and revised edition 1978
Ceramic Review Book of Clay Bodies and Glaze Recipes 1983

Clays and Glazes. The Ceramic Review Book of Clay Bodies and Glaze Recipes
First published 1988
Enlarged and revised 2001
ISBN 0 9504767 9 X

All information supplied by the potters concerned.
Photographs supplied by the potters concerned or Ceramic Review archive.

Edited by Emmanuel Cooper assisted by:
Emma Basham, Sally Boyle, Laurie Britton Newell, Rita Greenwood,
Kay Hussey and Julia Pitts

Designed by Richard Bonner-Morgan

Ceramic Review, 25 Fouberts Place, London W1F 7QF

© 2001 Ceramic Review.
No material may be reproduced without the Editor's permission.

Printed by VIP Print Ltd

Contents

Introduction 1
Health and Safety 1
Practical Notes 2
Raku/ Bodies, slips, glazes 5
Earthenware/ Bodies, slips, glazes 23
Mid-temperature Glazes 57
Stoneware and Porcelain/ Bodies, slips, glazes 103
Vapour Glazing, Salt and Soda/ Bodies, slips, glazes 283
Lustres 301
Egyptian Paste 309
Texture, Crystal and Colour 313
Temperature Conversion Tables 331
List of Suppliers 333
UK/USA Substitution Materials 335

List of Illustrations

Work illustrated may not be of detailed glazes

Raku Pages 71-75

Ian Byers	Harry Horlock Stringer	Paul Soldner
Eeles family	Anna Noël	
Susan Halls	David Roberts	

Earthenware Pages 76-89

Clive Bowen	Michael and Victoria Eden	David Miller
Alison Britton	Tessa Fuchs	Sara Robertson
Neil Brownsword	Jonathan Garratt	John Solly
Daphne Carnegy	Regina Heinz	Josie Walter
Simon Carroll	Walter Keeler	Mary Wondrausch
Bennett Cooper	Fenella Mallalieu	Betty Woodman
Stephen Dixon	Sophie MacCarthy	

Mid-temperature Pages 90-91

John Chalke
Carenza Hayhoe
Richard Zakin

Stoneware Pages 92-102/ 251-267

Mike Bailey and David Hewitt	Gilles Le Corre	Lucie Rie
Peter Beard	David Leach	Jim Robison
Terry Bell–Hughes	Eileen Lewenstein	Robert Sanderson
John Calver	Roger Lewis	Charles Stileman
Kyra Cane	Gillian Lowndes	Geoffrey Swindell
Dartington Pottery	Jane Maddison	Janice Tchalenko
Richard Dewar	Jim Malone	Martina Thomson
John Glick	John Maltby	Owen Thorpe
Ewen Henderson	Andrew McGarva	Peter Venning
Joanna Howells	Eric James Mellon	Edmund de Waal
John Jelfs	Ivo Mosley	John Ward
Jill Fanshawe Kato	Louis Mulcahy	Robin Welch
Chris Keenan	Matthias Ostermann	Geoffrey Whiting
Christy Keeney	Sara Radstone	

Vapour Glazing Pages 268-275

Michael Casson	Walter Keeler	Micki Schloessingk
Sheila Casson	Peter Meanley	Ruthanne Tudball
Jane Hamlyn	Marcus O'Mahony	
Lisa Hammond	Phil Rogers	

Lustre Pages 276-277

Alan Caiger–Smith
Margery Clinton
Sutton Taylor

Colour, Texture, Crystal Pages 278-282

Chris Carter	Damian Keefe	Aki Moriuchi
Emmanuel Cooper	Kate Malone	
Ashley Howard	Lesley McShea	

Introduction

This is a new and greatly enlarged edition of 'The Ceramic Review Book of Clay Bodies and Glaze Recipes'. Since the first edition of 'Glaze Recipes', culled from the pages of 'Ceramic Review', the collection has proved useful in providing sound, tried and tested recipes and has also encouraged potters to experiment with glazes and search for different effects.

Clay bodies and glaze recipes are two of the potters' fundamental means of expression. In their search for better and more reliable bodies and more interesting glazes, potters can turn with confidence to the experience of others. 'Ceramic Review', since it was first published thirty-one years ago, has encouraged potters to write about their own glazes and clay bodies and describe how they use them. This open sharing of information has made a wealth of practical experience widely available, and has helped both the beginner and the professional potter achieve more successful results. Such information has also enabled the highest technical standards to be achieved. It is in this spirit of open exchange, following on the success of previous editions, that this new book has been prepared.

Glazes, whether used on functional or decorative pieces, are an endless source of interest and fascination. Different glazes, as well as providing clean and hygienic surfaces, can emphasise the variations of shapes and surfaces with subtle or even flamboyant contrasts of colour, tone and texture, sometimes shiny, sometimes matt. Handsome glazes, however, are only as good as the bodies and forms they cover. The bodies detailed here provide a wide range of basic clay mixtures for all types of firings.

Potters who have contributed to this book were invited to revise or amend their previously published glazes (and bodies), many have supplied new recipes. Other recipes have come from council members of the Crafts Potters Association and from the early Newsletters of the Association. The editor would like to thank all the individual potters concerned for their generosity in allowing us to publish their hard-won recipes. Most of the mixtures and recipes have been well tried and tested by these potters, though none can be guaranteed to provide results identical to those obtained by the original potter. Most potters wisely point this out when sending in their information. For this reason, before preparing large quantities of different body mixtures or using the recipes on 'special' pieces of work it is sound practice to thoroughly test them yourself with your own materials in your own firing conditions to confirm that they do what you require. One additional inclusion in this edition is a reference for the appropriate article in 'Ceramic Review', where the information first appeared. This will enable potters wanting further information to check the full article. Two sections illustrate the work of 90 potters in full colour.

'Clays and Glazes' contains much practical information, it is a book we at 'Ceramic Review' hope will find a useful place in potters' workshops and studios. There are many, many years of pottery experience within these pages, and it is a tribute to the generosity and openness of potters today in making their imagination widely available.

Emmanuel Cooper

Health and Safety for Potters

Health and safety considerations in pottery fall into two parts – handling the materials, and formulating glazes to ensure they are safe to use for holding food and drink. Within the United Kingdom regulations concerning health and safety are constantly changing, and it is not possible here to give precise advice. The Health and Safety Executive issue guidelines and details of new regulations, and if in doubt contact them. One way of keeping up to date is to order 'Ceramic News', published by the Health and Safety Ceramic Industry Advisory Committee (Tel 01782 602 300), which, though aimed at industrial production, has much that is relevant to studio potters.

In general, most ceramic materials are safe to handle provided usual precaution are taken to prevent absorbing or inhaling them. Some oxides and materials are considered to be more harmful and with these greater care has to be taken. As a guiding principal, it is best to treat all materials as potentially harmful, and observe the following rules:

• Avoid inhaling dust. • Fettle pots when leatherhard rather than dry. • Avoid dropping clay on the floor where it gets trampled about. • Sweep with oiled sawdust. • Vacuum using approved equipment and filters. • Wet wipe surfaces.• Slip glaze materials into water slowly, do not drop them. • Wear a suitable face mask. • Wear a non-dust absorbent apron or overall or wash cotton daily. • Do not eat, drink or smoke in the studio. • Ensure there is adequate ventilation. • Wear protective gloves if worried.

Ready prepared glazes supplied by a manufacturer will usually indicate if the glaze is safe for use on pots intended for food and drink. An ideal surface for functional ware is smooth and shiny to avoid staining or retaining food, but other more matt surfaces can be used. For glazes prepared from recipe the problem of safety is more difficult. Glazes containing lead may, under some circumstances, be lead soluble in dilute acid solutions, such as tea or coffee. Lead is poisonous in its raw state, but when supplied in its fritted form it is safe to handle. When combined in a glaze, the lead is released and all glazes containing lead intended to hold food should be tested for lead solubility by a reputable laboratory offering such services. Glazes containing barium carbonate can also pose problems as they leach barium into stored liquids. There are as yet no accepted tests for barium release in the United Kingdom, but to be safe it is best to avoid using barium glazes on food vessels.

Spraying offers unique qualities, but the fine mist of glaze should not be inhaled. Follow full safety procedures: use a well ventilated spray booth which is vented to an outside area, or to a cleaning system. Wear a recommended respiratory mask.

Practical Notes

Glaze recipes themselves have great advantages over ready prepared mixtures such as those from potters merchants. They enable potters to see the materials present in the glaze and in what quantities, and from this information gain some idea of how the glaze will behave. For instance, the colour response from additions of metal oxides will be indicated by the major fluxes within the glaze. More importantly the recipe enables potters to adjust ingredients if faults occur. For example, the firing temperature can be raised by adding small quantities of china clay and flint. Conversely small additions of frits will lower the maturing point.

Recipes themselves must be used with caution because of variations that occur between different batches of the same materials, firing conditions and clay bodies used. For this reason they are an excellent starting point, but must be tested before success can be claimed.

Materials
There are often surprising variations from one batch of material to another. For instance, feldspars vary in analysis according to the source and supplier; while a material like wood ash needs to be tested each time as the composition of one batch will never be the same as another. Incidentally, when no particular feldspar is named in a recipe it is safe to assume that potash feldspar is required. All the frits mentioned in the recipes should be available from pottery suppliers in the U.K. whose addresses can be found at the end of the book. Where potters have stated the source of particular materials this information is included: where no suppliers are named or specific types of a material such as a named ball clay are given, potters must make their own choice.

Firing Conditions
Kiln atmosphere is one of the most important factors influencing glazes at stoneware temperatures: few glazes give the same results in oxidised and reduced conditions. But there are many other variations in firing programmes which can affect glaze quality – speed of firing, length of soak, size of kiln and so on. All these need to be taken into account to achieve a desired result. Fast-fire kilns may need to be slowed down to obtain a stronger body/glaze reaction.

Bodies
Many potters have given instructions on the best way to mix clay bodies. Basically, the clay powder is added to water and allowed to become thoroughly wetted before being pugged and wedged for use. Some potters like to make their clay into a slip and then dry this out slowly, others add sufficient water to make the clay plastic. It can be helpful when largish quantities of non-plastic material such as grog or sand are being added to plastic clay to first moisten them to avoid drying out the body.

The reaction that takes place between glaze and body occurs to a lesser degree at earthenware temperatures than at stoneware temperatures. Two main factors affecting the work of studio potters are the amount of iron present in the clay or slip and the size and quantity of any grog in the clay. Particularly affected are white glazes which at stoneware temperatures pick up the iron as spots which bleed into the glaze; at earthenware temperatures iron breaks through the white glaze at rims and edges.

Precautions and Mixing
It is a good rule of thumb to treat all glaze materials as definitely non-consumable and avoid either breathing in dust (this is especially important with quartz and flint) and avoid ingesting them by not eating or drinking in the studio. Add each weighed dry ingredient to a larger quantity of water than is eventually necessary; though this will result in a thin mixture, it helps to breakdown any lumps, reduces the dust and aides wetting the material. Gently slide rather than drop the powder into the water. Try to sandwich the plastic and non-plastic ingredients as far as possible to aid mixing. Hot water will quickly break up lumps and make mixing easier especially in cold weather. Leave the glaze to stand and slake as this makes sieving easier, then agitate with the hand to break up any other lumps. Pass the liquid twice through an 80's or 100's mesh sieve to ensure the ingredients are well mixed. Allow the glaze to settle before removing surplus water.

The consistency of a glaze will depend on whether it is to be applied by dipping, pouring or spraying, and it is also affected by whether the pot is biscuit fired, soft or hard, or is to be raw glazed. Generally speaking a glaze to be applied to an unfired pot needs to be thicker than a glaze used over biscuit; a glaze which is to be sprayed is best sieved through a 120's mesh and is slightly thinner in consistency.

As a rough guide a glaze for dipping medium-fired biscuit pots has the consistency of single cream and covers the hand fairly completely. Always stir the glaze thoroughly before use to ensure all the ingredients are evenly mixed. When frits are used constant stirring will be necessary to prevent them settling to the bottom of the bucket.

Incidentally a large bucket or barrel with an adequate quantity of glaze will make dipping a much easier process to carry out. Spraying should only be carried out when proper ventilation and an extraction booth are available.

Notes: Unless stated otherwise, all recipes are for use on fired wares. Some potters state if the glaze has been devised to be used raw i.e. on the unfired pot, though many glazes with a good proportion of ball clay can often be used raw. Firing temperatures are indicated with recipes and are by cone or by temperature. A comparison of temperatures for different cones – Staffordshire, Seger and Orton – is given at the end of the book. All temperatures are expressed in centigrade.

Raku Glazes

Glazes for raku melt at around 900-950°C and are usually based on the use of fritted materials such as lead or borax, which with small percentages of clay give suitable glazes. Other low temperature materials such as calcium borate frit are equally useful though such glazes usually take longer to melt and mature in the raku kiln. Raku is not often used for making functional wares. The body is porous and the surface may be textured. In addition, many attractive but potentially poisonous glaze effects can be obtained with, for example, the use of lead and copper. These materials should definitely be avoided on functional pots – especially those intended for holding drinks such as coffee, fruit juice etc.

When lead frits are used in the glaze extra care should be taken to avoid inhaling glaze dust. Never use raku covered with lead glazes for containing any food or drink.

Harriet E. Brisson CR 66

Body for Sawdust Firing, Raku and Stoneware Cone 8-10 Reduction
Fireclay 50
China clay 15
Ball clay 15
Grog 15
Talc 5

> Talc gives the clay body strength to withstand the thermal shock of sawdust and raku firing, but can be eliminated when firing to stoneware temperature. It is possible to bisque as high as cone 5 before raku firing if one desires a denser finished piece. However, the piece must be thoroughly preheated before being placed in the raku kiln. Some potters feel that this violates the integrity of raku; others find that it fulfils their purposes more satisfactorily. This body is excellent for handbuilding thick pieces and making flat tiles that do not readily warp. The grog can be decreased or eliminated when used for throwing. It fires to a cream colour in oxidation and a rich tan in reduction at cone 8-10.

Tom Buck CR 159

Red Lustre
Gerstley borate 50
Borax 50
Red copper oxide 10
Red iron oxide 10

> This is a version of Tomato Red by Carol Townsend who used Paul Soldner's 50/50 base glaze.

Gold Lustre
Gerstley borate 87
Nepheline syenite 13
Tin oxide 2.2
Bismuth subnitrate 4.4
Silver nitrate 4.4

> Similar to Robert Piepenberg's gold lustre and related to Soldner's 80/20 base.

Copper 80/20
Colemanite 80
Nepheline syenite 20
Copper carbonate 10
Red iron oxide 5

> Paul Soldner is usually credited with this glaze although Piepenberg and others have cited similar recipes.

Copper Sand
Colemanite 80
Bone ash 20
Copper carbonate 5
Cobalt carbonate 2.5

> Another off-shoot of Soldner's 80/20 glaze.

My Raku Base Glaze No.1
Borax (as 10H₂0) 43
Gerstley borate 34
Flint 15
Grolleg kaolin 8

My Raku Base Glaze No.2
Gerstley borate 43
Flint 19
Soda ash 15
Boracic acid 13
Grolleg kaolin 10

My Raku Base Glaze No.3
Gerstley borate 45
Ferro frit 3185 ....29.5
Pemco frit 2201 ....15.5
Grolleg kaolin 10

> Please note that gerstley borate is slightly soluble, more so in hot water and will cause problems: the glaze will 'floc' i.e. form a massive clump.

My Raku Base Glaze No.4
Pemco frit 2201 54
Potterycrafts P2957 ....27.5
Ferro frit 3185 12
Ferro frit 3819 ....6.5

Ian Byers   CR 102, 142, 155
(work illustrated)

Terra sigillata Slip
TWVD ball clay 2.5kg
Water..6.0kg
Sodium hexametaphosphate 25.0gm

> This recipe does not need to be levigated or ballmilled as the particle size is very fine. It can be stained with universal stains but these may need grinding in a mortar before addition to the clay base.

Raku Glaze Orton Cone 6
High alkaline frit 80
Whiting..8
Ball clay 4
Zinc oxide..4
Glaze suspender 4

> This glaze can be opacified with tin oxide or zirconium silicate 8-10%, or stained up with universal stains to give a range of colourful glazes.

Smoke Resist Slip
> A china clay and water slip can be used over fired slips and engobes to resist the effects of smoke on the surface of work. The work is painted with areas of slip then fired to about 700°C before smoking. After smoking the slip can be washed off.

Low Fire Alkaline Glaze 960°C
Potterycrafts high alkali frit P2962 72
Whiting..13
Ball clay 5
+ Glaze suspender 2%

For yellow add 6% Potterycrafts P4508 yellow.
For brown-purple add 8% manganese carbonate
For blue-black lustre add 4% copper oxide, 3% cobalt carbonate and 4% red iron
> Over-firing fades colour (lustre glaze needs reduction).

Orange Red Lead Base 960°C
Litharge 77
Flint 15
China clay..15
+ Chrome oxide 2%
> Do not reduce this glaze and note that litharge is poisonous to handle. This glaze can ONLY be used on non-functional objects.

Coloured Glazes for Raku

Alkaline Base Glaze Firing to 960°C
Potterycrafts high alkali frit P2962 100
Whiting..10
Zinc oxide..5
Ball clay 5
Clay suspender 5

Colours
1. White: add 8 parts tin oxide or 12 zirconium silicate
2. Turquoise: add 2.5 parts copper carbonate (bronze when reduced)
3. Green: add ½ part chrome oxide
4. Blue-black lustre: add 3 parts cobalt, 4 parts red iron and 4 copper carbonate
5. Purple: add 2 parts manganese dioxide plus ½ part cobalt carbonate
6. Silver lustre: (when reduced) add 2 parts silver nitrate and 1 part soda ash
> Underglaze colours or glaze stains can be added to the base to give a wider range of colour, but many colours fade if over-fired.

Eeles Family CR 178
(work illustrated)

Raku Clay Body
Ball clay 60
120 Molochite 30
Talc 10

Raku Glaze Clear
Borax frit..24
Alkaline frit 48
China clay..8

Quartz 20

An addition of tin oxide 5% will make a matt white raku glaze. We add copper oxide, silver oxide to give a lustre, between 3-5%. We also add a variety of glaze stains between 5% and 10% to achieve different colours. Our stains are from CTM Supplies, Exeter.

Copper Matt Glaze
Copper oxide 85
Alkaline frit 10
Bentonite 5

For best results fire between 960-1000°C. Experiment with post-fired reduction to find what suits your own tastes.

June Emmins CR 137

Persian Blue Raku Glaze
Sodium bicarbonate 40
Ferro frit 4108..20
Copper carbonate 2
Bentonite

Ferro frit 4108 is a leadless calcium borosilicate frit suitable for use in earthenware glazes 1040-1100°C and for promoting special effects in raku glazes.

Copper Matt Green Glaze
Copper carbonate 90
Ferro frit 4110..10
Bentonite 5

Ferro frit 4110 is a leadless soft sodium borosilicate frit for use in glazes 1000-1060°C. Numbers used for frit identification may vary in different countries but the descriptions included will identify the frit required.

Susan Halls CR 146, 177

Dry White Raku Slip Glaze 1000°C
Lead bisilicate 30
Borax frit..15
Tin oxide..3
China clay..30

Does not crackle but will be very reptilian where thick. Needs only a very light reduction in sawdust.

Harry Horlock Stringer CR 1
(work illustrated)

Taggs Yard Raku Glaze
Alkaline frit (soft)...48
Standard borax frit.......................................18
Bentonite 3

This is a simple and very reliable raku glaze which should be applied thickly either by dipping or with a soft brush. It has a wide range of temperatures but is most interesting if withdrawn immediately after the bubbling of the glaze is seen to be finished. At this point, if applied thickly, a grey-white, slightly matt glaze with good crazing is produced over a body made of North Devon ball clay 2 parts, to 1 part grog (by volume) or a porcelain body. The crazing is delineated in black if the pot is half immersed in sawdust almost immediately after being withdrawn from the kiln.

If the pot stays in the kiln for a longer period than that described above, a transparent shiny glaze is formed.

As materials differ between suppliers it pays to try them all before buying the 'big batch'. A turquoise glaze can be made by the addition of 3 parts copper carbonate to the above recipe. Try applying this over the other glaze, and in normal practice... only over a white body. Further experiments can be made with this basic glaze by adding manganese dioxide or iron oxide and, if you are rich, tin oxide.

William Hunt

Textured Coarse Raku Body Orton Cone 9
Perlite ....1 part by volume (13% by weight)
Any stoneware body (dry) ....1 part by volume (87% by weight)

This recipe and those containing still more perlite should exhibit resistance to thermal shock, will appear quite pebbly, and will be difficult or impossible to throw.

Coarse Throwable Body Orton Cone 8-9
Perlite ....1 part by volume (7% by weight)
Any stoneware body (dry) ....2 parts by volume (93% by weight)

This recipe has greatly reduced resistance to thermal shock, but does exhibit the pebbly or cratered surface typical of large perlite additions. It can be thrown on the wheel.

Himani Kapila   CR 187

Raku 960-1000°C Wood-fired in Reduction

Transparent
Alkaline frit 85
China clay..15

White
Alkaline frit 75
China clay..15
Tin oxide..10

Gold/Silver Lustre
Alkaline frit 75
China clay..15
Tin oxide..5
Silver nitrate..1

Turquoise
Alkaline frit 40
Sodium carbonate 12
China clay..12
Silica..34
Copper carbonate 2

Copper Ruby Lustre
Alkaline frit 70
China clay...................................10
Lead bisilicate 16
Copper carbonate 3
Lithium carbonate 4

Blue-black Lustre
Alkaline frit 70
Calcium carbonate 13
China clay.....................................5
Copper oxide 4
Manganese dioxide 3
Iron oxide 2
Bismuth subnitrate........................3

Green
Alkaline frit 85
China clay...................................10
Calcium carbonate 5
Copper 2

Name of some suppliers for chemicals and oxides in India:-
Chemicals de Centre, 3/15 Asaf Ali Road, New Delhi - 110 002
Branch Office: S - 162 Panchsheel Park, New Dehli - 110 017
The Pioneer Chemical Co., 313/314 Tilak Bazaar, Delhi - 110 006
For clays and glazes:
Stark & Co., 17 Najafgarh Road, Near Zakhira Chowk, New Dehli - 110 015

Walter Keeler CR 1, 112, 113, 152, 179

Raku Body
Fireclay 55
Ball clay 25
Grog 20
    This gives a rather coarse body suitable for higher temperatures.

Glaze
Alkaline frit 85
Whiting.......................................15
Ball clay 10

Copper (turquoise) 2-3%
Cobalt up to 0.5% blue (+ copper) up to 0.25% softer blue
Manganese 1-2% purple (+ cobalt 0.25% blue/purple)
Tin oxide 4% – white

Glaze
Lead frit (i.e. lead monosilicate) 82.5
Ball clay 17.5

Copper oxide 2-3% – green
Iron oxide 2-8% – cream-yellow-amber
Manganese – brown
Cobalt – heavy blue

Tin oxide could be used to opacify. On both these bases copper oxide decoration will give lustre when reduced. Other oxides can be used but with more unpredictable results.

John Mathieson CR 169

Raku Bodies

We are indebted to David Roberts and Tim Andrews for giving us two raku bodies which have become standard in this country – Potclays 1106 White St Thomas with grog, and a mix of T-material/porcelain (equal parts for throwing, 2:1 for handbuilding). Non-translucent porcelain works well, and cheaper alternatives to T-material are available eg. 'Y'-material from Potclays. However, many clays will work if grog is added – I have successfully used red earthenware in a raku firing.

Raku Glazes

As a general guide, any low to mid temperature frit plus 5-20% china clay and 1-2% bentonite will make a raku glaze. High alkali frit will tend to give a fine crazing, while borax frit will tend to be more open. Experimenting and asking questions are part of the process and contribute to the individuality of the work.

Different glazes in the same kiln can cause problems because of variations in maturing temperature. Using a torch to check for glaze melt is surprisingly effective. After turning off the burner, I wait for the glaze to start pinging before lifting the pot out of the kiln and placing it in fine sawdust. 'Spontex' scourers are excellent for cleaning glaze surfaces.

Harold McWhinnie

Raku Glazes

Crackle White
Calcium borate frit (Gerstley borate)..........80
Nepheline syenite 20
China clay..5
Tin oxide..1

Crackle White & Silver
Calcium borate frit (Gerstley borate)..........80
Nepheline syenite 20
China clay..5
Tin oxide..1
Silver nitrate..1

Crackle Yellow & Silver
Calcium borate frit (Gerstley borate)..........80
Nepheline syenite 20
Tin oxide..1
Yellow oxide 5
Silver nitrate..1
China clay..5

Crackle Pink & Silver
Calcium borate frit (Gerstley borate)..........80
Nepheline syenite 20
China clay..5
Tin oxide..1
Pink stain 5
Silver nitrate..1

Crackle Blue
Calcium borate frit (Gerstley borate)..........80
Nepheline syenite 20
China clay..5
Tin oxide..1
Rutile 3
Cobalt carbonate 1

Crackle Blue-Green
Calcium borate frit (Gerstley borate)..........80
Nepheline syenite 20
China clay..5
Tin oxide..1
Copper carbonate 3
Silver nitrate..1
Antimony oxide 3

Crackle Yellow
Calcium borate frit (Gerstley borate)..........80
Nepheline syenite 20
China clay..5
Tin oxide..1
Vanadium stain 5
Silver nitrate..1

David Miller CR 85

Raku Body for Throwing 1000°C
Fireclay...50
Fine plastic stoneware clay 20
Grog 25
Talc 10

Clay Body
Fireclay..50kg
Ball clay 15kg
Coarse Grog or Sand 25-30kg
Talc 15kg

The clay is mixed from powdered ingredients in a dough mixer.

Anna Noël CR 185
(work illustrated)

Clay
White stoneware and T-material 50/50

David Roberts CR 105, 137, 186
(work illustrated)

My general clay body is a blend of 2 parts T-material and 1 part porcelain which enables me to explore the way different strengths and patterns of carbonisation react to various surface treatments; surfaces can be burnished at the leatherhard stage, sanded when bone dry or ground and polished using wet and dry abrasive paper together with Diapads, both after the biscuit and the final raku firing. Biscuit firing is to Orton cone 6 which gives fairly strong body strength but is open enough for smoke to penetrate. The final raku firing takes place in a 'top hat' kiln to between 650°C and 1000°C depending on quality and strength of carbonisation required. The following slips and glazes control the strength and patterning of carbonisation.

Black and White Linear Patterns
Fine slip made from clay body sieved through 200 mesh mixed with gum arabic and painted on biscuit fired surface. This is removed after firing leaving lightly smoked surface, giving a contrast to heavily smoked, unprotected areas.

Resist or 'Peel Off' Slip
China clay .... 3 parts by volume
Flint ....2 parts

This is applied underneath a simple raku crackle glaze.

Raku Crackle Glaze
Alkaline frit 45
Soft borax frit 45
China clay....................................10

Raku Firing
After the required temperature is reached in the raku firing, the work is drawn from the kiln and smoked, using sawdust as the combustible in purpose-built metal containers. The firing temperature, the time between work being drawn from kiln and then placed in sawdust, the position of the work and the amount and grain size of sawdust all influence final surface quality. The work is cooled for approximately half an hour then removed from the smoking chamber, cleaned and, if necessary, ground and polished.

Copper Lustre 925°C
Calcium borate frit.......................35
Cookson's 'J' frit 35
China clay....................................20
Iron oxide 5
Copper oxide 5

What I believe may help in delivering a more permanent copper lustre is that at maturation (around 925°C) it was reduced heavily in the kiln for about 10 minutes before being smothered in sawdust immediately upon removal from the kiln. I must admit that I abandoned copper red glazes in my own work years ago because of suspicions over the stability of this type of glaze.

Crackle-White (open crazing)
Calcium borate frit 40
Borax frit (Potterycrafts 2955) 40
China clay...15
Tin oxide..5

Transparent Glaze I
Soft borax frit 85
China clay...15

Often used with added oxides and stains and as cover for pattern work.

Dry Copper Glaze
Borax frit...60
Powdered St Thomas body 30
Copper oxide 5
Red iron oxide 5

10-15 minutes heavy reduction in kiln increases durability of lustre.

Crackle-White (Finer Crazing)
High alkali frit 80
China clay...15
Tin oxide..5

Transparent Glaze II (Finer Crazing)
High alkali frit 85
China clay...15

NB Similar results can only be expected if used with same body and firing conditions as used by David Roberts.

Paul Soldner CR 109, 124, 173
(work illustrated)

Soldner's Low Fireclay Body – 1982
Plastic fireclay (Lincoln) .... Equal parts
Ball clay (Kentucky O.M. No. 4) ..Equal parts
Talc..Equal parts
Sand ....Equal parts
(good quality silica, mesh size: 20-60 average 30)

Add red clay for dark body, china clay for white body.

Sigillata Slip
China clay...50%
Ball clay 50%

Mix both with water to make a stiff slip, then deflocculate with sodium silicate. Let settle 24 hours, then use the part (liquid) near the top and brush it on. Very responsive to low fire salt firings.

Glaze No. 1
Colemanite 1
Borax 1
China clay 1

Glaze No. 2
Colemanite 80
Feldspar 20

White Slip
Colemanite 1
Silica 1
China clay 1
Ball clay 1

> P.S. I would 'caution' using colemanite. I would prefer to use gerstley borate – same elements but more dependable.
>
> I have found that 3% copper carbonate in the above white slip and post fire smoked plus a mild reoxidation at the end (in the smoking chamber), sometimes results in a beautiful yellow. With a glaze over it, it turns green as might be expected. This slip colour is quite dramatic in contrast to the white slip which remains shades of black.

R. Lynn Studham CR 80

Raku body

The clay bodies I have been using for raku are middle temperature range that become dense at cone 4. They are basically parian bodies that resemble porcelain. Bisque firing is done to cone 4 prior to the raku glaze firing. The higher bisque produces a less fragile piece with the same quality associated with the raku technique. The clay bodies allow a tremendous amount of flexibility from the very thin thrown piece to the heavier sculptured works.

C/04-4
E.P.K. kaolin 38
Potash feldspar 32
Flint 25
Bentonite 3
Whiting 1
Zinc oxide 1

C/4
E.P.K. Kaolin 40
Nepheline syenite 24
Flint 20
Kentucky ball clay 4 10
Cornwall stone 6

> Up to 25% silica sand (50 mesh) is kneaded into the clay depending upon the method of production. The thinner thrown pieces have less sand than the heavier sculptured pieces.

Raku Base Glazes Cone 08/04

Glaze No. 1
Borax 50
Potash feldspar 20
Ferro frit 3110 20
Kaolin 10
+ Bentonite 3%

Glaze No. 2
Colemanite 70
Potash feldspar 30
+ Bentonite 3%

Glaze No. 3
Ferro frit 3134 48
Colemanite 47
Kaolin 5
+ Bentonite 3%

Glaze No. 4
Colemanite 48
Borax 52
+ Bentonite 3%

Colourants

Black lustre
Red iron oxide 4%
Copper oxide black 4%
Cobalt carbonate 3%

Copper blue
Copper oxide black 2%

White
Tin oxide 5%

Blue-mauve
Cobalt carbonate 2%
Manganese dioxide 3%

Silver yellow/gold
Silver nitrate 6%

Mottled blue
Cobalt carbonate 1%
Rutile 3%

Grey-yellow
Nickel oxide 3%
Potassium bichromate 3%

Brown lustre
Red iron oxide 4%

All pots were fired in a raku kiln fueled with wood. Pieces were exposed to varying degrees of reduction. The heavier the reduction the more lustrous and iridescent the colours. The reduction materials used included sawdust, wood shavings, dry leaves, pine needles and straw. Results vary depending on the quantity of reduction material used and the placing of the pot in the material.

Suppliers

Tucker's Pottery Supply Inc., 111 Esna Park Drive, Unit 9, Markham, Ontario. L3R 1H2, Canada

The Pottery Supply House Ltd., 2070 Speers Road, Oakville, Ontario, L6J 5A2, Canada

Jonathan Switzman

GS Raku Turquoise Crackle Cone 06
P2962 High alkali frit 94
China clay..................3
Bentonite 3
Calcium chloride 0.05
Copper oxide 5
Tin oxide..................3

> Soft turquoise blue green with orange red if reduced. Note: Add the bentonite to water by combining with china clay first.
>
> Possible health hazards: P2962 high alkali frit: slightly soluble and therefore caustic. Copper oxide: respiratory irritant, damages vital organs. Avoid inhalation or ingestion. Significantly alters lead release if used in lead based glazes.

Baggy House Crackle Glaze Cone 07
P2962 High alkali frit 57.18
P2954 Calcium borate frit 2.26
Grolleg china clay 16.46
Whiting..................3.5
Lithium carbonate 5.54
Zinc oxide..................0.72
Flint 14.33
Copper carbonate 5
Red iron oxide 2.5

> Medium/large crackle, bright turquoise blue, shiny. Just matures at 980-960°C with 40 minute soak. Only use on tiles/flat surfaces.

Chrome Tin Red 2 Cone 012
Lead bisilicate 70.8
Whiting..................2.7
Potash feldspar 3.9
China clay..................5.4
Flint 11.6
Chromium oxide 4.2
Tin oxide..................1.4

> Rich red-orange, slightly matt due to lime and chrome content. Fire fast to 850°C and cool rapidly.
>
> Possible health hazards: lead bisilicate classed as toxic. Chromium oxide: all chromium compounds should be viewed as potentially carcinogenic.

Gold Silver Lustre Glaze Cone 06
Lead sesquisilicate 45
Borax frit..................45
China clay..................10
Silver nitrate..................1

Soda ash 1
Bismuth subnitrate...1

Gold with some purple flashes. Keep in a sealed container. Wear gloves and eye protection when applying.

Possible health hazards: silver nitrate/bismuth subnitrate: harmful: skin irritant, can damage eyes. Wear eye and skin protection when handling.

Soda ash: caustic. Will cause irritation and burns to skin tissue. Avoid contact with eyes, skin and by inhalation. Wear gloves and HSE approved respirator. Eye protection is necessary if splashing is a risk.

JS Metallic Speckle Green Cone 03
Lead bisilicate 43.81
Ball clay SMD...25.71
Whiting...17.15
Flint 8.57
Copper oxide 2.86
Iron oxide spangles 0.95
Red iron oxide 0.95

A rich apple green with metallic speckles. Sieve the glaze but add the iron unsieved. Definitely not food safe.

Possible health hazards: Lead bisilicate. Copper oxide harmful, respiratory irritant, damages vital organs, avoid inhalation or ingestion, significantly alters lead release if used in lead based glazes. Not food safe.

Metallic Black Cone 04-9
High alkali frit 20
Copper carbonate 60
Cobalt carbonate 10
Nickel oxide 10

Dry metallic blue-metallic black lizard skin at 1000°C, matt metallic blue black with copper black spots at 1280°C.

Possible health hazards: high alkali frit slightly soluble and caustic. Nickel oxide can cause allergic skin reactions.

Borax Project Glaze Cone 02
P2959 Borax frit high temperature 60
Ball clay hymod SMD 20
Whiting...20

A tile glaze developed at Goldsmiths' College for student project work and colour development. Best fired on horizontal surfaces. Develops soft milky colours.

Roz O'Connor Matt Clear Cone 3
Lead bisilicate 61
China clay..25
Cornish stone 9
Whiting...5

Satin matt semi opaque glaze. Use over stains and slips. Fire with a 20 minute plus soak for satin surface.

Petalite Matt Cone 06
Petalite 28.18
Flint 41.84
Lithium carbonate 28.83

Bentonite 1.14

Produces vibrant colour with dry surfaces i.e. vivid chrome greens with chrome oxide, bright 'earth colours' with stains.

Sarene's Amber Heavy Iron Cone 02
Lead sesquisilicate 65
P1312 Red earthenware 25
Cornish stone 5
Whiting 5
Red iron oxide 4

A rich toffee-brown classic lead glaze. Can be used with or without the iron addition.
Possible health hazards: lead sesquisilicate: toxic, avoid ingestion, not food safe.

Black Vitreous Slip Cone 01
Lead bisilicate 34.84
P1312 Red earthenware 37.19
China clay 17.13
Cornish stone 5.12
Whiting 5.72
Manganese dioxide 6
Ferric oxide 7.6
Copper oxide 0.3
Cobalt oxide 7.88

Opaque black-blue. Surface texture matt slip or engobe. Not food safe.

Blue Zinc Crystal Glaze Cone 04
Lead bisilicate 50.8
P2953 Borax frit general purpose 34.6
Zinc oxide 8.3
Titanium dioxide 6.3
Cobalt carbonate 1
Nickel oxide 2

Possible health hazards: lead bisilicate. Nickel oxide can cause allergic skin reactions.

Allison Weightman CR 138

Leonie White Glaze
Standard alkaline frit 70
Calcium borate frit 30
Feldspar 10
Ball clay (hyplas) 10
Tin oxide 10

At 1050°C it produces a lovely small cracked white glaze.

Streaky Glaze with Amazing Lustre
Calcium borate frit 40
Alkaline frit 40
China clay 15
Iron oxide 3
Copper oxide 4

John Wheeldon CR 154

Raku Glaze 1040°C

Copper oxide 100
Frit 10
Bentonite 10
Polycel 1

   A copper matt.

Earthenware
950-1150°C
Bodies, Slips, Glazes

In this section potters give the clay bodies they make up themselves, either from dry materials or from blending different prepared bodies together. Most potters give the method of mixing they use, but in general outline this is done by adding dry ingredients to water, bearing in mind that most plastic bodies have a 20% water content. Small quantities can be mixed by hand, however for larger quantities a machine such as a 'dough mixer' is useful. Bodies can also be mixed by the slop method in any suitable container and then dried out to workable consistency. Most bodies benefit from storage, though the use of a de-airing pug mill will remove small air bubbles and greatly aid plasticity. As with glaze recipes potters should test body mixtures thoroughly before making up large amounts.

Most glazes falling into the firing range 950-1150°C are classified as earthenware glazes and like raku glazes usually incorporate commercially available fritted materials. Fritting renders lead safe to handle and alkalies in a non-soluble form. Most manufacturers supply their own particular frit mixtures and give analyses of the contents in their catalogues. For UK/USA substitutes see the end of the book.

Generally lead frits should be used with caution on vessels which are to be used for holding food and drink and copper oxide should never be added to lead glazes in these circumstances. Glazes based on alkaline and borax frits are safe for food and drink containers. All glazes containing lead should be tested for lead release by a qualified laboratory.

Lead Poisoning – The Danger of Lead in Glazes
Glazes containing lead must be treated with care. Unless the lead content is properly balanced within the glaze and the glaze then tested for lead release, it is best to avoid putting lead glazes on vessels intended for the preparation or serving of food or drink.

Gordon Baldwin CR 158, 179

Shiny Glaze Orton Cones 03, 02, 01, 1 or 2
Lead bisilicate 70
China stone 20
Clay 10

Matt Glaze Orton Cones 03, 02, 01, 1 or 2
Lead bisilicate 61
China stone 9
Clay..20
Whiting..5

Paul Barron

Transparent Coloured Glazes 1140-1200°C

Base Glaze
Harrison Mayer 216 (formerly JC983)......100

Add the following for colour glazes:

Rich Green
TWVD ball clay 11
Copper oxide 4

Olive Green
TWVD ball clay 11
Copper oxide 2
Iron oxide 3

> For application on commercial while bodies maturing at 1140°C. Best for use over cut and/or relief decoration. This glaze is 'hardened' so, applied fairly thinly to raw clay or soft biscuit, glaze and body can mature together at 1140°C avoiding crazing. These proportions of oxide give a medium tone. The oxides will disperse well in the glaze except for cobalt. This should be ground with the following glaze...

HM 216 10
Cobalt oxide 1

> ...for 2 hours, preferably in a ball mill, e.g. for 0.5% cobalt add 5% dry weight of compound to 95 parts of clear glaze such as HM 216, etc.

Glazes 1100°C
Podmores 'T' frit P2250 72
Cornish stone 23
Bentonite 5

Fired to 1100°C to avoid later scumming by uncombined alkali salts. This glaze may be very effectively coloured, the following oxide additions give a medium tone if applied at 3mm thickness:

Ultramarine (blue) + cobalt oxide 0.25
Cobalt (blue) + cobalt oxide 0.1
Copper oxide 1.0
Copper oxide 1.0

Turquiose (blue) + copper oxide 2.0
Viridian (dark green) + copper oxide 6.0
Purple (aubergine) + manganese dioxide 4.0
Yellow (cool) + uranium oxide 6.0
Yellow (walm) + iron oxide 8.0

> A transparent glaze for horizontal surfaces only, excellent with William de Morgan type underglaze painting, the oxides giving brilliant colours. Use over a white body or slip and apply very thickly, 3 mm at least using a trailer to flow on if necessary or spray. Much bulk is lost in the firing. The glaze crazes heavily adding to the brilliance of the effect.

Reg Batchelor CR 147

Coloured bodies
To use in a typical clay/quartz/feldspar body

Pale pink, going to tan brown at 5%:
Black iron oxide 2
Black:
Black iron oxide 8
Manganese dioxide 3
Cobalt oxide 1
Light grey with specks:
Manganese dioxide 2.5
Iron chromate 2
Grey-brown:
Iron chromate 6
Grey-brown:
Copper oxide 2
Red iron oxide 2
Tan, darkening to 6%:
Rutile 3
Buff with specks:
Ilmenite 6
Light brown with specks, dark brown with specks at 6%(RB):
Manganese dioxide 3
Pale olive green, darkening to a charcoal at 5%:
Black copper oxide.. 2-5
Grey-green to olive green at 5%:
Chromium oxide 3

Peter Beard CR 109

Clear Glaze 1100°C oxidation
High alkaline frit 65
Nepheline syenite 15
China clay 10
Flint 5
Whiting 5

> I fire this clear glaze to 1280°C oxidation to which one can add anything that gives colour and in many combinations. I use it in combination with my other glazes. At 1280°C it runs a lot and is not good on its own at this temperature.

Clive Bowen CR 131, 149
(work illustrated)

Clay
Fremington – washed for slipware
Fremington – unwashed for garden pots

Slips

White
Peters Marland stoneware clay shredded (120 sieve)

Red
Own clay from field, vitrifies 1200°C

Black
Fremington clay 8lb
Iron oxide 1lb
Manganese dioxide 1lb

Glazes

Clear (outside only)
Galena 18
Clay 9
Flint 3

Yellow
Lead bisilicate 36lb
Clay 14lb
Flint 1.5lb
Iron oxide 6oz
Bentonite 8oz

Brown
Lead bisilicate 36lb
Clay 14lb
Flint 1.5lb
Iron oxide 2lb
Bentonite 8oz

Alison Britton CR 107, 129, 170, 173
(work illustrated)

Dora Billington's Lead Sesquisilicate Matt Glaze 1100°C
Lead sesquisilicate 47.1
Whiting 10
China clay 16
Potash feldspar 25.5
  Best when soaked at top temperature.

Neil Brownsword CR 183
(work illustrated)

Base Glaze 800-1000°C
Lead oxide 80
Nepheline syenite 20

    Chrome oxide is added at 0.1% for yellows and 4% for reds. Glaze has a range of 800-1000°C, I usually fire at 920°C.

    Caution: Lead oxide should be handled with great care.

Alan Caiger-Smith CR 130, 141

Earthenware Clay
Fremington clay is used for the body.
For ovenware 15% of silver sand and grog, in equal portions, is added.

Tin Glaze Cone 04-03
Lead bisilicate 62
Cornish stone 13
China clay..5
Borax frit...10
Tin oxide..10

    A wide range of colours can be painted on the glaze before firing.

Reliable Clear Glaze Cone 04-03
Lead bisilicate 74
Ball clay 13
Flint 9
Whiting..4

    Best in wood-firing, but all right oxidised.

White Tin Glaze 1050°C
Lead bisilicate 62
Cornish stone 13
China clay..5
Borax frit...10
Tin oxide..10

    This tin glaze has proved useful to me for many years and could be a helpful starting point for others. It has good colour-carrying qualities except for iron-browns and is best fired at about 1050°C.

Maiolica Colours

Blue-green
Copper oxide 130
Cobalt oxide 45

Flecky Blue-green
Copper oxide 60
Cobalt oxide 22
llmenite..30

Black
Manganese dioxide 6
Cobalt oxide 1

Bronze-green
Iron oxide 90
Copper oxide 10

Brown
Iron oxide 8
Cobalt oxide 1

Yellow
Antimonate of lead 35
Lead bisilicate 25
Iron oxide 5

Glaze for Lustre Decoration 1050°C
Lead bisilicate 29.9
Borax frit 44.2
China clay 2.6
Zinc oxide 5.2
Flint 6.7
Zirconium silicate 10.0
Barium carbonate 0.7
Tin oxide 9.0

This glaze, in current use, suits many different lustres.

Simple Pigment Lustres

Red
Copper carbonate 52
Red ochre 98

This is better calcined to low red heat and milled for one hour.

Silver Lustre
Silver carbonate 20
Red ochre 100

Daphne Carnegy CR 129
(work illustrated)

Body
Valentine's Standard red

Glaze Orton Cone 02
Lead bisilicate 60
Standard borax frit 9
Cornish stone 15
China clay 5
Tin oxide 7
Zirconium silicate 7

Zinc oxide...2
Bentonite 2

> Based on an original recipe by Alan Caiger-Smith. I fire to Orton Cone 02 but the glaze has a wide range of 1060-1160°C.
>
> For painting I use both oxides and commercial underglaze colours. The commercial stains on their own are rather bland and oxides alone give a somewhat limited palette; so they complement each other. They can also be intermixed with good results. The proportions of the mixtures vary according to mood and I like to retain some element of unpredictability. Those oxides that are fluxes, such as cobalt, copper and manganese are mixed with a little china clay to give more stability; underglaze colours and those oxides which tend to be refractory and rough on the surface of the glaze, are mixed with a little of the base glaze or with straight lead bisilicate to assist fusion.

Simon Carroll CR 175
(work illustrated)

Clay
Valentine's standard red, with a bit of grog

Slip

White
Ball clay 60
China clay...40
> Sieved through 80's mesh.

Red
Sieved Valentine's body

Black
Red slip with 10% manganese dioxide

Glazes 1060°C
Lead sesquisilicate 80
Ball clay 20
plus
Red iron oxide 0-6%
or
Tin oxide...10%

> Firings are to Cone 04, 1060°C with a soak in a propane fired kiln based on a salt kiln design by Mick Casson. The atmosphere in the kiln is on the borderline between oxidation and reduction.

Kenneth Clark

Glazes using Lead Frits 1060-1080°C
Lead bisilicate 72.8
China clay..12.1
China stone 13.5
Flint 1.6

Lead sesquisilicate 52.8
Feldspar 31.1
Whiting......................................5.6
China clay...................................7.2
Flint 3.3

Lead sesquisilicate 75.5
China clay..................................18.7
Flint 5.8

Bennett Cooper CR 138
(work illustrated)

Body
Potclays ogden red 1137 ....50kg
Potclays fireclay 1276/3 ....25kg
Slops (from previous mix)...................35kg
Grog 30-80 ....3-10kg
Flint 3kg
    If salts are a problem in the water add 0.5-1% barium carbonate with the slops.

Base Slip
HVAR ball clay..............................15
China clay...................................2
Potash feldspar..............................6

Blue Slip
1 pint white slip plus 25gm cobalt oxide

Blue-green Slip
1 pint white slip plus 25gm cobalt oxide and 4gm chrome oxide

Transparent Glaze 1160-80°C
Lead bisilicate 65
China clay..................................10
Potash feldspar.............................15
Whiting......................................5
Flint 5
    Oxidised, soak for one hour.

Emmanuel Cooper CR 136, 160

Opalescent 1080-1150°C
Alkaline frit (P2962).......................86
Calcium borate frit..........................8
China clay...................................6
    A bright opalescent blue with chun effects over red clays.
Additions
Bright turquoise:
Copper oxide 1-5%
Mid blue:

Cobalt oxide 1-5%
Iron oxide 1%
Grey-beige:
Iron oxide 5%

Suzi Cree

Clear Glaze 1040-1080°C
Lead bisilicate 70
Local lime-rich earthenware clay 10
Cornish stone 4
Whiting..2
Bentonite 1
HVAR ball clay..5

Honey Glaze 1040-1100°C
Lead bisilicate 68
Local earthenware clay 26
Cornish stone 2
Whiting..2

Clear Glaze 1040-1080°C
Galena...45
HVAR ball clay...17.5
Cornish stone 2
Bentonite 3

    Galena glaze: only to be used on surfaces that do not come into contact with food. The addition of 2.5 iron oxide makes a good yellow glaze.

Coxwold Pottery (Peter and Jill Dick) CR 126

Standard Slips Around 1080°C
White:
HVAR ball clay
Green:
HVAR ball clay plus copper oxide 7.5%
Dark blue:
HVAR ball clay plus cobalt oxide 2.5%
Medium blue:
HVAR ball clay plus cobalt oxide 1.25%
Pale blue:
HVAR ball clay plus cobalt oxide 0.62%
Black:
Red slip (Potclays 1137).............................30 litres
+
Manganese dioxide 720gm
Red iron oxide 360gm
Crocus martis 360gm
    Fired in an electric kiln.

Standard Clear Glaze 1080°C
Lead bisilicate 75.4
HVAR ball clay...4.96
China clay..4.96
Bentonite 2.48
Cornish stone 7.94
Whiting..2.97
Quartz..1.29

Stephen Dixon CR 139
(work illustrated)

Bronze-brown Clay
Vingerling sculptors red clay......................25
Vingerling modelling black clay 25
White St. Thomas body 25
Craft crank 25

Cream Coloured Clay
White St. Thomas body 50
Craft crank body..50

Low Shrinkage White Clay
ST Material (Commercial Clays, Sandbach Road, Stoke-on-Trent)
   Bisque to 1140°C.

Matt White base Glaze 1180°C
Lead bisilicate frit 17
Nepheline syenite 15
China clay..21
Flint 15
Zinc oxide..10
Whiting..22

Transparent Shiny Base Glaze 1120°C
Lead bisilicate frit 44
Flint 17
Petalite 11
China clay..11
Barium carbonate 11
Whiting..6

Transparent Satin 1120°C Oxidising
Lead bisilicate 64
Cornish stone 10
China clay..20
Whiting..6

Michael and Victoria Eden CR 180
(work illustrated)

Slips
Basic White Slip:
Hyplas 71 ball clay
> This has a good resistance to peeling but is more buff than true white. Prepare with a paint mixing attachment on an electric drill as it will then pass easily through an 80s sieve.

Coloured slips add:
Blue:
Cobalt oxide 3.5%
Green:
Copper oxide 2.5%
Tan:
White slip 50%
Red body clay 50%
Black:
Add to a slip made from a red clay body:
Iron oxide 3%
Cobalt oxide 2%
Manganese dioxide 2%

> Where commercial stains are used, add 10-15% of stain to white slip. Potters who use these glaze recipes should always have them tested for lead release as variations in materials or firing technique could affect the levels of lead release.

Clear Glaze 1060-1080°C (with 30 min soak)
Lead sesquisilicate 20.0kg
China clay...4.8kg
Flint 1.6kg

> This is enough for a binful. Add approximately 2 teaspoons of calcium chloride in a saturated solution to deter settling. This glaze, which came from David Green, has passed current British and American lead release standards over our slips, including the copper one. It has a good colour response; we add the following:

Golden orange:
Iron oxide 4%
Strong blue:
Cobalt oxide 1%
Green:
Copper oxide 2.5%

Galena Glaze 1060-1080°C
Galena ....18 parts
Clay..9 parts
Flint ....3 parts

> Clive Bowen's recipe. Use on the outside of pots only, or on pieces not intended for food.

Honey Glaze 1060-1080°C
Lead sesquisilicate .... 3 parts
Red clay .... 1 part

> Use the same body as that of the pot to ensure a good glaze fit. With the addition of a little bentonite this glaze will work well raw.

Clear Glaze 1100-1115°C
Lead bisilicate 11.25kg
Cornish stone 3.0kg
China clay 1.5kg
Bentonite 1.5kg

> Add calcium chloride as with the other clear glaze. This is an excellent raw glaze; very craze resistant so useful for cookwares. It does not produce a good green when used with copper, but passes British and American lead release standards, as does the honey glaze.
>
> Most work is fired in an electric kiln. The lead sesquisilicate clear glaze to 1180°C and its coloured versions to +/– 1065°C. For wood-firing, the glazes which respond best are the orange and clear lead sesquisilicate glazes which are fired to cone 04. The blue can look dull and the green muddy depending on kiln atmosphere and temperature.

Derek Emms CR 123

Transparent Earthenware 1050-1060°C
Lead bisilicate 70
Low expansion frit (P2246) 15
China clay 15

> Add 2-4% red iron for light to dark honey.

Blue Flash Glaze 1120-1140°C
Alkaline frit 32
Feldspar 48
Whiting 12
China clay 8

> Creditied to Heber Mathews. Fired about 1120-1140°C (oxidised) and over iron bearing bodies, iron oxide and iron slips produce alkaline blue flushes.

Miguel Espinosa

Clear Glaze 1135°C
Ferro standard borax frit 36.00
Alkaline frit 10.25
Wollastonite 5.25
Barium carbonate 6.25
Zinc oxide 3.25
China clay 16.00
Quartz 23.00

Up to 1140°C
Alkaline frit 30.75
Wollastonite 12.25
Barium carbonate 11.50

Zinc oxide..4.00
China clay..10.50
Quartz..31.00
With added oxides

Zinc Turquoise 1120°C
Feldspar 34.50
Ferro standard borax frit 15.50
Wollastonite 10.00
Barium carbonate..7.75
Zinc oxide..6.00
China clay..4.00
Quartz..19.25
Copper carbonate 3.00

Clive Fiddis

Alkaline White Tin Glaze 1060°C
Borax frit 78
China clay..10
Tin oxide..8
Zirconium oxide...4

> This glaze produces a white shiny surface, pinholing can be lessened by 'soaking' the kiln at 1060°C for forty-five minutes.

Alan Frewin

Once Fired Slipware 1140°C
Lead bisilicate
(or lead frit with low melting point)..........48
Clay*..47
Whiting...5

> * C H Brannam, Barnstaple for red clay with low melting temperature.
> As a rough guide the maturing temperature depends on the type of clay and lead frit used. The whiting is not essential but helps to increase the firing range, i.e. the range between under and over firing. Red clay will make the glaze show yellow over a white slip.

Tessa Fuchs
(work illustrated)

White Silky Matt Earthenware Glaze 1080°C
Lead sesquisilicate 47
Whiting...10
Feldspar 25
China clay..16

> I use this glaze on all my sculptural work. Cone 04 in an electric kiln. Needs soaking for one hour. It is very good over oxides. You can achieve good colour glazes by adding 5-10 % glaze stains.

David Garland CR 105

A Favourite Glaze
Lead bisilicate 75
White earthenware clay 25
    2 or 3 % of red clay can be added to 'warm up' the glaze and help to flux it.

Jonathan Garratt CR 177
(work illustrated)

Clay Body 1040-1100°C Wood-fired
Delivered from the pig farm 2km away. It is dug from just below the leaf litter and contains not only roots and gravel, but a high proportion of fine silt and occasional big sandstones.
For strength add ball clay 10%
For plant pots, 'garden punctuation' pieces add sand
For fuming on surface place galvanized nails and staples etc.

Honey Glaze 1040-1100°C
Lead bisilicate 75
Fremington clay 25
Red iron oxide 3

Clear Glaze 1040-1100°C
Lead bisilicate 75
Hyplas 71 ball clay 19
Dolomite 4
Potash feldspar 2

    Both are raw glazes, applied to leatherhard pots after slipping. I tend to use a white slip thickly under the honey glaze, and thinly under the clear for best effects of the rouletting. I use fired copper plumbing pipe, ground down to a powder and mixed 1:2 with yellow ochre for green pigment. The blue is cobalt oxide 4: red clay body 6. They are both used under the glaze. Wood-fired.

Paul Gooderham

Deep Green Glaze 900°C
Lead bisilicate 100
Copper oxide 10

Pink-brown Glaze 900°C
Lead bisilicate 70
China clay..3
Flint 27

David Green

Glazes Containing Lead Oxide

Lead Oxide as the Only Flux 1080°C
Lead sesquisilicate 75.2
China clay..18.6
Flint 5.8

Lead Oxide with Alkalis 1080°C
Lead sesquisilicate 61.2
Soda feldspar 36.8
Flint 2.1

Lead Oxide with Alkaline Earths 1080°C
Lead bisilicate 68
China clay 12
Cornish stone 15
Whiting..5

1080°C
Lead bisilicate 70
Fremington clay 30

Lead and Boric Oxide 1080°C
Lead bisilicate 39.8
Flint 11.0
Potash feldspar..32.3
Whiting..5.8
Frit (P2244)..12.0

Lead and Zinc Oxide 1080°C
Lead sesquisilicate 55.2
China clay..25.5
Zinc oxide..10.0
Whiting..5.3
Flint 4.0

Alkali and Boric Oxides 1080°C
Frit (P2244)..16.4
Frit (P2250)..27.8
Frit (W1461) 31.4
China clay..24.5

Alkaline Earth and Boric Oxide 1080°C
Frit (P2244)..29.8
Feldspar 40 1
Whiting..7.2
China clay...3.7
Flint 19.0

Zinc and Boric Oxide 1080°C
Frit (W1460) 27.1
Zinc oxide...7.7
Whiting...12.7
China clay..15.5
Flint 37.0

Bill Hall CR 147, 158

Coloured Clay Bodies
Colourants (all with 100 parts clay):
Mid to dark grey with a touch of brown unglazed:
Cobalt oxide 0.5
Iron oxide 3.0
Mid tone greyish:
Cobalt oxide 0.25
Nickel oxide 0.50
Mid tone chromium-green:
Cobalt oxide 0.25
Chrome oxide 0.50
Mid tone to light tone brown:
Cobalt oxide 0.25
Iron oxide 1.00
Light rich brown:
Copper carbonate 1
Mid to dark green-blue:
Cobalt 1
Nickel oxide 1
Mid brown:
Chromium oxide 0.5
Iron oxide 2.0
Dark green-blue:
Copper carbonate 3.0
Cobalt oxide 1.5
Dark brown:
Copper carbonate 2
Iron oxide 3
Chromium oxide 1
Mid chromium green:
Cobalt oxide 0.5
Chromium oxide 1.0
Dark chromium green:
Chromium oxide 3
Cobalt oxide 1
Very dark green:
Chromium oxide 3
Copper carbonate 3
Mid brown:
Iron oxide 2
Chromium 1

Regina Heinz CR 178
(work illustrated)

Lithium Glaze 1025-1035°C
China clay..30
Whiting..30
Potash feldspar 10
Lithium carbonate 10

Fritted Slip
China clay..50
Ball clay 50
High alkaline frit 30

> All glaze firings are in an electric kiln in an oxidising atmosphere to 1035°C with half an hour's soak. At this temperature the lithium glaze is under-fired, the lithium grains just start to melt and create an interesting speckle effect that adds depth and variation to the coloured surface.

Harry Horlock Stringer

Taggs Yard Production Potters White Tin Glaze 1120°C
Electric Kiln
Lead bisiliate (Potterycraft) 26
Borax frit (Potterycraft P2245).....................7
China clay...4
North Devon ball clay 6
Bentonite 1.5
Tin oxide...3

> This glaze seldom ever crazes over Sadlers teapot body from Stoke-on-Trent. It has a rich reaction with copper oxide and is pleasant with most others. Best fired to 1120°C when throwing lines in the red clay break through in a rich red colour as the glaze runs thinner. Greens of an interesting variety can be obtained by putting the above glaze over this slip:- Sieve 1.75 gallons of your red slip through an 80 mesh lawn (this makes nearly a normal plastic bucket full) at dipping consistency (double cream). Mix the following with a small amount of hot water and add to the slip. <u>Do not sieve</u> after adding the oxides or you will sieve out the speckle effect

Copper oxide 16oz
Iron oxide (not precipitated) 24oz
Granular manganese dioxide......................6oz

A Speckle Slip 1120°C Oxidised
To a two gallon bucket of sieved (80 mesh) red clay slip add unsieved:
Red iron oxide (not precipitated) 2lb
Granular manganese dioxide......................0.5lb
Manganese dioxide 0.5lb

> Never sieve again or out go your speckles. Instead give it 30 seconds with a paint stirrer fixed into an electric hand drill. This goes for all your slips. A good texture under a tin glaze. NB. 2% of bentonite in all slips and glazes makes for happy potters.

John Huggins

Plant Pot Body
I use two local brickyard clays to which I add extra sand.

Honey Glaze 1060-1080°C
Lead bisilicate 80
Red clay 20
Flint 5
Red iron oxide 3
Bentonite 3

> Applied thickly to leatherhard or biscuit ware this recipe gives a rich deep honey glaze, especially over white slip.

Clear Glaze 1060-1080°C
Lead bisilicate 80
SMD ball clay 20
Flint 5

> Applied thinly to leatherhard or biscuit ware this recipe gives a good clear glaze especially for use over coloured slips. It gives white slip a rather creamy quality.

Woody Hughes CR 127

04 White Slip (For Wet to Leatherheard Clay)
China clay..12.5
Calcined china clay 12.5
Ferro 3124 (alkaline/borax frit) 20
Talc 5
Flint 20
Zircopax 5
OM4 Ball clay...25

Archie Bray Black Slip Cone 04-10
Redart clay 50
OM4 ball clay...25
Manganese dioxide 15
Black stain 12
Black iron oxide 5
Barium carbonate ....pinch

Oxidation Glazes Cone 04-02
Base Glaze 1
Ferro 3124 (alkaline borax frit) 45
Ferrro 3304 (lead frit)................................45
China clay..10
+ Copper carbonate...................................2% – green
   Iron oxide...3% – yellow
   Colbalt carbonate.................................0.5-1% – blue

Base Glaze 2
Ferro 3124 (Alkaline/borax frit)..................75

Lithium carbonate 3.8
Nepheline syenite 9.4
China clay..9.4
Flint 2
Bentonite 2

Woody's Blue
Ferro 3124 (alkaline/borax frit) 80
Talc 13
China clay..7
Copper carbonate 2%

Water Blue
Gerstley borate (calcium borate frit) 5.8
China clay..7.2
Ferro 3110 (alkaline/calcium frit) 76.9
Flint 10.1
Copper carbonate 3-6%

Batz Majolica White
Ferro 3124 (alkaline/borax frit) 100
Barium carbonate...4
China clay..15
Zircon 24

123 Higby Clear
Flint ....1 part
China clay..2 parts
Colemanite (calcium borate frit) ....3 parts

Otto Texture
White lead* 73.75
Feldspar 23.75
Barium carbonate...11.25
China clay..5
Cornwall stone 5

*This is a poisonous glaze. White lead must be handled with great care. Try substituting lead monosilicate.

Additions:
Chrome 6%
Rutile 6-10%
Copper carbonate 3-6%
colbalt carbonate 1-5%
Iron oxide 3-5%

Majolica (Alfred)
Ferro frit (alkaline/borax frit)......................80
Ferro frit (lead frit) 65
China clay..5
Zircopax 7
Tin oxide..2
Rutile 0.1
F/4 Kona 32

Redart is a highly plastic clay with a high iron content; it is usually used to produce earthenware bodies. Substitute any red clay. F-4 Kona is a soda feldspar with the formular $Na_2O\ Al_2O_3\ 6SiO_2$.

Stephanie Kalan

Base Glazes for Chrome-tin Pinks and Reds 1000-1200°C
Lead bisilicate 42
Whiting..10
Feldspar 23
China clay...7
Flint 18
Lead bisilicate 46
Whiting..10
Feldspar 7
China clay...9
Boric acid 8
Flint 20

Lead bisilicate 29
Whiting..9
Borax..23
Feldspar 7
China clay...9
Flint 23

Feldspar 32
Lead bisilicate 10
Whiting..20
China clay...7
Flint 27
Boric acid 4

All glazes need the addition of Chrome-tin glaze stain in amounts from 2-10%.

Calcium Matt Glazes 1060°C
Feldspar 45
Dolomite 7
Lead bisilicate 13
Whiting..20
Flint 15

Feldspar 17
Dolomite 6
Whiting..15
Lead bisilicate 32
China clay...8
Flint 22

Alumina Matt Glaze 1140°C (approx.)
Lead bisilicate 40
Feldspar 24
Whiting..13

China clay 18
Flint 5

Barium Matt Glaze 1140°C
Lead bisilicate 12
Zinc oxide 3
Feldspar 30
Barium carbonate 24
Whiting 11
China clay 9
Flint 11

Mary Lambert CR 119, 120

Green Slip
FP101 DBG 4lb
Dry red body 1lb
Copper carbonate 3oz
    For a brighter, paler green, omit the red body.

Black Slip
Dry red body 6lb
Manganese dioxide 6oz
Iron oxide 4oz
Cobalt oxide 1oz
    Omission of the cobalt results in a warmer black.

Blue Slip
FP101 DBG 8lb
Cobalt oxide 2oz

Martin Lewis CR 146

Barium carbonate 9
Lithium carbonate 7
Calcined china clay 7
Whiting 19.5
Lead sesquisilicate 57.5
    Plus various amounts of oxide, firing to between 750-1080°C depending on colour response and degree of mattness.

Roger Lewis CR 179

Transparent Earthenware 1050°C
Borax frit (Select FR002) 80
Whiting 5
China clay 15
(Inside as above + copper carbonate)
    Earthenware is biscuit fired to 1120°C before airbrushing with underglaze colours that are then sprayed with borax glaze, fired to 1050°C. The firing is fast to 900°C and then slow

to the top temperature with a 30 minute soak. It is then cooled slowly down to 950°C. The firing sequence affects the final result considerably. (I prefer the colours to run slightly and the glaze to pick up a slight opalescent cast from the dark blue and black stains.)

Sophie MacCarthy CR 156
(work illustrated)

My base slip is made from a combination of Special Stoneware and Studio White E/W passed through an 80 mesh sieve. To this I add a range of oxides and body stains from Potterycrafts and Ceramatech. I do not measure precise quantities, preferring to act instinctively as one would to a certain extent with cooking. I fire to 1020°C bisque.

Transparent Glaze 1100°C
Lead bisilicate 80
China clay..10
Flint 10
    With a 20 minute soak.

Fenella Mallalieu CR 143
(work illustrated)

Glazes 1060°C

Orange Cone 04 1060°C
Lead sesquisilicate 75
Whiting..4
China clay..17
Flint 6
Iron oxide 4
(2 for yellow)

Sea-green
Lead bisilicate 70
Cornish stone 20
China clay..10
Iron oxide 2.5
Cobalt carbonate 0.6

Blue Cone 04 1060°C
Lead sesquisilicate 70
Soda feldspar 10
High alkaline frit 3.5
Whiting..3
China clay..15
Flint 4
Cobalt carbonate 1
    Do not overfire.

John Mathieson CR 169

Matt Off-white Glaze 1110°C
Lead sesquisilicate 100
China clay..40
Whiting..15
Tin oxide..10

    Good with oxide decoration. Red clay will burn through where the glaze is thin. Suzi Cree's Honey Glaze works well with Potclays 1135 Red S/E body in place of Local Earthenware Clay.

David Miller CR 85, 118, 186
(work illustrated)

Red Earthenware Clay
Argile de Provence from Salernes.
Dept. – Var supplied by Ceradel, France.

White Slip
Hyplas 71 ....7kg
China clay (Grolleg) 2kg
Flint 1kg

Matt 1120°C with 45min Soak
Lead bisilicate frit 56
China clay..25
Flint 4
Whiting..5
Zinc oxide..10

Shiny 1085°C with 45min Soak
Lead bisilicate frit 7000gm
Feldspar 400gm
Whiting...200gm
Hyplas 71 ....500gm
White earthenware..................................1000gm
'Sifralo' bentonite.....................................100gm

    Both glazes are fired in an electric kiln.

Nora and Naomi (Israel) CR 86, 117, 162, 182

Kaolin Negev S/5 ....35%
Red Motza clay..35%
Mixed grog 30%

    This is a rather common local mixture (Negev clay is a kind of rather impure kaolin and Motza Red clay is a reddish earthenware) which is used for wheel work when the grog is very fine, and for handbuilding with rough grog.

Matthias Ostermann CR 123

Maiolica Glaze Orton Cone 05 1046°C Electric Kiln
Frit 3124 (Ferro) 60
Frit 3195 (Ferro) 10
Ball clay 6.5
Kaolin 6.5
Silica 4
Whiting 2
Zircopax 11

> For saturated coloured glaze: six parts wet glaze to one part dry colour stain with no extra frit addition. For in-glaze painting (on surface of raw glaze) equal part frit to colour stain and water; reduced frit will create more matt surfaces.

Anthony Phillips CR 123, 124

Slips
Slips made with 60% ball clay (e.g. SMD ot Hyplas 71 or DBG) and 40% china clay.
Body stains, glaze stains, underglaze colours and oxides are used to add colour.

Clear Glaze
Lead bisilicate 57
Borax frit (P2953 Potterycrafts) 25.6
China clay 10.3
Quartz or flint 7.1
Bentonite 2

> Fired to 1080-1120°C in electric kiln.

White Slip
Ball clay (P3354 Potterycrafts) 60
China clay 40

> This slip is suitable for the addition of oxides and body stains. It can be used on red earthenware clay or white earthenware clay, the latter biscuit fired to about 1170°C.
> To avoid the slip and glaze shivering after firing, the slip should be applied when the clay body is at the soft leatherhard stage. Rims and edges which dry first on a pot should be wetted if necessary before applying the slip. If the pot is in danger of collapse after slipping put it on front of a fan heater for a while.

Matt Glaze
Lead bisilicate 36
Borax frit (P2953 Potterycrafts) 17
China clay 15
Whiting 9
Potash feldspar 24
Bentonite 2

> Fired to 1080-1100°C in electric kiln.

Glaze
Lead bisilicate 57
Borax frit 25.6

China clay 10.3
Flint 7.1
Bentonite 2
    Fired to 1105°C.

John Pollex   CR 132, 146

Coloured Slips
5% body stain per container e.g. in a 450gm container dilute 20gm of body stain in approximately 0.5cm of water. To this add white slip.

White Slip
Feldspar 2lb
China clay... 3.5lb
Blue ball clay (Medcol) 10.5lb

Black Slip
Red earthenware body 8lb
Potash feldspar 1lb
China clay... 8oz
Red iron oxide 1lb 8oz

Transparent Glaze for Slipware
Lead sesquisilicate 74
China clay... 12
Potash feldspar 5
Flint 7
Whiting... 2

Lucie Rie   CR 134, 150, 163, 165

Transparent
Lead bisilicate 1000
Feldspar 150
    The glaze may be improved by substituting part of the feldspar by china clay.

Opaque
Lead bisilicate 1200
Zinc oxide... 200
Feldspar 150
Tin oxide.. 130

Semi Opaque
Lead bisilicate 95
Cornish stone 20
Barite (barium sulphate) 2
China clay.. 10
Zinc oxide.. 10
Tin oxide.. 10

ZNN
Lead bisilicate 142.5
Cornish stone 30
Barite 3
China clay..15
Zinc oxide..15
Tin oxide...15

Sara Robertson CR 181

Basic White Slip
White ball clay..60
China clay...40

> My approach to colour is that of a painter and I often mix underglaze powder into white slip until the colour looks right. I paint slip onto newspaper and make lines and marks by drawing into it with a metal tool. I then paint over this with another slip which becomes the colour of the lines. The images print back to front when transferred onto the clay. I work with three clear glazes given to me by Nigel Wood.

High Lead 1080-1100°C
Lead sesquisilicate 74
Cornish stone 15
China clay...7
Flint or quartz 4

> I use this glaze for its warm rich colours and lush, shiny surface.

Eggshell Matt 1080-1100°C
Lead bisilicate 62
Cornish stone 9
Whiting..11
China clay...21

> I like glaze for its subtle, non-reflective surface and more muted colours.

Clear Leadless 1040-1120°C
Calcium borate frit......................................70
SMD ball clay..30

> This glaze creates clean, crisp colours and a softness in the black lines. I biscuit fire to 1000°C and glaze fire to 1100°C using an electric kiln.

Anita Sattentau-Scott CR 146

Earthenware Glazes 1020-1050°C

Transparent
Lead bisilicate 41
Standard borax frit.....................................50
China clay...9

> Opalescent wilh very small additions of iron, or over red clay.

Transparent
Lead bisilicate 85

Cornish stone 15
   Suitable for additions of commercial glaze stains, and some colouring oxides. Cobalt oxide gives unsightly spots.

Glossy White
Lead bisilicate 66
Standard borax frit 15
China clay...4
Tin oxide..10
Zinc oxide...5
   Delicate pink/mauves will small additions of manganese compounds.

White
Lead bisilicate 42.5
Standard borax frit 22
China clay...15
Flint 7.5
Tin oxide..4.5
Zinc oxide...8.5
   Amazing Chinese blues with very small additions of cobalt carbonate.

Matt White
Lead bisilicate 42
Standard borax frit 30
China clay...5
Tin oxide..5
Zinc oxide...18

Cream
Lead bisilicate 48
Standard borax frit 32
Zinc oxide...10
Rutile (light) 10
   Dark 'Aventurine' brown with 3% addition of manganese oxide. Cool slowly.
   These six glazes give reliable results at 1020-1050°C. The suggested additions or other alterations may render them unsuitable for domestic use. Any low temperature glaze which is intended for table or ovenware should be tested at a laboratory authorised to carry out British Standard safety tests. Colouring oxides may be added to any of the glazes. Copper compounds will give a toxic release in all of them. Chrome will give only browns in zinc-bearing glazes. Large quantities of colouring oxides will reduce the maturing temperature and the glaze will run.

Sarah Scampton CR 123

Glaze 1020-1060°C

Flint	54
Lithium carbonate	30
China clay	10.5
Bentonite	1
Copper carbonate*	3

*(or any oxide for colour, optional)

> A lower temperature results in a more matt surface. At the higher temperature it becomes shinier.

Sarah-Jane Selwood CR 148

Porcelain Glaze Recipes

Blue Crackle Celadon

Potash feldspar	55
Whiting	8
Barium carbonate	15
China clay	5
Flint	17
Iron oxide	1.5

White Satin Matt

Potash feldspar	25
Cornish stone	20
Whiting	10
Dolomite	10
Talc	8
China clay	20
Flint	7

> I have an 8 cubic foot gas kiln. I bisque to 1020°C, the glaze firing is to 1260-1280°C. I start lightly reducing at 1000°C increasing to a fairly heavy reduction by 1200°C, soaking for 45 minutes when cone 8 bends.

Alan Sidney

Off-white Semi-matt High Fired Earthenware Orton Cone 01

Lead bisilicate	100
China clay	50
Whiting	25
Tin oxide	5
Dolomite	5
Vanadium pentoxide	2
Bentonite	1

> To this can be added copper oxide and cobalt oxide. I use this glaze over Potclays 1129 St Paul's Clay, with which body the iron breaks thorough on edges. The glaze also works well with underglaze colours.

Clive Simmonds

Deep Brown Glaze for use on Flat Surface 1100°C
G92 (from C.J. Baines) 13
F1739 (from C.J. Baines) 16
Black copper oxide..2
Naturally red iron oxide 6
Crocus martis 6

Frosted Green Glaze for use on Flat Surface 1100°C
Lead bisilicate 96
Black copper oxide..1.5
Dark rutile 7
Bentonite 1.5

> Rutile causes attractive crystalline reactions. Alkali frit P2250 when substituted for the lead frit will give a powerful blue turquoise.

Peter Smith

Bodies for a coal buring fired to a nominal 1080°C

> These bodies are designed to withstand direct flame impingement and are capable of being fired to much higher temperatures than 1080°C. Wherever possible the clays are mixed as thick slips and the grit is wedged into the body near the time of use.

Body 1
Staffordshire red clay....................................3
Dobles fireclay 1
Ball clay 0.5
Grit – 10 mesh 10%
Grit – 3/16 mesh + 10 mesh 10%

Body 4
Ball clay 2
Staffordshire red clay....................................1
Dobles fireclay 1
Grit – 10 mesh 5%
Grit – 3/16 mesh + 10 mesh 10%

Body 6
Ball clay 2
Thistle fireclay 1
Dobles fireclay 0.5
Grit – 3/16 mesh + 10 mesh 10%

> The grit is the stated fraction of the rock out of which china clay is washed and consists mainly of quartz and mica with some iron bearing materials.

Suppliers
Thistle fireclay ex. – GR Stein, Bonnybridge, Scotland
Dobles fireclay ex. – Dobles, St Agnes, Cornwall
Other clays – Usual suppliers
Grit – Local china clay pit that I collect myself

John Solly CR 166
(work illustrated)

White Slip
Ball clay and china clay 50/50

Blue Slip
Ball clay 97
Cobalt oxide 2
Manganese dioxide 1

Green Slip
Ball clay 97
Copper oxide 2.5
Red iron oxide 0.5

Black Slip
Dry red body 92
Manganese dioxide 6
Cobalt oxide 2

Tan Slip Mix
Red clay 33.3
Ball clay 66.6

All permutate well with the three standard glazes.

Transparent Shiny 1060-1100°C
Lead bisilicate or borax frit 39
Feldspar 27
Whiting 5
China clay 6
Flint or quartz 23
+ 10% tin oxide for maiolica, when the glaze will fire to 1140°C.

Transparent Hard Shiny (Good for Slipware)
Lead bisilicate or borax frit 52
China clay 16
Cornish stone 27
Whiting 5
    Usually soaked for about half hour (12 cu. ft. kiln)

Transparent Clear Glaze 1120-1140°C
Borax frit (or Lead bisilicate) 60
China clay 14
Cornish stone 21
Whiting 5
+ Red iron oxide for 'honey' 5%
+ Copper oxide for 'green' 2.5%
    Usually soaked for about half hour (12 cu. ft. kiln)

Mark Stanczyk CR 102

Multi-purpose Body Oxidation 1140-1160°C (Raku 1000-1140°C)
T-material 72
Red clay 7
Talc 10
Bone ash 3
Sand/molochite/or
grog to your requirements 8

>Measures in dry weight. The additional ingredients effectively lower the maturing temperature from 1280-1300°C to 1140-1160°C yet maintain the virtues of high tensile working strength, and fired durability. It is an exceptional body for multiple-firings and more experimental slip and glaze applications.
>
>It is best to thoroughly dry out T-material and breakdown before combining it with the red clay and slaking down for 24hrs.
>
>Bone ash and talc should be wet ground/ball milled into a thick slip before adding them to the other ingredients.

Bronze Slip (for Patination) 1100-1160°C
Manganese dioxide (coarse).....................100
Copper oxide (black) 24
Red clay 10
Soda ash 4

>If applied too thickly or overly multiple-fired the metal will begin to be affected by gravity and move, eating its way through the body. For this reason always remove (before firing) any metal based slips that accidentally get onto kiln furniture and brickwork. The above ingredients can be varied considerably to create a variety of effects from a golden bronze-antique finish to a cracked matt-black surface ideal for patination.
>
>As with any 'given' recipe which has been created for personal imagery the above should be considered as merely starting for your own developments and experiments.

Peter Venning

Dartington Mock Celadon 1120-1160°C
Any leadless, transparent,
earthenware glaze 44
Nepheline syenite 20
Whiting..8
China clay..10
Flint 5
Dolomite 5
Zircon silicate 8
Copper carbonate...2
Cobalt carbonate 0.25

>Designed for engraved decoration on white or pale bodies. Juggle the oxides for other tints. A little iron will soften the colour, 3-4% will give Northern Celadon.

Blue Mottle Glaze 1100-1160°C
Any leadless, transparent,
earthenware glaze 75
Nepheline syenite 15

Rutile 6
Ilmenite (fine)...2
Copper carbonate 3
Cobalt carbonate 2

> Best around 1140°C and particularly good over manganese tinted body (i.e. Potclays Chocolate Black) which gives rich reaction. Soak a little, followed by controlled cooling down to 800/750°C.

James F. Walford CR 124

Earthenware 1100°C
Feldspar 48
Whiting...12
Quartz..8
Standard borax frit...32

> A very useful glaze, given to me by my one-time teacher, the late Heber Mathews, with the addition of frit. The advantage is that one can devise a glaze for any intermediate temperature by adjusting the frit proportion. This is a low temperature glaze which somehow achieves a stoneware quality. It is in fact based on one of his standard stoneware glazes for 1280°C as follows:-

Feldspar 70
Whiting...18
Quartz..12

Glaze 1100°C
Standard borax frit...50
Feldspar 25
Quartz..10
Ball clay 15

> This is my own 1100°C recipe; a good all-purpose glaze.

Jane Waller CR 114, 144, 145, 147

Lead Bisilicate Glaze 1080-1100°C
Lead bisilicate 64
China stone 9.4
China clay..21
Whiting..5-10

Annie Turner's Matt Glaze 1140°C
Lead bisilicate 26
Borax frit (any)...36
Cornish stone 12
Ball clay 4

> Apply not too thick, not too thin.

Josie Walter CR 147, 149
(work illustrated)

Light Honey Glaze for Slipware Orton Cone 03
Lead bisilicate 75
Borax frit..5
Potash feldspar 10
Red clay (Potclays 1135/2).........................10
Bentonite 3

Transparent Glaze Orton Cone 03
Lead bisilicate 75
Borax frit..5
Potash feldspar 10
Ball clay 10
Bentonite 3

Decorating Glaze
Lead bisilicate 72
Whiting...5
Potash feldspar 16
China clay..5
Bentonite 3

Green
+ Chrome oxide...1
Brown
+ Manganese dioxide 4
Tan
+ Iron oxide 6

Mary Wondrausch CR 164
(work illustrated)

Clear Glaze 1070°C Orton Cone 05
Lead sesquisilicate 75
China clay (WBB)..18
Flint 6

Additions of 1 or 2% iron oxide gives pale and dark honey glaze. Fired for 12 hours at Sunvic 70, soaked 1 hour, 24 hours to cool.

Betty Woodman CR 183
(work illustrated)

Basic White Earthenware Slip
Silica..36
Feldspar 24
Kaolin 24
Ball clay 24
Frit 3124 12

Opax 12
This slip is for use on biscuit fired clay. For coloured slip add 12-15% stain.

Underglaze Colours
1 tablespoon of commercial colour to 2 tablespoons of colemanite

Leadless Glaze (Italy)
C.F.18 100
(An Italian non-lead frit available from Colorobia, Montelupo, Italy)
Colemanite 10
Talc 5
Bentonite 2

Lead Glaze
Lead carbonate 66
Kaolin 4
Silica 30
Bentonite 3

These glazes are applied to raw, dry clay. Firing is to 980°C. Betty Woodman uses different materials in the USA and Italy.

The lead glazes are unsuitable for use with food.

Clear Lead Glaze (USA)
Lead carbonate 63
Calcium carbonate 6.1
Kaolin 8.5
Silica 26
Bentonite 3

This glaze is suitable for gas or electric firing to Orton cone 04, 1050°C.

Mid-temperature Glazes
1180-1220°C
Oxidation

With growing concerns about fuel conservation and energy saving, increasing numbers of potters are looking to the mid temperature 1180-1220°C for effects that often have the qualities of higher fired wares. Interest in this area is growing rapidly and it is a range in which there are still many discoveries to be made.

John Chalke CR 116, 149, 154
(work illustrated)

Smooth Ivory Matt Cone 6-7 Oxidation
Nepheline syenite (Ontario) 56.8
Whiting..11.8
Zinc oxide (raw)..10.9
Kaolin 18.9
Flint 1.6
+ Vanadium pentoxide 5.8%

Barbara Colls CR 25

Matt Turquoise Cone 6 Oxidation
Barium carbonate...20
Soda feldspar 60
Dolomite 20
Bentonite 1
Copper carbonate 2.5

    Good over speckled bodies. Runs on porcelain. Glaze fairly thickly but watch the foot rims.

Edgar Delsaer

Raw Glazes Cone 5-6 Reduction Firing 950°C

Dry Matt Beige-yellow
Calcium borate frit 15
Dolomite 40
DBG ball clay 45
Bentonite 2
Rutile 4
+ Cobalt carbonate ....0.5% – blue

Spotted Satinee Light Brown
Cornish stone 15
Wollastonite 38
DBG ball clay 32
Coarse ilmenite 15
Bentonite 2

Opaque Ginger
Lithium carbonate 3
Calcium borate frit 20
Bone ash 6
Dry red earthenware clay 60
Flint 11
Bentonite 2

Matt Satinee Ash Glaze

Nepheline syenite 35
Talc 15
Mixed wood ash (sieved not washed)........30
DBG ball clay 20
Bentonite 3
Crocus martis 5

Light brown with dark specks.

These glazes are used for once firing (raw glaze). I do not bisque my work. Medium reduction from ±950°C till the end with no oxidation. The firing range of the glazes at this temperature is very short, only half a cone difference is allowed.

Geoffrey Eastop

Granular White 1200-1220°C Oxidation

Feldspar 58
Whiting..24
China clay..10
Flint 6
Titanium oxide 5
Zinc oxide..3

Fire slowly in middle period 1050-1150°C. Apply fairly thickly. Broken white with opalescence. Good over slips and oxides.

Carenza Hayhoe CR 181
(work illustrated)

Glaze No.7.11 Shell Pink

Nepheline syenite 35
HVAR ball clay..10
Bentonite 2
Whiting..15
Quartz..19
Frit 2268 calcium borate 9
Tin oxide..10

Glaze No. 7.55.1 Pale Blue Talc Vellum

Nepheline syenite 20
HVAR ball clay..20
Whiting..10
Talc 30
Zinc oxide..20
Cobalt oxide 0.25%

Glaze No. 7.29 Green-Black Matt

Nepheline syenite 35
HVAR ball clay..12
Flint 19
Whiting..17
Magnesium carbonate 7

Tin oxide 10
Copper oxide 2%

Glaze No. Mixed Ash 1 with Copper Oxide
Nepheline syenite 35
HVAR ball clay 6
China clay 6
Quartz 19
Whiting 15
Mixed ash 19
Copper oxide 1%

Glaze No. 8.78 Dark Glossy
Soda feldspar 25
HVAR ball clay 25
Quartz 25
Dolomite 15
Bone ash 5
Lithium carbonate 5
Red iron oxide 10%
   Brown-black with a blue haze.

Glaze No. 8.41.11 Peacock Blue
Potash feldspar 40
HVAR ball clay 15
Quartz 20
Whiting 15
Zinc oxide 10
Titanium dioxide 10%
Cobalt oxide 0.75%
Copper oxide 1%

Starter Kit

Robin Hopper's Basic Recipe for Cone 6
Any feldspar 35
Any ball clay 12
Whiting 17
Flint/quartz 19
Any flux 17

   Zinc, barium carbonate and boric oxide are the three main mid-temperature fluxes. If you are raring to go and don't know where to begin try the following recipes which previously appeared in 'London Potters Newsletter' No. 71 June/July 1999 in 'It's All Greek to Me III'.

Clear Glaze
Nepheline syenite 40
HVAR ball clay 5
China clay 8
Whiting 16
Flint 21
Zinc oxide 10
   Apply thinly.

Semi Matt

Cornish stone 50
HVAR ball clay 23
Bentonite 2
Whiting..25

    Good with any colour oxides or 10% tin oxide.

Dry Smooth

Nepheline syenite 35
HVAR ball clay 12
Whiting..17
Flint 19
Bone ash 3.4
Talc 13.6

    Based on Robin Hopper's 17% any flux recipe. For shiny crazed glazes try calcium borate frit as part or all of your 17%. For dramatic colour response try barium carbonate on its own or in combination. Interesting results can be obtained from adding a little ash to a dull test. Tip all tests and scrapings into one bucket and you may have end up with a magic mix. I have one at the moment which is white with gold flecks – sadly I shall never be able to repeat it.

    Firing: 4 cubic foot top loading electric kiln. Bisque to 980°C. Glaze 150°C per hour to 1190°C with 30 minutes soak.

Sylvia Hyman

Oxidation Cone 4-6 Apricot

Nepheline syenite 36.9
Wollastonite 14.5
Barium carbonate...14.5
Gerstley borate (calcium borate frit) 9.7
China clay...9.7
Flint 10
Lithium carbonate 4.7
Mason stain No. 6121 ....15%

Oxidation Cone 4-6 Crimson

Nepheline syenite 37.2
Wollastonite 14.6
Barium carbonate...14.6
Gerstley borate (calcium borate frit) 9.8
China clay...9.8
Flint 10.1
Lithium carbonate 3.9
Mason stain no. 6006...................................10%

Oxidation Cone 4-6 Turquoise

Nepheline syenite 43
O.M. No. 4 ball clay 6
Barium carbonate...33
Flint 7
Lithium carbonate 11
Copper carbonate 2%

Oxidation Cone 4-6 Dark Purple
F4 Feldspar (soda) 37
Kaolin 9
Whiting 9
Talc 18
Flint 19
Lithium carbonate 8
Rutile 0.6%
Cobalt oxide 2.0%

To all glazes add:
Bentonite 2%
Few drops of CMC
Epsom salts ....1 tsp. per 100gm

Katharine Pleydell-Bouverie

Off White Glaze 1190°-1200°C Oxidation
Petalite 8
Soda feldspar 12
Potash feldspar 6
Whiting 12
Mixed ash 12
Quartz 10
China clay 8

Barbara Tipton CR 125

Porcelain Slip Base Cone 6
Kona F4 feldspar 15
Nepheline syenite 10
No. 6 Tile clay (or Grolleg) 45
Tennessee 7 (or 5) ball clay 15
Flint 15

> This has proved to be a reliable slip on any of the cone 6-9 porcelains I have used over the years. (Actually its a cone 8-9 porcelain I used before switching to lower firing temperatures). Additions of the following Mason stains will allow a fairly varied palette, though any stain can be used.

Peacock 6336 ....6%
Mazarine 6300 ....6%
MnAlCo lavender 6319 ....8%
Saturn orange 6121 ....8%
Black 6600 ....6%
MnAl pink 6020 ....8%
Vanadium yellow 6404 ....6%

Slip Variation Cone 6
Porcelain slip base 68
Nepheline syenite 28.4
Lithium carbonate 3.6

This slip is a more textured, slightly glossy variation.

Transparent Base Glaze Cone 6
Kona feldspar (potash) 40
Gerstley borate 15
Whiting..15
No.6 Tile clay (china clay)..........................15
Flint 15

Unless applied very thinly, this glaze does not craze on my commercial cone 6 porcelain body. By itself, it is useful over slip or underglaze-decorated functional ware; as a base for experiment it has yielded several interesting surfaces, one being the following recipe:

Orange Glaze Cone 6
Transparent base glaze................................77
Rutile 23

A matt, slightly crawled glaze.

Edwin Todd

Matt Glaze Tan Shading to Brown Cones 5-7
Lead bisilicate 610
Nepheline syenite 90
Kaolin 221
Whiting..50
Rutile 34

For white add:
Tin oxide..41
Zircopax 41

Another Interesting Glaze, Fat White Shading to Tan
Cryolite 28
Lithium carbonate 32
Barium carbonate..40
Zinc oxide..16
Nepheline syenite 248
Flint 12
Tin oxide..8
Zircopax 24

All our glazes are oxidised fired.

Gordon Baldwin's earthenware matt glaze (see earthenware chapter) can be amended to a white matt to fire at standard cone 5 by adding the following materials:
China clay...10
Rutile 3
Tin oxide..3
Zircopax 3

Maribel Todd

Opaque Glaze Orton Cone 1-9
Colemanite 550
Cornish stone 1440
Kaolin 100
Steatite 382

Richard Zakin CR 74
(work illustrated)

Medium Temperature Glazes 1222°C Oxidation

Pumice Glaze
Barium carbonate 6
Gerstley borate (calcium borate frit) 12
Ground pumice 40
Wollastonite 10
Zinc oxide 2
Ball clay 12
Silica 18
    A shiny, transparent glaze, abrasion resistant.

Satin Matt I
Barium carbonate 10
Gerstley borate (calcium borate frit) 20
Nepheline syenite 30
Wollastonite 20
Zirconium silicate opacifier 10
Ball clay 10
    A soft opaque matt.

Drummond Base
Wollastonite 30
Soda feldspar 22
Spodumene 12
Kaolin 10
Barium carbonate 10
Opax 8
Flint 6
Bone ash 2
    A translucent satin base.

Troy IV Base
Nepheline syenite 30
Wollastonite 20
Ball clay 20
Gerstley borate (calcium borate frit) 10
Barium carbonate 10
Zirconium opacifier 10
    A translucent satin matt.

Gower Base

Nepheline syenite 33
Barium carbonate 24
Flint 23
Gerstley borate (calcium borate frit) 10
Ball clay 6
Whiting 3
Magnesium carbonate 1
Iron oxide 0.6

A shiny translucent glaze, very smooth, hard and abrasion resistant. (The iron is part of the base formula. Other colourants or more iron may be added.)

Coburg Base

Potash feldspar 41
Whiting 15
Barium carbonate 14
Kaolin 13
Zirconium opacifier 9
Gerstley borate (calcium borate frit) 8

A satin matt opaque glaze base.

Karen's Base Glaze

Nepheline syenite 40
Dolomite 20
Flint 20
Kaolin 10
Bone ash 6
Zinc oxide 4

A frosty translucent glaze.

Cardington Base

Nepheline syenite 37
Barium carbonate 24
Flint 15
Gerstley borate (Calcium borate frit) 14
Ball clay 5
Dolomite 4
Iron oxide 0.6

A broken textured satin matt glaze in many ways similar to the Gower base glaze. The 0.6% iron oxide is part of the base formula.

Huntley Engobe

Kaolin 36
Nepheline syenite 25
Flint 18
Dolomite 10
Gerstley borate (calcium borate frit) 6
Zirconium opacifier 5

Brutus Base I

Albany slip clay 43
Wollastonite 38
Whiting 15

Lithium carbonate 2
Bone ash 2

This glaze works best over other glazes. It encourages rich, broken textures.

Brutus Base II
Wollastonite 45
Albany slip clay 41
Spodumene 11
Bone ash 3

This too works best over other glazes, encouraging rich, broken textures and modulations.

K15 Glaze
Nepheline syenite 40
Dolomite 18
Flint 18
China clay 12
Bone ash 6
Lithium carbonate 2
Zinc oxide 4
+ Copper carbonate 2

Carbonate Variation
Nepheline syenite 35
Barium carbonate 22
Flint 14
Gerstley borate (calcium borate frit) 12
Zirconium opacifier 9
Ball clay 5
Lithium carbonate 2.5
Zinc oxide 0.3
+ Cobalt oxide 1.5
  Rutile 1

A rich royal blue.

Coburg Variation
Potash feldspar 40
Whiting 15
Barium carbonate 14
China clay 12
'Opax' (zirconium silicate) 9
Gerstley borate (calcium borate frit) 7
Lithium carbonate 2.5
Zinc oxide 0.3
+ Copper carbonate 2

A lime green colour.

Gower II Variation
Nepheline syenite 30
Flint 20
Barium carbonate 18
Gerstley borate (calcium borate frit) 10
Zirconium opacifier 9
Ball clay 6

Whiting 4
Lithium carbonate 2.5
Zinc oxide 0.5
+ Copper carbonate 2
   A soft, cool, green-coloured glaze.

Brantingham Copper Blue
Nepheline syenite 34
China clay 24
Talc 24
Tin oxide 8
Gerstley borate (calcium borate frit) 6
Zinc oxide 2
Lithium carbonate 2
+ Copper carbonate 2.5
   A mossy green. This is a rather frosty looking glaze with a subtle visual texture.

Troy I Variation
Nepheline syenite 30
Wollastonite 20
Gerstley borate (calcium borate frit) 18
Ball clay 10
Barium carbonate 10
'Opax' (zirconium silicate) 9
Lithium carbonate 2.5
Zinc oxide 0.5
+ Cobalt oxide 1
for a clear medium blue or:
Iron oxide 2
Rutile 2
   This is a very durable glaze with a strongly patterned visual texture. It can be used over other glazes for increased texture possibilities.

Sabbattis GK 3X Variation
Wollastonite 30
Soda feldspar 22
China clay 12
Barium carbonate 16
Zirconium opacifier 9
Flint 2
Bone ash 2
Lithium carbonate 2.5
Zinc oxide 0.5
+ Cobalt oxide 1%
   A rich medium blue.

Westdale Glaze I
Nepheline syenite 30
Ball clay 20
Wollastonite 18
Gerstley borate (calcium borate frit) 10
Barium carbonate 10
Zirconium opacifier 7

Zinc oxide..........3
Lithium carbonate 2
+ Copper carbonate..........2%
   A clear strong green.

Westdale Glaze II
Nepheline syenite 30
Wollastonite 20
Ball clay 20
Gerstley borate (calcium borate frit) 9
Barium carbonate 8
Zirconium opacifier 10
Lithium carbonate 2.5
Zinc oxide..........0.5
+ Copper carbonate..........2
   This is a rich, translucent, green-coloured glaze with good surface texture.

Satin Matt II
Barium carbonate
Gerstley borate (calcium borate frit) 16
Nepheline syenite 28
Wollastonite 11
Zirconium silicate opacifier 20
Kaolin 10
Silica..........5
   An opaque satin glaze.

Chenies Base
Soda feldspar 31
Spodumene 15
Barium carbonate 15
Gerstley borate (calcium borate frit) 8
Magnesium carbonate 7
Whiting..........6
Kaolin 6
   A satin matt translucent glaze base.

Stonewares 1220°C Oxidation

Light Buff Body
Stoneware clay 45
Kaolin 35
Nepheline syenite 5
Wollastonite 5
Flint 5
Ball clay 5

Dolomite White Body
Kaolin 30
Velvacast 18
Flint 16
Nepheline syenite 14
Dolomite 8

Potash feldspar 7
Ball clay 7

> N.B. Velvacast is a coarse particled Kaolin (mean particle size 3.5-4.5 microns rather than the 1.0-1.3 microns of the Kaolin). This gives some particle size variation in the body. The clay was originally intended for mouldmakers (hence the name), again because of its large particle size. Any English china clay will make a suitable alternative and, having a slight plasticity and a low titanium content, may even be better.

UBI White Fireclay
Kaolin 45
Potash feldspar 20
Ball clay 15
Fireclay 15
Flint 5

August Tan Fireclay
Plastic fireclay 55
Potash feldspar 14
Flint 11
Fireclay 10
Red clay (terracotta) 5
Ball clay 5

> Test these with your own fireclay before using them. The fireclay I use is high in silica (70%). If your test is immature, use a different fireclay or add more potash feldspar. I make my clay bodies using the dewatering method. I dry the clay in large bisque fired bowls or between newspapers. The latter method sounds messy but with care it is not. After the bodies are dewatered they are wedged. At this time I add plain, unflavoured yogurt (the natural variety with no added gelatin). The yogurt bacteria grow very nicely in clay, especially in a warm environment such as is found near the kiln.

Anna Noël – Animal, modelled, smoke fired.

Ian Byers – Cup and Stand, high alkaline glaze with oxides and stains, raku, post firing reduction.

Eeles family – Bottle, wood–fired raku with brushed pattern and copper matt glaze, 980°C.

Harry Horlock Stringer – detail, raku–fired glaze with post reduction copper oxide.

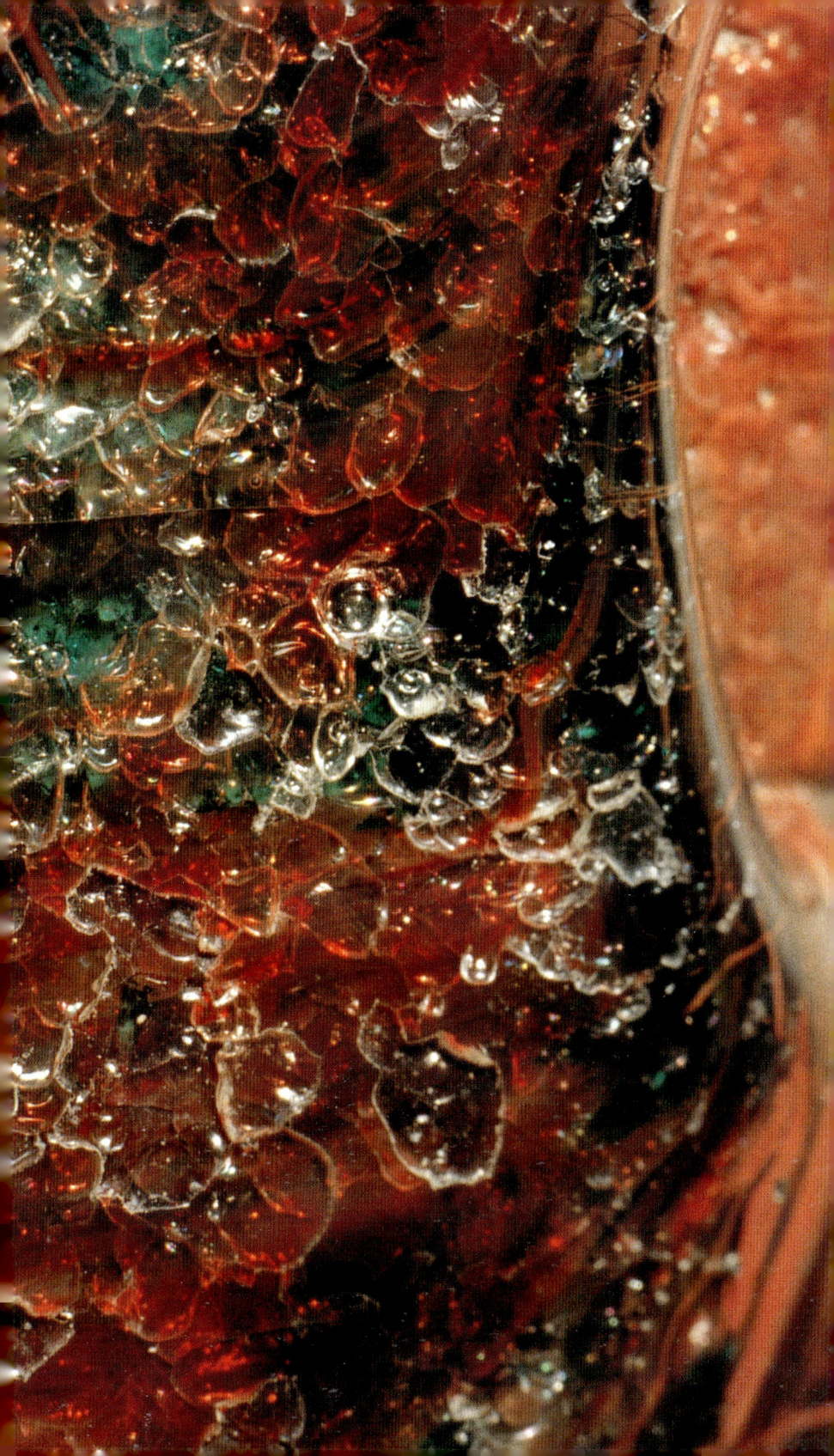

David Roberts – Vessel with pedestal, hand built, raku with resist slip decoration.

Susan Halls – Dinosaur, modelled.

Opposite Page **Paul Soldner** – Vessel form, hand built with raku glaze.

Neil Brownsword – She Wants Your Junk, 1998, ceramic collage (earthenware), metal, found object, H42cm. Photograph Andrew Pritchard

Simon Carroll – Vessel, thrown and hand built with slips and oxides and clear glaze.

Alison Britton – Pleated Yellow Pot, hand built, clear glaze over colours, H48cm. Photograph Phil Sayer

Bennett Cooper – Pressed and thrown dishes, 1999, clear glaze over decoration, earthenware, Ø30-46cm.

Tessa Fuchs – Toucan Tree, sprayed stained earthenware glazes, cone 04, electric kiln.

Clive Bowen – Two Jugs, thrown, with slip and oxide decoration under clear glaze.

Daphne Carnegy – Plate, thrown with painted decoration and white tin glaze.

Stephen Dixon – Living in the Past, 1993. Bronze brown and cream coloured clays, matt white and transparent shiny base glaze with oxides and stains, 1180°C. Photograph Len Grant

Sara Robertson – Detail 'Love Letters', 2000. Ceramic wall dish, Ø55cm.

Walter Keeler – Sauce Boat and two Jugs, 1999. Thrown and hand built with oxides and clear earthenware glaze.

Mary Wondrausch – Quince Plate, slip trailed and scratched with painted slips and oxides under clear glaze, Ø35cm.

Sophie MacCarthy – Trellis, thrown and decorated, clear earthenware glaze, Ø41cm.

Betty Woodman – Assembled Vessel Form with oxide decoration under clear earthenware glaze.

Michael and Victoria Eden – Curved dish, L28cm.

John Solly – Dish, clear glaze over green glaze over black, blue, white and brown slips, 1140°C.

Josie Walter – Pasta Bowls (detail), transparent earthenware glaze with coloured glazes over white slip (WBB Puraflo TWVD 90, Flint 10). Photograph Ian Jeffery

Fenella Mallalieu – Harlequin Pasta Bowls, lead glazed earthenware, cone 04, Ø21cm.

David Miller – Oval Vessel, with wire cut rim, H17cm, W24cm. Photograph Bruno Flament

Jonathan Garratt – Disc, zinc fumed, 1080°C, wood–fired.

Regina Heinz – Weathered (detail), ceramic wall piece, soft slab construction, brushed lithium glaze, iron oxide, biscuit slip, 1035°C, 46 x 34 x 4cm. Photograph Alfred Petri

Carenza Hayhoe – Peacock Bowl.

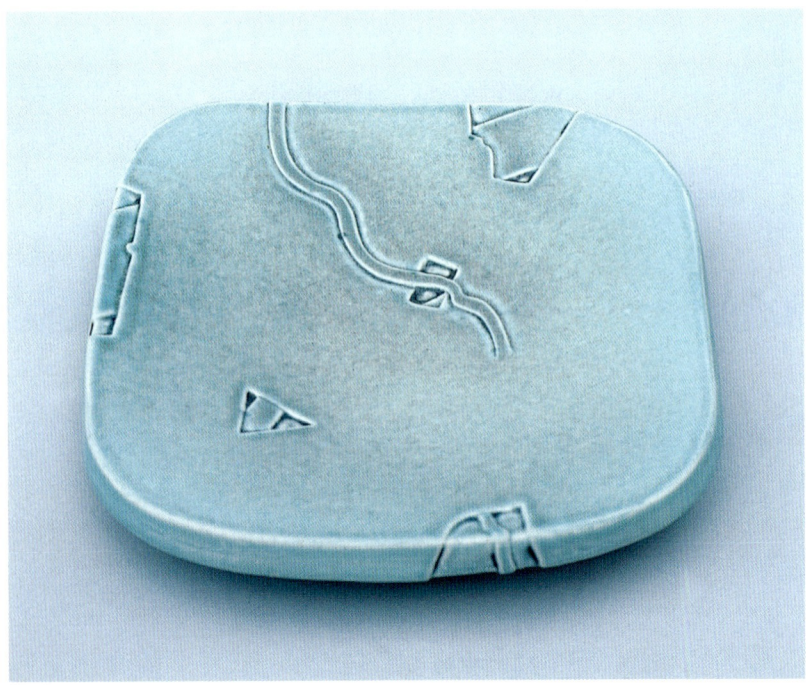

Richard Zakin – Dish, press moulded with lithium glaze.

John Chalke – Nail Head, Ø51cm.

Peter Beard – Arch, slab built, glazes 3 and 4, H40cm.

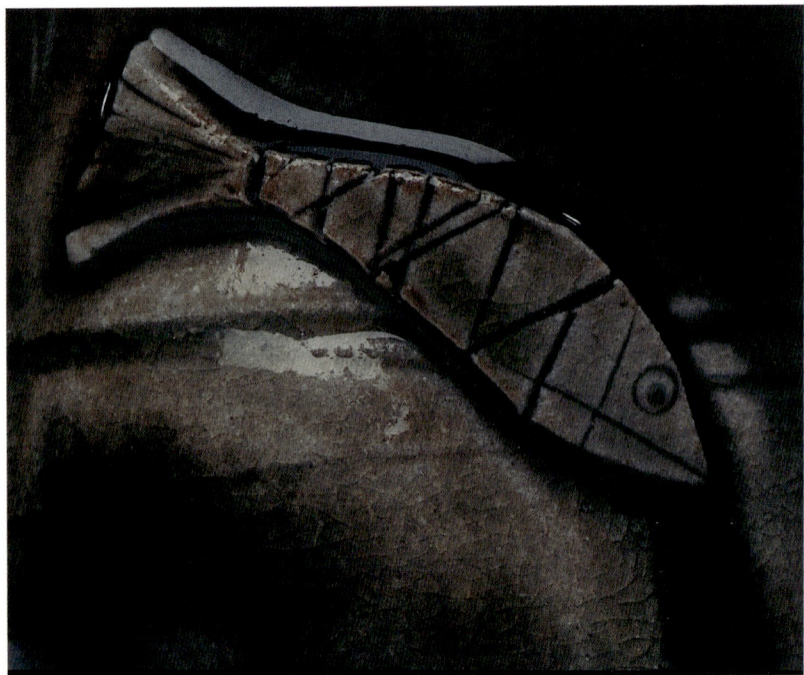

Terry Bell–Hughes – Mug, (detail). Thrown and modelled wih reduction fired fluid ash glaze, 1300°C.

Photograph Dewi Tannatt Lloyd

Mike Bailey and David Hewitt – Test tiles. Clockwise top left: green-brown, orange-red, oil spot, blue-grey.

John Calver – Vase, H20cm. Thrown Potclays White St Thomas body, chattered decoration with sponge floral motifs using rutile slip and iron slip, covered with glaze No. 3, reduction fired in oil kiln, Orton cone 10–11.

Kyra Cane – Four Pots, 2000. Black underglaze and nickel oxide brush decoration with GK2 white glaze, H44cm Photograph Mike Simmons

Opposite Page **Dartington Pottery** – Toucan jugs (detail), 2000. Celadon glaze.

Richard Dewar – Footed Dish with Handles. Lavender glaze (No. 2) inside; outside decorated with the two slips plus cobalt carbonate/rutle to give green. The orange is an industrial stain, the blue/black cobalt in water.

Opposite Page **Ewen Henderson** – Tall Vessel, hand built, stoneware.

Eileen Lewenstein – Wave Dish, press moulded stoneware with slip, oxide and glaze decoration, W29cm.

Jill Fanshaw Kato – Dove Sculpture, undercoat of white slip Photograph Setsuo Kato

Opposite Page **John Jelfs** – Vase, stoneware, H20cm.

Christy Keeney – Two Heads, stoneware.

Gilles le Corre – Large Platter, Ø34cm. Stoneware with white base glaze with blue and green glazes trailed on top, Orton cone 10. Photogragh Chris Honeywell

David Leach – Bottle. Thrown with temmoku glaze and iron/ilmenite decoration.

Roger Lewis – Cube Box. Semi-gloss, Orton cone 8, glaze on outside.

Gillian Lowndes – Loofahs (wall piece), 1994.

Stoneware and Porcelain
1220-1280°C
Oxidation and Reduction
Bodies, Slips, Glazes

Glazes for use over 1220°C are usually classified as stoneware. Most of the glazes work well on both porcelain and stoneware bodies but will give different results. Some potters point out which glazes they have tested and found successful for porcelain. Because of the large variation between different stoneware bodies, glazes react to give different effects. This is particularly evident at temperatures over 1260°C when body and glaze interaction increases. This can result in a wide variation of effects ranging from dry glazes where the body has 'sucked' in the glazes, to runny effects caused by a highly vitrified body. Sometimes a thicker application of glaze will help.

Potters are warned to test all glazes on the clay body they use with the ingredients they select and in their own kilns. Only then can the recipe be said to be 'fail safe'.

Billy Adams CR 144

Glaze 1080°C
Nepheline syenite 20
Barium carbonate..35
Lithium carbonate 10
Flint 11
China clay..19

> I apply this and then rub most of it off, allowing it to glaze the cracks only, and therefore the base colour still shows through.

Paula Appleby

Stoneware Body 1260°C Oxidation
Potclays DB...3
St Thomas White 1

Mick Arnup

Standard Stoneware Body Reduction
> I use Potclays 1104 body, which gives the glaze results.

Body for Very Large Pots
Potclays 1104 (plastic) 60
Leeds fireclay (dry) 30
Feldspar (dry) 10
Silver sand (dry)..10

1280°C Reduction Glaze
Whinstone cyclone dust 15
Ash tree ash 25
Nepheline syenite 30
Ball clay (TWVD or similar) 30

> Produces a very sound orange-brown glaze in reduction. We have six elderly ash trees and a supply of Whinstone dust from a good neighbour who is a quarryman. This dolorite is a 'waste product' of the quarry crushers, but I think any basic rock dust would produce interesting glazes.

Ash Ash Glaze
Ash tree ash 38
Nepheline syenite 35
Talc 14
China clay...13

> This makes a rich mid brown textured glaze when reduced.

Silky Green Stoneware 1260°C
Potash feldspar...34
Flint 26
Whiting..18
Ball clay (SM)...13

Talc 9
Iron oxide 1.25

    An oxidising/neutral atmosphere at 1260°C will produce the special soft green of this recipe. A reduced 1280°C will give a bright mid celadon.

Chris Aston CR 96

Stoneware Bodies 1260-1280°C

Speckled Light Brown
HVAR 50
BBV 25
Nepheline syenite 325 mesh 9
Quartz 200 mesh 13
Fireclay grog 60's-85's 10
Red iron oxide 0.5

White Stoneware
HVAR 40
EWVA 40
Nepheline syenite 325 mesh 8
Quartz 200 mesh 12

    Particularly good for throwing due to the highly plastic EWVA clay.

Orange Brown Speckle
HVAR 50
BBV 25
Quartz 200 mesh 15
Nepheline syenite 325 mesh 9
Barium carbonate..2
Black iron oxide 0.5-1

    The barium carbonate makes the clay appear more opaque and imparts an opaque orange effect when iron oxide is contained in the clay.

High Silica Stoneware
HVAR 50
BBV 25
Quartz 200 mesh 15
Nepheline syenite 325 mesh 5
Red iron oxide (optional)...............................0.5

    A hard, dense clay body with good chip resistance.

Materials: HVAR, BBV, EWVA, are all ball clays from Watts Blake Bearne, Newton Abbot, Devon. Quartz 200 mesh silica flour from British Industrial Sands. Nepheline syenite is North Cape nepheline syenite from British Industrial Sands. All clays are mixed in a blunger, passed through vibratory sieve 60 mesh, filter pressed and pugged.

Calcium Magnesium Matt Glaze
Soda feldspar 23
Talc 14
China clay..30

Whiting 16
Quartz 18

Milky Satin Glaze
Soda feldspar 36
Wollastonite 26
China clay 22
Quartz 15

Magnesia Semi Opaque
Soda feldspar 44
Talc 8
China clay 20
Wollastonite 16
Quartz 12

Iron Red with Flecks
Soda feldspar 32
Whiting 18
China clay 35
Quartz 26
Red iron oxide 12
Titanium dioxide 3
Dolomite 18
Bone ash 8

Prone to running. Needs to be applied thinly.

Mixing by hand: Firing 1260-1280°C 85 cu.ft. Kerosene oil-fired kiln 19 hours heating, 36 hours cooling.

Materials: soda feldspar from Colin McNeal, Stoke on Trent. China clay from E.C.C. Meledor powder.

Mike Bailey & David Hewitt CR 147, 158
(work illustrated)

Two Oil Spot Glazes Cone 8 Oxidised

	No.1	No.2
Potash feldspar	11.7	25.7
Soda feldspar	17.4	36.2
China clay	28.4	17.4
Dolomite	6.4	6.9
Whiting	–	1.2
Flint or quartz	17.1	7.2
High alkaline frit	13.0	–
Red iron oxide	5.4	5.4
Barium carbonate	0.4	–
Lithium carbonate	0.3	–

A Bright Oil-spot Temmoku Cone 8 Oxidation
Potash feldspar 25
Soda feldspar 35
F3110 (High soda frit from Ferro) 5

Dolomite 5
Talc 5
China clay 15
Flint or quartz 8
Bentonite 2
Red iron oxide 6

Opaque Crystalline Blue Cone 8 Oxidation or Reduction
Potash feldspar 42.6
Dolomite 13
Whiting 14.6
China clay 3.8
Flint or quartz 16
Cobalt carbonate 0.6
Red iron oxide 1.5
Manganese dioxide 1.5
Zirconium silicate 12

The zirconium silicate can be left out to give a blue-grey glaze. This glaze is fairly sensitive to temperature; fired lower it stays opaque, fired higher it loses the crystals and becomes transparent.

Satin Grey Cone 9 Reduction
Potash feldspar 41.4
Dolomite 6.4
Whiting 9.5
China clay 21.5
Flint or quartz 21.5

A quiet glaze with a good colour response to oxides and coloured slips.

Bright Orange Red Cone 8 Oxidation
Potash feldspar 40.6
Talc 9.4
Bone ash 12.8
Lithium carbonate 2.2
TWVA ball clay 12.8
Flint or quartz 12.8
Red iron oxide 9.4

The lithium and bone ash have an amazing effect on the iron producing a bright orange glaze. A red iron oxide progression in this glaze goes from a black with red spots, through to red, then orange and finally khaki.

Variegated Green-brown Cone 8 Oxidation
Potash feldspar 38
Dolomite 16
Whiting 13
China clay 6
TWVA ball clay 6
Flint or quartz 14
Red iron oxide 5
Copper oxide 2

This is a high calcium glaze giving a broken texture ranging from golden brown to greeny brown. Looks good on models of monsters etc.

Gordon Baldwin CR 158, 179

Dolomite Based Glaze Orton Cone 7 Oxidation
Potash feldspar 41.5
Dolomite 7
Whiting 23
Clay 19.5
Flint 9
+ 6% Tin oxide or 20% Zircon (Dispersion)

    Same glaze base without tin oxide or Zircon is used combined with oxides (4% iron or 1% cobalt carbonate or 2% copper carbonate) or glaze stains (5-10%) to get colour effects.

Clear Shiny Glaze for Porcelain Orton Cone 7
Potash feldspar 57.59
Whiting 16.56
Clay 6.20
Flint 14.48
Zinc oxide 5.17

Barium Glaze Orton Cone 8
Nepheline syenite 70
Dolomite 5
Clay 10
Flint 10
Barium carbonate 20

Paul Barron

Temmoku Type for Raw Glazing Cone 9 Reduction
Potash feldspar 55
London clay 35
Whiting 10
Red iron oxide 2.5

    Use medium to thick. Cone 7 (genuine black matt) – Cone 10 (brown-black). Optimum temperature Cone 9.

    The clay is local, lowest level of the London beds, just over the chalk. Other red clays might be used but addition of flint at expense of whiting might be necessary. Iron is critical as with all temmoku to obtain the rust-black mutation, and will depend on brand and amount in body. For glazing biscuit calcine half the clay or, if thick, it will crawl.

Val Barry (Valerie Fox)

Satin Black – Staffordshire Cone 7a
Potash feldspar 42
Dolomite 13
Fireclay 8
Barium carbonate 2
Flint 20
Manganese dioxide 2

Cobalt oxide 3
Chrome oxide 1
Red iron oxide 4

White with Small Crystals – Staffordshire Cone 7a
Potash feldspar 18
China clay 31
Whiting 12
Quartz 15
Zinc oxide 23

Dark Speckled Brown – Staffordshire Cone 7a
Potash feldspar 50
Dolomite 25
Fireclay 13
Flint 15
Titanium dioxide 9
Manganese dioxide 9

All these glazes can be used on once fired ware.

Peter Beard CR 109
(work illustrated)

Clay 1280°C Oxidation
T-material (from most suppliers)
Scarva Earthstone range, all 3 grades (Scarva Pottery Supplies)

I mix these clays together in various combinations depending on the scale of work and whether it is thrown or slab built. I tend to use the two finer grades of the Scarva clays mixed 50/50 for throwing. Fired colour is pale which is a good ground for brighter colours.

I also use bone china from Les Bainbridge Ceramics, The Crescent, Heath Grove, Loggerheads, Market Drayton, TE9 4PE Tel/Fax: 01630 673762

Gold Glaze Cone 7 Oxidation
Manganese dioxide 7
Dry red clay 3
Copper oxide 1

Apply with a brush in several layers. China clay can be used instead of red clay. Runs very easily so test carefully.

Matt Black Oxide Cover Cone 7-10 Oxidation or Reduction
Copper oxide 1
Manganese dioxide 1
Red iron oxide 2

Apply with brush. In reduction tends to boil if thick which can be very interesting.

Dry Barium Glaze Base Cone 7-10 Oxidation or Reduction
Barium carbonate 33
Nepheline syenite 52
China clay 15.7

Add oxides for colour. Not for domestic ware; must be applied very carefully to avoid runs which show badly.

Useful supplier of clay and glaze materials:
Degg Industrial Minerals, Adderley Hill, Brookhouse Road, Cheadle, Stoke-on-Trent, ST10 2NJ Tel 01538 752236 Fax 01538 757350

Terry Bell-Hughes CR 170
(work illustrated)

Chun Type 1300°C Reduction
Potash feldspar 48
Flint 32
Whiting 16
Bone ash 4
Red iron oxide 1

Good over slips thinnish. When applied thicker it is bluer and more opaque.

Temmoku 1280°C Reduction
Potash feldspar 48
Flint 32
Whiting 16
China clay 6
Red iron oxide 11

Good over red slip medium thickness.

Ash Glaze 1280-1300°C Reduction
Wood ash 48
Potash feldspar 32
China clay 8
Ball clay 8

Dependent on ash. Good over slips medium thickness. Thicker tends to opalescence.

Shino Type 1280°C Reduction
Nepheline syenite 80
Ball clay 20

Orange rust where thin to hard white where thicker, good over slips. Dependent on type of ball clay. Reduction starts at cone 6 and continues to cone 9.

Suzanne Bergne

Matt-glaze Base for Strong Colour Reaction Cone 9-10 Electric Kiln
Nepheline syenite 56
Barium carbonate 25
Ball clay 6
Flint 7
Lithium carbonate 3
Bentonite 3

Any oxide addition will produce a strong colour. For example:
Copper carbonate 3   strong turquoise
Copper carbonate 1   light turquoise with

+ Rutile 6   a yellow speckle
Cobalt carbonate 1   electric violet blue
Copper carbonate ....0.5   Light green
+ Chrome oxide..0.5

Audrey Blackman CR 56

Impervious Stoneware 1140-1160°C Oxidation
Ball clay 13
Cornish stone 2
Bentonite 1
Sand 1

> Katharine Pleydell-Bouverie gave me this recipe to which, with her help, I added oxides to give me a range of coloured bodies for inlay or marbling.

Porcelain 1270-1280°C Electric Kiln
Super Standard Porcelain China Clay........50
Westone – H
(Sodium-activated white Texas bentonite) ..5
FF feldspar 27
Quartz (M 300)..17
Whiting..1

> This is a dry-weight recipe, but the china clay is normally supplied at about 10% moisture, so 55 parts should be taken to get 50 parts dry. M 300 quartz from Sibelco was used, but any good quality potters quartz should do. If the body shows signs of sagging at high temperature, leave out the whiting, and even try feldspar 25%, quartz 20%.

David & Sally Body CR 134

Glaze No.1 1300°C Reduction
China clay..22
Feldspar 39
Ash 22

Glaze No.2 1300°C
China clay 110
Calcinated china clay...............................110
FFF feldspar 412
Borax frit..50
Whiting...132
Talc 11
Bone ash 11
Bentonite 33
Flint 11

To this recipe I add:
Zirconium silicate 60

> The zirconium whitens the glaze and retards the blushing from the copper oxide as without it the glaze can be very grey/red – a plum red matt glaze – especially if heavily reduced.

A Plum-red Matt Glaze
To the basic glaze with no zirconium silicate I add:
Tin oxide 3
Copper carbonate 0.25

Colours
The following colours I use are mixed with 0.5 pint of base glaze and the oxides and stains are measured out with a Cow & Gate baby milk measuring spoon equal to 10 gm approx. (really high tech). Stains from Potterycrafts.

Dark Green
Chrome oxide ....2 spoons
Light Green
Chrome oxide ....0.25 spoon
Canary yellow stain ....4 spoons
Dark Blue
Cobalt carbonate ....0.25 spoon
Jay blue stain ....2 spoons
Light Blue
Jay blue stain ....1 spoon
Pink
Rosso orange-red stain ....1 spoon
Black
Cobalt carbonate ....2 spoons
Iron chromate ....1 spoon
Manganese dioxide ....1 spoon
For the grey-blue dots on my pots
Cobalt carbonate ....0.25 spoon
Rutile light ....2 spoons

Alan H. Bolton

Clear Glaze Cone 9 Oxidation
Potash feldspar 40
Whiting 22
Quartz 30
China clay 8

With the following additions:
Light Green
Copper carbonate 3
Light Honey (now used as a celadon in reduction)
Red iron oxide 3
Subtle Blue
Red iron oxide 0.5
Cobalt oxide (or carbonate) 0.5

Matt Green Cone 9 Reduction
Potash feldspar 45
Whiting 25
China clay 25
Talc 5

Copper carbonate 1
Red iron oxide 1
   Must not be underfired
   Also my thanks to Mick Casson as his temmoku glaze is now my main glaze although I have found 10% red iron oxide acceptable.

Harriet E. Brisson

Textured Red Orton Cone 9
Feldspar 261-F 41.7
Kaolin 1.7
Flint 26.1
Whiting...7
Gerstley borate 8.7
Dolomite...8.7
Zinc oxide..6.1
Tin oxide..2.6
Copper carbonate 0.45

Deep Red Orton Cone 9
Nepheline syenite 42.4
Feldspar 261-F 9.1
Kaolin 2
Flint 22.7
Gerstley borate 13.2
Whiting...10.6
Copper carbonate 0.3
Tin oxide..1

Peach Bloom Orton Cone 9
Feldspar C–6 ....34.6
Feldspar 261–F 43.2
Gerstley borate 10.6
Whiting...11.6
Copper carbonate 0.3
Tin oxide..1
   Calcium borate frit can be substituted weight for weight for gerstley borate.

Bill Brown

Ilmenite Glaze Orton Cone 9 Reduction
Feldspar 58
Dolomite..20
Talc 15
Ball clay 10
Ilmenite 0.5%
   Ochre coloured glaze. Buttery texture. Apply thickly.

Clear Glaze for Porcelain Orton Cone 9-10
Feldspar 33
Flint 33

China clay 17
Whiting 17
> Apply thinly over underglaze decoration. Can also be used at normal thickness with 0.5-3% iron for a smooth, bright celadon.

Ash Glaze Orton Cone 9 Reduction or Oxidation
Cornish stone 40
Wood ash 30
China clay 15
Whiting 15
> Fires to a dry-textured surface with colour changing due to thickness of application. Add 2.5% iron oxide for red-yellow break up. 1% cobalt for blue-green.

Celadon Orton Cone 9 Reduction
Feldspar 50
Flint 6
Whiting 14
China clay 14
Ball clay 6
Zinc oxide..8
Red iron oxide ....0.5 - 3%
> Fires pale blue to jade green, depending on the percentage of iron used. Mainly used on porcelain.

Michael Buckland

Copper Red Glaze 1300°C Reduction
Feldspar 51
Calcium borate frit 6.5
Dolomite 2.5
Whiting 9
Zinc oxide..2
Flint 29
Red iron oxide 1
Tin oxide..3
> The pot to be glazed should first be covered with a thin clear glaze, the copper red then being applied on top of this. When firing a good reduction must be maintained from 850°C until the maturing temperature of 1300°C is reached.

Matt Chun Blue 1300°C Oxidation and Reduction
Feldspar 37
China clay 30
Basic slag 3
Dolomite 9
Whiting 13
Flint 9
> This glaze works in both oxidised and reduced conditions but surface textures will differ under different atmospheres.

Christopher Buras

A Rainbow Raw Glaze 1250°C Electric Kiln
Ball clay 10
Petalite 2 0
Potash feldspar 40
Quartz 10
Dolomite (best quality) 10
Bentonite 5

With the addition of commercial glaze stain (up to 10%) this basic recipe gives a full palette of colour. This can be applied with a brush, poured or dipped in the standard way to a bone dry raw pot.

Ian Byers CR 142, 155

Rouge Red 1260°C Oxidation Orton Cone 8
Barium carbonate 41.7
Zinc oxide 11.1
Soda feldspar 31.7
Lithium carbonate 1.7
China clay 9.5
Flint 4.3
Nickel oxide 2%

Dry smooth glaze over white stoneware or porcelain.

Purple Red Brown and Yellow Glaze 1240-1260°C Oxidation
Soda feldspar 42.3
Flint 8.2
Zinc oxide 18
Barium carbonate 31.5
Nickel oxide 2%

Semi shiny over white stoneware. This glaze is very variable, but gives purple red where thick, brown yellow where thin. Runs if thickly applied or overfired. Beware shelves! The colour response is dependent upon a high barium and low alumina or clay content. Variations in colour can be tried keeping the alkaline content high but substituting some barium for lithium carbonate.

Mauve 1260°C Oxidation
Potash feldspar 20
Soda feldspar 18
Whiting 16
Zinc oxide 5
Barium carbonate 5
Magnesium carbonate 20
Flint 16
Cobalt carbonate 2%

Mauve where thick and crystalline blue where thinner.

Crystalline Glaze Silver Grey 1260°C Oxidation
Potash feldspar 52
Fluorspar 8

Flint 9
Zinc oxide..24
China clay...7

> Best over porcelain. Gives silver grey crystals in transparent base which can be tinted by light sprays of oxides e.g. copper and rutile give green crystals.

John Calver CR 128
(work illustrated)

Glaze No.1 Transparent, High Gloss
Potash feldspar 30.4
China clay...................................20.9
Whiting..10.4
Flint 23.5
Colemanite 4.4
Barium carbonate 5.2
Bone ash 5.2

Glaze No.2 Transparent Satin
Potash feldspar 29.2
Dolomite 16.7
China clay...................................25
Whiting...4.1
Flint 25

Glaze No.3 Smooth Matt
Potash feldspar 32.2
China clay...................................16.6
Whiting..20.5
Flint 19.5
Talc 11.2

> These three glazes are poured in two layers. First – glaze No.3, some areas with a double thickness. Second layer – glazes No.1 and No.2 with partial overlaps. Glaze No.1 over a double thickness of No.3 gives a bright but opaque titanium blue, while over a single thickness of No.3 the result is a transparent glossy amber glaze which highlights impressed patterns and reacts well with slips. Glaze No.2 over a single thickness of No.3 gives a translucent mottled dark grey which blends well with the other surfaces.

Rutile slip
Red earthenware clay..................30
Potash feldspar 40
Rutile 20
Black iron oxide 10

> Used with sponge stamps over paper resist decoration.

Iron Slip
Red earthenware clay..................50
Black iron oxide 50

> Used for banding and over paper resist decoration.

Kyra Cane CR 187
(work illustrated)

GK2 Cone 10 Reduction
Potash feldspar 48
Whiting...20
China clay...22
Flint 10
Titanium dioxide 8

> I have been working with GK2 for fifteen years and it still reveals surprises depending on the exact thickness and firing cycle. Usually I add black underglaze, building up layers of subtle colours. It has a smooth silky surface and responds well to oxides and underglazes.

Matt White Cone 9
Potash feldspar 50
Whiting...3
Dolomite...22
China clay...25

Michael Casson CR 106, 126, 189

Standard Body 1260-1300°C Reduction
HVAR ball clay (WBB) 86
Leeds fireclay 74
Potclays red Keuper marl............................30
Potash feldspar 10
80's mesh quartz 10
Silica sand (Aylesbury) 15

> This is modified with the addition of grog for throwing certain shapes and sizes.

Stoneware Body 1280-1300°C
Leeds fireclay 32
HVAR ball clay..50
Red iron oxide 1.5
Sand 6
Molochite 200-80 (Whitfield Minerals)........6
Potash feldspar 6

> A 'toasted' body, best in reduction but will oxidise.

Porcelain Body 1280°C
ECC porcelain china clay 4
Potash feldspar 2
Fine mesh flint (at least 300 mesh).............1
+ Bentonite 3-5%
(depending on type and iron content)

> Sieve separately and together, stir every day for a week, re-sieve, dry off and leave as long as possible – a year or more. Deflocculated this makes a fine casting slip.

Magnesium Glaze 1280°C Reduction
Cornish stone 33
Whiting...7

Ball clay 4
Magnesium carbonate 2
China clay 6
Iron oxide 1.5-3
    Minus the iron makes white, semi-opaque glaze at 1300°C.

Ash Glaze 1250-1280°C Reduction
Ash 50
Ball clay 25
China clay 25
    More ball clay, less china clay increases the shine slightly. Try adding 10-20% talc or dolomite for different effects.

Temmoku 1260-1300°C Reduction
Cornish stone 85
Whiting 15
China clay 8
Iron spangles 5
Crushed iron scales 5

Dolomite Glaze 1280°C Reduction
Potash feldspar 100
Soda feldspar 100
China clay 100
Whiting 14
Dolomite 80
Tin oxide 1

Slips
(a) SMD ball clay 50
     China clay 50
        Good under ash glazes in oil or gas kiln.

(b) AT ball clay – dark coloured slip

Sheila Casson   CR 106

Vitreous Slip 1280°C Reduction
Cornish stone 60
Ball clay 35
China clay 5
+ Red iron oxide up to 100
    Good under or over glazes thick or thin. This can be mixed half and half with red clay for variations, or 0.25 cobalt gives good blues. Used to spray and overspray to decorate porcelain bowls. The decorative technique included inlay, paper and latex resist and sgraffito.

Magnesium Glaze 1280°C Reduction
Cornish stone 63
Whiting 13
Hyplas 71 ball clay 8
China clay 12
Magnesium carbonate (light) 4

Dolomite and Tin Glaze 1280°C Reduction
Potash feldspar 24
Soda feldspar 24
China clay...24
Dolomite 21
Whiting..3
Tin oxide...4

Jenny Clarke

Semi-Matt White Cone 8-9 Oxidation
Potash feldspar 50
Dolomite 18
China clay...22
Quartz...3.5
Bone ash 3

This glaze makes a good dark brown with the addition of iron oxide.

Elm Ash Glaze Cone 8 Oxidation
Elm ash 40
Feldspar 30
Ball clay 25
Flint 5
Iron oxide 2

Derek Clarkson   CR 107, 137

My glaze firings take approx. 5 hrs with continuous strong reduction from 960°C until end of firing to 1300°C. No end soak or oxidising period (12 cu.ft. kiln)

Titanium Aventurine Glaze
Potash feldspar 32
China clay...28
Flint 11
Whiting..20
Talc 3
Titanium dioxide 6

Matt pinkish grey with off white speckle on light bodies; good on porcelain. Tan with cream speckle on more irony bodies. Gives well spread speckles where thin; a solid mass where thick. Any applied pigments will bleed.

Temmoku Glaze – Variation Emms Recipe
Potash feldspar 62
China clay...6
Quartz...14.5
Whiting..11
Red iron oxide 6.5

Good shiny black breaking to bright rust where thin. Pigments used for rust brush decor. Ilmenite, iron or titanium. Fired in hottest part of kiln and on Potclays 1118 (smooth body with touch of iron).

Wood Ash Glaze – Variation Emms Recipe

Cornwall stone 51
Ball clay 23
China clay...5
Whiting 3
Talc 5
Wood ash 13

> Waxy cream colour – slight variations with different ash source. Apply generously. Good on most bodies from coarse irony to porcelain. Sharp definition with pigment decoration.

Copper Red Glaze

Soda feldspar 42
China clay...5
Flint 19
Whiting 14
Alkaline frit 14
Tin oxide...5
Copper carbonate 1

> Shiny rich medium dark red. Needs to be applied fairly generously for good red but then inclined to move and craze. (Remember fluxes and moves more on porcelain but excellent colour). Fired in coolest part of kiln.

Russell Collins CR 77

Stoneware Body

Clay is prepared from dry ball clay SMD with an addition of 1% red iron oxide and 13% of 80's mesh quartz and 13% grog 60's to dust, ground firebrick.

SMD ....50 kg
Red iron oxide ....1 lb
Quartz ....13 lb
Grog ....13 lb

> Reduction fired in oil kiln 1280°C soaking for one hour in neutral atmosphere.

White Matt Opaque Glaze 1280°C Reduction

Cornish stone 60
Talc 10
China clay..30
Whiting 15
Quartz...8

Temmoku 1280°C Reduction

Potash feldspar 15
Cornish stone 35
China clay...6.75
Quartz..18.75
Whiting 15
Red iron oxide 5.5
Iron spangles 3

Shiny White 1280-1300°C (Porcelain)
Potash feldspar 30
Quartz 39
Whiting 18
China clay 11

Semi-Matt Opaque Grey-Green 1280°C
Potash feldspar 85
Whiting 15
Quartz 8
Red clay 35
Zircon 2

Delan Cookson

Pale Ochre Rust 1280°C Reduction
Mixed wood ash 70
China clay 60
> The wood ash should be sieved dry through a 60-mesh sieve prior to weighing. The glaze should be applied thickly.

Darker Ochre Rust 1280°C Oxidation
Mixed wood ash 25
China clay 40
Feldspar 40
Whiting 30
Iron oxide 6
> The colour of this glaze depends on thickness: thick – ochre; medium – rust red; thin – brown.

Dolomite Glaze 1280°C Reduction
Feldspar 49
China clay 25
Dolomite 22
Whiting 4
> A semi-matt white glaze which needs a fairly thick application, works well on buff and porcelain bodies. Can also be used in oxidation.

Emmanuel Cooper CR 121, 136, 160, 175

Stoneware Speckle Body 1260°C Oxidation
White stoneware clay 80
Potclays grog (60's) 10
Potclays Ironstone Speckle body 10

Basic Bronze 1200-1260°C
Black coppper oxide 2.5
Manganese dioxide 48
China clay 15
Ball clay 12

Gold Pigment 1230-1260°C
Manganese dioxide 43
Copper oxide 5
Cobalt oxide 5
Red clay 57
Ball clay 4
Quartz 5
    Thickness of application determines degree of gold.

Chrome Pink No.1 1260°C Electric Kiln
Cornish stone (or Cornwall stone) 50
Whiting 30
Flint 5
China clay 15
+ Tin oxide 5%
    Chrome oxide 0.2%
    A smooth bright pink. A larger amount of chrome will darken the red to a crimson.

Chrome Pink 2
Soda feldspar 62
Whiting 28
China clay 10
+ Tin oxide 6%
    Chrome oxide 0.5%
    A dryish matt pink.

Copper Red Reduction
Feldspar 57
Barium carbonate 18
Dolomite 5
Flint 10
China clay 5
+ Copper carbonate 1.5%
    Tin oxide 2.5%
    A strong reduction is required.

Barium Glaze 1250-1260°C Electric Kiln
Feldspar 35
Barium carbonate 40
Zinc oxide 15
China clay 5
Flint 5
    Not suitable for tableware.

Joanna Constantinidis CR 152

Stoneware Clay
Usually a blend of Potclays White Stoneware body and T-material; sometimes an iron bearing clay may be added.
Biscuit fired at 1000°C.

Glaze No.1 1300°C Reduction
Cornish stone 20
Whiting..23
China clay...30
Quartz...27

Glaze No.2 1300°C Reduction
Whiting..100
China clay 100
Cornish stone 100
Quartz...100
Talc 20
Firing takes 10-12 hours starting reduction at 1000°C.

John Corr CR 132

Celadons

CEL B, C & D Cones 9-10 Reduction
Finer Finish Feldspar (FFF) 81.4
Whiting...6.3
Flint 12.3
B, C & D + 0.5, 1 & 1.5% black iron oxide respectively.

CEL E Cones 9-10 Reduction
Finer Finish Feldspar (FFF) 62
Whiting...11.2
Flint 26.8
+ Red iron oxide 0.5%

CEL F Cones 9-10 Reduction
Finer Finish Feldspar (FFF) 65
Wollastonite 27.5
Flint 7.5
+ Red iron oxide 1.6%

CEL G Cones 9-10 Reduction
Finer Finish Feldspar (FFF) 82
Whiting...16
Flint 2
+ Black iron oxide 0.8%

Copper Reds

BR1 Cone 10 Reduction
Finer Finish Feldspar (FFF) 19.4
Soda ash (sodium carbonate) 12.6
Calcium borate frit 12.8
Wollastonite 11.7
China clay..32.6
Flint 10.9
+ Copper carbonate 0.1%
+ Tin oxide 0.3%

BR1 (alternative)
Nepheline syenite 42.4
Soda ash (sodium carbonate) 1.6
Calcium borate frit 13.5
Whiting..10.5
China clay..6
Flint 26
+ Copper carbonate 0.3%
+ Tin oxide 1%

BR7A Cones 9-10 Reduction
Finer Finish Feldspar (FFF) 49.6
Calcium borate frit 11.2
Whiting..12.7
China clay..23
Flint 3.5
+ Copper carbonate 0.1%
+ Tin oxide 0.3%

BR7S Cones 9-10 Reduction
Finer Finish Feldspar (FFF) 51.2
Calcium borate frit 11.6
Wollastonite 15.2
China clay..12.2
Flint 9.8
+ Copper carbonate 0.1%
+ Tin oxide 0.3%

Jun Glazes

Jun C Cones 9-10 Reduction
Finer Finish Feldspar (FFF) 42.5
Calcium borate frit 10
Whiting..15.6
China clay..1.6
Flint 25.5
Talc 4.8
+ Bone ash 2%

Jun D Cones 9-10 Reduction
Finer Finish Feldspar (FFF) 56.7
Whiting...13
China clay...1.5
Flint 22.4
Talc...6.4
+ Bone ash..2%

Cameron Covert CR 71

Porcelain Body Orton Cone 8-11
Edgar Plastic Kaolin (china clay)................40
Ball clay O. M. No. 4 ....8.9
Flint 17.7
Nepheline syenite 31.6
Bentonite 2.2

Very good for firing crystalline glazes in an electric kiln.

Dartington Pottery CR 116, 150
(work illustrated)

Base White Glaze 1280°C Reduction
Potash feldspar...50
Quartz..22.7
China clay..13.6
Whiting..9.1
Talc..4.5

Yellow 1280°C Reduction
Potash feldspar..44.9
Whiting...3
Barium carbonate.......................................20
China clay..7
Talc..7.2
Zirconium silicate 14.9
Red iron oxide 3

Janice Blue 1280°C Reduction
Potash feldspar..36.1
Whiting...19.3
Talc..14.5
China clay..9.64
Ball clay 7.23
Quartz...7.23
Cobalt carbonate 2.41
Red iron oxide 3.61

Tav's Green Celadon 1280°C Reduction
Potash feldspar..35.8
China clay..4.97
Quartz..22.4

Calcium borate frit 3.98
Talc 3.98
Red iron oxide 1.49
Wollastonite 10.4
Chrome oxide 0.05
Tin oxide 1.98
Strontium carbonate 14.9

Clive Davies CR 119

Body
Hyplas 130
China clay 20
Molochite 20
Flint 30
Bentonite 2

Cream Base Glaze 1280-1300°C Reduction
Nepheline syenite 60
Flint 20
AT ball clay 20
Dolomite 20
Zirconium silicate 20

Green Glaze
Feldspar 85
Whiting 15
Chrome 3

Red Glaze (JT)
Potash feldspar 300
Borax frit 35
Whiting 45
Copper oxide 1
Tin oxide 3

White Base Glaze
Cornish stone 60
China clay 20
Talc 20
Whiting 20
Zirconium silicate 20

Black Glaze
Cornish stone 80
Whiting 15
China clay 3
Black stain 7

Blue Glaze (JT)
Potash feldspar 35
Whiting 16

Talc 12
China clay 8
Bal clay 6
Quartz 6
Cobalt oxide 2
Iron oxide 3

John Davies

Stoneware Body Oxidation and Reduction

Hyplas 67 ball clay, powdered (ECC) 100kg
R B ball clay, lump
(ECC, now No. 1 ball clay) 25
A62F fireclay, ground fine (Acme Marls) ..15
White siliceous sand, washed and graded
20's-40's (Stoddards, Burslem) 15
Feldspar (water-ground) 15

A nice 'tanned' hue in oxidation, but is at its best in a reducing fire. The 'dark' clay I use is, or was, called RB ball clay, a bright red clay from Dorset. Some years ago I bought several tons from Pike Bros., now part of the English China Clays (ECC), and still have a lot left. I understand that it can still be had from ECC, although they no longer list it for sale, but you can go and fetch it yourself from the mine. Other clays listed are readily available and suppliers are in brackets.

To mix you need either a blunger and something large enough to hold a large quantity, like an old baker's dough-mixer, or a large sheet of builders polythene spread out on the ground (under cover), and you can tread it by foot. Pour into the blunger 10 gallons of water and to it add the RB, broken into pieces about the size of walnuts. When it is all a good thick slip, transfer it to the mixer, which should be clean and without any other material at this stage. To this slip add the dry powdered clays, sand and feldspar and mix until all is of a heavy, though quite wet, even consistency. The body will now require some drying before throwing and will need to be stored for at least a year, to allow the enzymes to get to work.

Wood Ash Glaze Cone 9-10 Reduction

Soda feldspar 35
Mixed ash 35
China clay 15
Talc 10
Quartz 10

Used over low-iron bodies, gives a nice warm ochre green colour. Used over high-iron bodies, gives a splendid golden-green colour and will turn blue where thickest.
Note: for use as a once fired (raw) glaze, substitute the china clay for a high alumina ball clay (e.g. TWVD) and add Bentonite 4.

Celadon Glaze Cone 8-9 Reduction

Potash feldspar 41.75
Quartz 27
Limestone 17.5
China clay 13
Ochre 3

Needs thick application, best over high iron bodies. Is also useful as a porcelain glaze. Gives a pleasant pale green (not greyish), and a nice fat quality.

Opaque Bluish Glaze Cone 6-8 Reduction
Potash feldspar 40
Quartz 30
Limestone 20
Boro-calcite frit 10
(Calcium borate frit)
Black iron oxide 1

A glaze for the cooler parts of the kiln. We all have them. Beware! Very fluid above cone 8. Nice soft quality, grey-blue colour at cone 6-8. Iron oxide decoration over this glaze can be quite spectacular.

Mary Davies

Japanese Glaze from Mr Sinnai in Mashiko 1280°C Reduction
Feldspar 20.7
Whiting...8.2
Barium carbonate 2.8
Kaolin 2.7
Flint 14.4
Talc 1.7
Titanium dioxide 1.7
Rice straw ash ....0.5 (90% Silica)
Copper oxide 0.05
Tin oxide...1.7

Wood fired kiln gave results of green-red-blue patches. Gas kiln gave results of blue and pink. This was Mr Sinnai's result. Mine have been disappointing on porcelain. It works better on an iron bearing clay and can be very rich, nearing purple/red at times, on stoneware in a heavy reduction.

Paul Davis   CR 135

Chun Glaze Cone 10 Reduction
Potash feldspar 39.35
Whiting...13.54
China clay...1.8
Magnesium carbonate 0.9
Bone ash 1.2
Flint 33.1
Barium carbonate 9.1
Iron oxide 0.5

For porcelain clay.

Copper Red Brush Mix for Top of Chun Cone 10 Reduction
Soda ash 12.1
Barium carbonate 22.6
Gerstley borate frit 15.6
Flint 34.6
Tin oxide..10
Black copper oxide 7.5

Shino Glaze Cone 10 Reduction
Nepheline syenite 47.6
Spodumene 31.8
Zircon opacifier 4.8
Alumina hydrate 12
Salt 2
Bentonite 4
    For stoneware clays.

Celadon Cone 10 Reduction
Potash feldspar 33.9
Whiting..13.26
Talc 3.9
Flint 26.6
Bone ash 0.1
Red iron oxide 1.1
China clay..5
    For porcelain.

Sally Dawson

Temmoku 1280°C Oxidation
Cornish stone 88
Whiting..12
Red iron oxide 8

Dolomite Off White Matt 1280°C Oxidation
Cornish stone 48
Dolomite 21
Whiting..4
China clay..24
Bone ash 3-5
    Cornish stone in both these glazes must be the green sort.

Richard Dewar   CR 185
(work illustrated)

All interiors are glazed at leatherhard stage with one of the following glazes:

Glaze No.1 1320°C Reduction
AT Ball clay (ECC) 1
Nepheline syenite 1

Glaze No.2 1320°C Reduction
China stone 8
Calcium carbonate 2
Lavender ash 1
Rutile 0.5
Cobalt carbonate 0.1

Firing

All pieces are once-fired to 1320°C in a two cubic metre, down-draught oil kiln. The firing takes twenty four hours and includes four hours reduction and two hours salting.

Slips

I use many slips but two of my favourites are:

Kaolin (china clay) 1
Powdered porcelain 1
Ball clay 1

Kaolin (china clay) 3
Ball clay 2
Nepheline syenite 2

Brian Dewbury

Originating at Harrow School of Art in the 1960s, this clay body is well known:
SMD ball clay 52
AT ball clay 26
Leighton Buzzard sand 20
Red iron oxide 2

Iron Slip
Red clay (Sharnbrook) 72
Red iron oxide 28

Black Slip
Red clay (Sharnbrook) 64
Flint 16
Red iron oxide 8
Manganese dioxide 8
Cobalt carbonate 4

59B Glaze
Nepheline syenite 23
Whiting 4.5
Spodumene 10
Dolomite 10
Talc 9
Ash (Dutch Elm) 20
AT ball clay 8
China clay 12.5
Quartz 3
Cobalt carbonate 0.5
Recorded range 1050-1310°C

Colour	Temperature
Lilac – a dry skin	1140°C
Mauve lilac – smooth melted	1190°C
Blue – mauve speckle	1220°C

Similar – slight orange speckle ....1260°C
Stronger blue, more gloss ....1290°C
Similar, more fluid ....1310°C

Notes: good temperature range from 1200-1300°C

Ash Glaze
Ash (Dutch Elm) 25
Cornish stone 10
China clay 25
AT ball clay 10
Flint 25
  Fired at 1280°C.

Results are as follows:

Base Glaze		Grey white	even colour	medium gloss
Base glaze over Iron slip		Broken orange	uneven	medium gloss
A Adding Iron oxide	5%	Pale grey green	even	medium gloss
B Adding Iron oxide	6%	Grey-green	even	gloss
C Adding Iron oxide	7%	Dark rich amber green	even	gloss
D Adding Iron oxide	8%	Dark green brown	even	gloss
E Adding Iron oxide	9%	Beige black	uneven	gloss
F Adding Iron oxide	10%	Iron black slight crystalline	even	gloss
G Adding Iron oxide	15%	Lustrous iron	even	gloss
H Adding Iron oxide	20%	Browner iron	even	gloss

Crackle 3B
Potash feldspar 35
Ash (Dutch Elm) 40
AT ball clay 5
China clay 15
Zirconium oxide 5
+ Chromium oxide 2%

No.162 1260°C
Nepheline syenite 29
Spodumene 20
Whiting 3
China clay 3
Dolomite 23
Base – cold grey-white 25

Variations with additions
A + Tin oxide..............5% opaque matt white
B + Copper carbonate ....0.5% broken blue grey
C + Copper carbonate ....1% warmer blue grey orange
D + Copper carbonate ....2% broken darker blue grey
E + Manganese dioxide ....1% silver grey blue

No.139 1260°C

Nepheline syenite 20
Potash feldspar 15
Whiting 15
Talc 17
China clay 10
Ball clay 11
Red clay (Sharnbrook) 12
Base – yellow-orange brown.

Variations
A + Tin oxide ..... 5%   warm ochre
B + Copper carbonate ..... 0.5%   redder ochre
C + Copper carbonate ..... 1%   similar
D + Black nickel oxide ..... 1%   brown ochre

No.151 1260°C

Nepheline syenite 45
Colemanite 10
Dolomite 19
Barium carbonate 5
Whiting 3
Quartz 28
Base – transparent cream grey crackle.

Variations
+ Tin oxide ..... 5%   glossy white
+ Copper carbonate ..... 0.5%   glossy pale turquoise blue
+ Copper carbonate ..... 2%   glossy turquoise green
+ Manganese dioxide ..... 1%   glossy green speckle
+ Nickel dioxide ..... 1%   darker green speckle

No. 165 1260°C

Potash feldspar 43
Whiting 3
Spodumene 10.5
Colemanite 18
Barium carbonate 10.5
Quartz 15
Base – transparent grey

Variations
+ Copper carbonate ..... 1%   lustrous turquoise blue
+ Nickel oxide ..... 1%   lustrous green

Mike Dodd   CR 107

For Raw Glazing

Local earthenware or iron clay (low firing) 1
Potash feldspar 1
Wood ash mixed 1

Different combinations will give matt or runny results. Local granite dust, river iron, chalk, ochres, flint, feldspar, and wood ash, ball clay, local earthenware clay and china clay is all we use for glazes. Some common sense, luck and experiment is for me the best and most reliable recipe and great fun.

Jack Doherty CR 171

Coloured Porcelain Body

I mix about 5kg of each colour using dry clay, usually scraps from turning. If I want an even colour the stain or oxide is sieved but I find, increasingly, that I enjoy the textural quality produced by adding unsieved material in small quantities. I add the following amounts to achieve desired colours:

Rutile ....2.5% Speckled grey
Manganese carbonate unsieved....................5%   Speckled yellow
Deancroft Salmon stain ....1%   Pale pink

Dark Green Stain

Chrome oxide 25
Cobalt oxide 10
Alumina 25
Iron oxide 30
Manganese dioxide 15

Will produce a rich blue-green through to black depending on percentage used, i.e. 3%-8%. Reduction fired in propane kiln to 1300°C, reducing from 900°C until the end of the firing.

Glazes 1300°C Reduction

No.1
Talc 24
Feldspar 27
China clay..22
Whiting..13
Flint 22

No.2
Feldspar 48
Whiting..20
China clay..20
Flint 10
Titanium dioxide 6

Fired in propane kiln, reducing from 900°C until end of firing.

Gulielma Dowrick CR 172, 182, 184

High Calcium

Gerstley borate 8.4
Nepheline syenite 10.3
Potash feldspar..6.4
Silica..32.3
Lithium carbonate 1.5
Whiting..24

Grolleg china clay 17.1
Copper carbonate 3
    Shiny crazed. (Calcium borate frit can be used as a substitute for gerstley borate).

Bernard Leach Base
Potash feldspar 40
Silica 30
Whiting 20
Grolleg china clay 10
Titanium dioxide 10
Copper carbonate 2
    Low sheen. Not crazed.

Canberra Calcium Matt
Potash feldspar 33
Whiting 33
Grolleg china clay 33
Copper carbonate 3
    Dry, smooth where thick.

Greg Daley Base
(High calcium)
Nepheline syenite 30
Whiting 26
Silica 30
Ekalite kaolin 14
Copper carbonate 2
    Crazed. Smooth satin.

Variation on Greg Daley Base
Nepheline syenite 27
Whiting 23.4
Silica 27
Ekalite kaolin 12.6
Titanium dioxide 10
Copper carbonate 2
    Not crazed. Smooth satin. Pinholed where thick.

Emmanuel Cooper's Shiny Craze Free Clear
Cornish stone 40
Whiting 15
Zinc oxide 10
China clay 15
Silica or flint 20
Copper carbonate 3
    Crawls where thick.

Satin Version
Cornish stone 40.9
Whiting 14.9
Zinc oxide 10
China clay 25.9
Silica 8.3

Copper carbonate 2
    Crawls where thick.

Emmanuel Cooper's Base High Zinc
Nepheline syenite 75.6
Silica...0.3
Bentonite 0.5
Calcined zinc oxide 23.6
Nickel oxide 1.5
Epsom salts (if needed) 0.2
    Super smooth.

Melanie's Magnesium
Potash feldspar...28
Whiting..12.2
Talc 16.6
Grolleg china clay 15.5
Silica...27.7
Copper carbonate 2
    Waxy smooth, craze free.

Titanium Variation
Potash feldspar......................................25.2
Whiting..11
Talc 14.9
Grolleg china clay 14
Silica...24.9
Titanium dioxide 10
Copper carbonate 2
    Smooth satin, craze free.

Cobalt Titanium Green
Nepheline syenite 14.4
Magnesite*..1.3
Whiting..18.6
Silica...25
Grolleg china clay 37.4
Lithium carbonate 3.4
Titanium dioxide 5
Cobalt carbonate 3
*heavy magnesium carbonate

2A
Gerstley borate 8.3
Potash feldspar.......................................10.3
Whiting..12.5
Lithium carbonate 0.9
China clay...37.8
Silica...30
Chrome oxide 0.5

2B
Gerstley borate 7.1
Potash feldspar 9
Lithium carbonate 0.7
Whiting 10.8
China clay 32.5
Silica 39.8
Chrome oxide 0.5

Firing
All the above glazes are fired to the point of cone 9 touching the shelf, having soaked from cone 8 beginning to bend, for the sake of the high calcium glazes. Not all glazes need firing precisely to a cone position. The high calcium glazes require this, but the rest of the glazes are probably more tolerant.

Satin Orton Cone 4 Gas Oxidation
Gerstley borate 5.1
Cornish stone 34.5
Lithium carbonate 1.5
Whiting/calcite 7.8
Zinc oxide (calcined) 5.5
Talc 8.2
China clay 22.4
Silica/flint 15
Tin oxide 2
Zirconium oxide 2
   Calcium borate frit can be substituted for gerstley borate.

Satin Orton Cone 6-7 Electric
Gerstley borate 7.3
Cornish stone 36
Lithium carbonate 0.9
Whiting/calcite 7.4
Zinc oxide (raw) 3.7
Talc 6.2
China clay 14
Silica/flint 24.5
Tin oxide 2

Craze Free Clear Orton Cone 9
Cornish stone 40
Whiting/calcite 15
Zinc oxide (raw) 10
China clay 15
Silica 20

Satin Matt Orton Cone 9
Cornish stone 40.9
Whiting/calcite 14.9
Zinc oxide 10
China clay 25.9
Silica 8.3

Ruth Duckworth

Ash Glaze 1260°C Oxidation
Ash 60
Feldspar 80

Basically what I do is to use very thin layers of oxide and several glazes over each other. Most glazes I use are very simple concoctions of my own such as a mixture of ash and feldspar.

Glaze No.2 1260°C Oxidation
Feldspar 40
Whiting..30
Kaolin 20

Fishscale Cone 9 Oxidation
Clinchfield potash feldspar 40.7
Whiting..13.3
Kaolin 6.8
Spodumene 15.5
Fluorspar 4.7
Bone ash 6.3
Bentonite 3

For cone 6 use nepheline syenite instead of feldspar.

Elizabeth Duncombe

Stoneware 1250°C Reduction
Feldspar 30
Flint 15
Whiting..20
China clay...40
Iron oxide 12

Very good matt glaze, must be thick, fired to 1250°C in reduction atmospheres.

Stoneware 1250°C Reduction
Flint 32
Whiting..20
Feldspar 33
China clay...15
Zinc oxide...3
Tin oxide..4

Shiny white glaze, good over iron decoration 1250°C reduction.

Stoneware 1250°C Oxidation
Cornish stone 45
Whiting..20
China clay...25
Copper carbonate 3
Cobalt oxide 0.5
Nickel oxide 0.5

Geoffrey Eastop CR 121, 131

Porcelain Casting Slip 1260°C
China clay 13lb
Flint 4.5lb
Potash feldspar 7.25lb
BBV ball clay 3lb
Bentonite 0.5lb
Sodium sillicate 140°C TW 32gm
Water..12 pints

> Dissolve sodium silicate into 1 pt hot water; add to remaining water in a bucket. Mix dry ingredients by hand in another bucket and add gradually to the water stirring continuously (with a mixer if available). Sieve through 60's. If necessary to improve flow add further solution 1 pt hot water 2 gm sodium silicate.

Variegated Green 1260-1280°C Oxidation
Cornish stone 43
Whiting...22
China clay...23
Flint 3
Synthetic red iron oxide 1
Cobalt oxide 0.6
Titanium oxide...7

> Semi-matt green – breaks to flecks of violet and pale blue grey when thicker.

Stony Cream 1260-1280°C Oxidation
Feldspar 47
Whiting...23
China clay...16
Flint 17
Rutile 7.5

> Stony-waxy – reacts well over iron glazes.

Stove Black Vitreous Slip 1250-1260°C
Potclays white earthenware
1140/2 (powdered) 150
Whiting...75
Manganese oxide 15
Chrome oxide 9
Red iron oxide 30

Billy Eccles CR 183

Dry Glaze Cone 8/9 Reduction
Potash feldspar 45
China clay...36
Whiting...9
Quartz...10

Eeles Family

Yellow Glaze Slipware Type 1280°C Reduction
Greensand, i.e. 'Glauconite' 40
China clay...4
Feldspar 34
Whiting..22
Red iron oxide 5

Celadon 1280°C Reduction
Acid granite 71.25
Whiting..15
Red clay 7.5
Quartz...6.25

A typical light green celadon as compiled by Michael Cardew using acid granite of this type.

Semi-matt Pale Celadon 1280°C Reduction
Acid granite 60
Whiting..16.12
Quartz...6.12
China clay..18.25

Penlee Stone Glaze 1280°C Reduction
BBV ball clay 31
Penlee Stone 30
Whiting..6
Quartz...25.5
Iron oxide 6
Manganese dioxide 2.4
Cobalt oxide 0.2

Andesite Glaze 1260°C Reduction
Andesite 33
Feldspar 27
Whiting..16
China clay..10
Quartz...14
Red iron oxide 7

A black glaze of the Hares Fur type.

Chun 1280°C Reduction
Borax frit...10
Feldspar 52.7
Talc 7.3
Wollastonite 15
Quartz...16.75
Bone ash 1
+ Red iron oxide 1%

Celadon (Satin Matt) 1280°C Reduction
Acid granite 60
Whiting 16.12
China clay 18.25
Flint or quartz 6.12

Iron Glaze 1280°C Reduction
Basic rock 60
Whiting 9
Bentonite or plastic clay 4
Flint or quartz 27

Lis Ehrenreich CR 176

Agnete Glaze
Straw ash 65
Beech ash 85
Feldspar 140
Borax 160
Quartz 10
Ball clay 60

Firing in my electric kiln, reducing very heavily from 900°C to a top temperature of 1180°C, I obtain my very rough surface.

Kelding Glaze
Straw ash (1) 70
Straw ash (2) 80
Feldspar 140
Red earthenware clay 60
Borax 160

Siddig El'Nigoumi

Hard Greenish-blue Stable Glaze 1250-1300°C Reduction
Feldspar 40
China clay 38
Whiting 20
Cobalt oxide 1
Red iron oxide 1

Use very thickly in the slip trailer for decoration on biscuited ware. The same glaze should then be thinned to a watery consistency and used as a glaze to cover the decoration. This should give a dark background in contrast to the colour of the decoration, which will be greenish-blue.

Stoneware Glaze 1250-1280°C Reduction
Feldspar 39
China clay 23
Whiting 18
Flint 11
Ball clay 6
Talc 11

Alumina matt glaze for tableware. Use medium thickness. If colour is desired use 2-4% red iron oxide. This glaze is also suitable for porcelain.

Derek Emms CR 123, 124, 146

Blue-green Celadon 1280°C Orton Cone 9
China clay..10
Wollastonite 20
Flint 30
W/G feldspar...40
Talc 5
Molochite 5
Zinc oxide..5
Synthetic red iron oxide 0.5

This produced a slightly opaque glaze but when ball-milled for four hours it became clear and transparent enough to show fine engraving through it. Increase iron oxide to 2% for green celadon.

A Zinc Oxide-free Version 1280°C Orton Cone 9
China clay..10
Wollastonite 20
Flint 30
W/G feldspar...40
Talc 5
Molochite (200s) 5
Calcium borate 5
Synthetic red iron oxide 0.5

Basic Transparent 1270-1280°C Oxidation
HT borax frit (low expansion)....................35
Cornish stone 50
Flint 5
China clay..5
Whiting..5

Glaze stains can be successfully added to give soft transparent colours. The addition of 10% red iron oxide produces a passable oxidised temmoku when applied fairly thinly. This glaze is for oxidised firing on porcelain bodies.

Chun 1270-1280°C
Colemanite (Calcium borate frit).................1
China clay..2
Whiting..20
Quartz..30
Feldspar 43
Talc 5
Red iron oxide 1

To develop the red from copper, typical of the Chinese Chuns a slip was made up of a white earthenware clay + copper oxide 3%.

Copper Red Glaze 1280°C Reduction
Standard borax frit.....................................15
Soda feldspar 45

Whiting..........15
China clay..........5
Flint..........20
+ Tin oxide..........5%
+ Copper carbonate..........0.5%

> A small amount of copper will produce good strong reds. In an oxidised stoneware firing this glaze produces a pleasant pale green glaze. Add 200's mesh molochite and bentonite 2% to reduce crazing on porcelain.

Temmoku No.1 1280°C Reduction
FFF feldspar..........62
Whiting..........10
Flint..........19
Ball clay (HVAR)..........9
Red iron oxide..........8

Temmoku No.2 1280°C Reduction
FFF feldspar..........59
Whiting..........10
Flint..........23
Ball clay (HVAR)..........8
Red iron oxide..........8

> This glaze gives a good black even when applied fairly thinly and is therefore good for the ilmenite pigment mentioned earlier.

Temmoku No.3 1280°C Reduction
FFF potash feldspar..........45
Whiting..........12
Quartz..........43
Red iron oxide..........8

> The addition of 3-4% China clay improves the suspension in the glaze tub. This glaze is a very black glaze which does not 'break to rust' as readily as the previous two recipes but is good for decorating on. When high fired it develops an inky blue-black quality.

> All these glazes are fired in reduction atmosphere, starting reduction around 960°C and continuing to the end of firing.

Blue Pigment
Red clay..........92
Cobalt oxide (or carbonate)..........4
Manganese dioxide..........4

> This is a very flexible pigment which can be used in a variety of ways. Under earthenware glazes it produces a dense black slip (for slipware) whilst at stoneware temperatures the cobalt predominates and it becomes blue. It can be painted on the raw clay, on biscuit or on top of the unfired glaze.

Porcelain Glaze 1280°C Reduction
China clay..........15
Molochite (fine)..........14
Feldspar..........25
Quartz..........26
Whiting..........21

> This has a semi-matt surface which can be made into a semi-matt celadon by the addition

of 1-2% red iron oxide.

Chun 1280°C Reduction
Wood ash 20
Feldspar 20
Granite dust 20
Flint 20
Clay...20

If this glaze fires glassy with perhaps tinges of blue pooling in the bottom of bowls it has been overfired and a lower temperature should be tried.

Chun 1280°C Reduction
Feldspar 36
Quartz...26
Granite dust 22
Whiting...13
Dolomite 3
Bone ash 1

Celadon 1260-1280°C Reduction
China clay...10
Whiting...20
Flint 30
Feldspar 40
+ Talc 5
Red iron oxide 1

This gives a good blue Celadon over white firing stoneware clays. The clay however needs to be highly siliceous (e.g. some of the white earthenware bodies) or crazing will occur.

1280°C Reduction
A darkish blue glaze using ilmenite (which is of course ferrous titanate)
China clay...9
Whiting..17.5
Flint 26.5
Feldspar 35.5
Talc 4.5
Ilmenite (fine)...7

Try varying the amount of ilmenite in the recipe e.g. 2, 4 and 6 parts.

Sky Blue
Borax frit..10
Whiting...20
Flint 30
Feldspar 40
China clay...2
Talc 5
Black iron oxide 1

Fire 1270-1280°C in reduction. Experiment with different borax frits but I suggest a high temperature, low expansion frit, which will help to reduce crazing on a highly siliceous body.

Ivan Englund CR 110

Stoneware Nickel Yellow Glaze
Potash feldspar 29
Soda feldspar 20
Dolomite 23
Whiting..4
Bentonite 13
Titanium dioxide 9
Nickel oxide 2

    My work is all once fired so is glazed on the leatherhard ware but this glaze would no doubt work equally well for biscuit ware if kaolin was substituted for bentonite.

Celadon Glaze 1250°C Reduction
Avgrain (any granite
or mixture of granites) 63
Whiting..17
Flint 8
Bentonite 12

    A raw glaze. Mix materials dry before adding water: soak overnight, limit amount of water added as surplus cannot be poured off because glaze will stay in suspension.

Matt Pale Blue Nickel Glaze 1250°C
Feldspar 54
Whiting..8
Barium carbonate 24
China clay..5
Zinc oxide..7
Nickel oxide 2

    This glaze gives a matt pale blue which is best below 1250°C. Above that temperature it starts to go transparent in a smeary sort of way. As I once fire all my work I substitute bentonite for the china clay and add another 8% which makes it a good raw glaze.

Jill Fanshawe Kato CR 158
(work illustrated)

White Slip
DBG ball clay 1
China clay..1

    Add underglaze stains or oxides in small amounts.

Oatmeal Matt 1280°C
Potash feldspar 41
Red earthenware clay................................13
China clay..13
Flint 3
Dolomite 30

    Add underglaze stains or oxides in small amounts.

Holden Transparent 1280°C
Ball clay (DBG)..35

Whiting 25
Potash feldspar 8
Flint 25
Talc 6
+ Copper oxide ....4% for green
+ Red iron oxide ....6% for brown
    Can be used as raw glaze.

J. V. Faragher

Two matt glazes 1260-1280°C cone 9 down oxidation or reduction. Both these are in constant use, are reliable and are good for adding stains or oxides.

Matt 1
Potash feldspar 28
Dolomite 14
Own body or ball clay 25
Silica 20
Magnesium silicate (talc) 22
Zinc oxide 10
Red iron oxide or red earthenware clay 2-5%

Sculptural Porcelain Cone 10-12
Feldspar 25
Kaolin G1 50
Flint 20
Aluminium silicate 5
+ Chamotte 200 mesh 5
Chamotte 2mm/4mm 5

Jorge Fernandez Chiti   CR 120

Transparent 1230°C
Feldspar 53
Whiting 6.5
Barium carbonate 13
Quartz 18.5
China clay 4.5
Ball clay 4.5
Good for added oxides:
Nickel oxide ....1.5% red
Manganese dioxide ....1%   pink
Copper carbonate ....3%   green

Temmoku 1250°C
Quartz 5
Feldspar 50
Whiting 15
Ball clay 15
Iron oxide 5

Cobalt oxide 5
Manganese dioxide 5

Celadon 1250°C
Feldspar 83.4
Zinc oxide 7.3
Whiting 9.3
Iron oxide 1.5
    Via 'El Libro del Ceramista' (Argentina).

Murray Fieldhouse

Celadon Glaze 1250-1260°C Reduction
Potash feldspar 37.48
Whiting 12.11
Barium carbonate 10.63
Zinc oxide 2.16
China clay 3.48
Flint 31.57
Red iron oxide 2.57
    Suitable for cold parts of kiln. Green on stoneware, blue on Leach porcelain.

Vivienne Foley

Jade Green 1260-1280°C Oxidation
Barium carbonate 22
Feldspar 55
Flint 10
China clay 10
Dolomite 5
Copper oxide 2
    Softened with green underglaze stain. The refractory qualities of this glaze can be exaggerated with a further addition of 10% barium and 5% bone ash to produce a fine crackle glaze that is attractive with manganese, giving pale lilac. Additions of tin oxide, zinc oxide or alumina hydrate will increase depth and help to eliminate crystalline effects, but they have an adverse effect on some colouring oxides, e.g. nickel. (Lithium carbonate can be used in small amounts as an auxiliary flux to improve brightness and extend the firing range.) Further adjustments to texture and colour can be made with small additions of silicon carbide.

The following list of colours were achieved by adding 2% oxide to the Jade Green Glaze (without the copper oxide and green underglaze stain.)

Chrome oxide	moss green
Copper oxide	bright greenish-turquoise
Nickel oxide	mushroom brown
Red iron oxide	yellowish cream
Manganese dioxide	brown-mauve
Cobalt dioxide	bright blue, (+ 2 pts copper oxide, royal blue)
Black stain (8%)	deep blue black

Robert Fournier

Ash Glaze 1260°C Oxidation
Feldspar 51.5
Ash (hardwood) 31
Flint 8.25
China clay...6.25
Bentonite 3
Red iron oxide 7.5
Synthetic iron oxide 7.5

> Fires red/brown/black according to ash, sometimes with yellow spots. If glaze turns out dark and dead-looking, dilute with glaze mixture without iron until colour is satisfactory.

Slightly Speckled Buff 1260°C Oxidation
Feldspar 28
China clay...13.5
Dolomite 18
Ash (hardwood) 18.5
Tin oxide...8
Red clay 7
Alkaline frit 7

Neal French

Clay Matt 1260°C Oxidation
China clay...70
Ball clay 20
Whiting...70

Oxide additions
1 Vanadium pentoxide................................7 stoneware bodies
2 Red iron oxide ....5 stoneware bodies
3 Light rutile...5 porcelain on stoneware
4 copper oxide ....2 porcelain

Brown Matt 1260°C Oxidation or Reduction
Potash feldspar...80
Flint 20
No.4 ball clay (Hymod SMD) 15
China clay...20
Barium carbonate.......................................40
Manganese dioxide 5
Vanadium pentoxide 10

David Frith CR 164

Body
Hyplas 71 ball clay 69
China clay...23
Silica sand 60's 8

Standard Stoneware Body Recipe

BBV ball clay	39.86%	1.5 cwt
AT ball clay	26.57.%	1 cwt
High silica fireclay	13.29%	0.5 cwt
Grog	19.93%	0.75 cwt
Red iron oxide	0.36%	1.5 lb

    BBV ball clay: white firing with large particle size.
    AT ball clay: low in silica with high percentage of iron.
    HS ball clay: used to adjust silica content of body and also for the iron content.
    Grog: either ground bisque ware or silica and 60s mesh.

Pale Green Celadon Reduction

Cornish stone	80
China clay	10
Whiting	10
Talc	6
Black iron oxide	1

Deep Green Celadon Reduction

Cornish stone	56
Wollastonite	20
Ball clay	20
Red iron oxide	1.5

Temmoku Reduction

Feldspar	73
Ball clay	10
Whiting	8.5
Quartz	3
Red iron oxide	7.5

Glazes which are used for trailing are the same as those base glazes but unmilled.

Blue Overglaze

Feldspar	55
Flint	20.5
Whiting	15
Barium carbonate	2.5
Zinc oxide	2.5
Iron oxide	2
Cobalt	0.5
Bentonite	1.5

Khaki Overglaze

Feldspar	30
Dolomite	6
Whiting	1.5
China clay	20
Quartz	35
Red iron oxide	7

Blue Painting Pigment
Dry red clay 100
Cobalt oxide 4
Manganese oxide 4

Various trailing pigments based on: Feldspar 80 China clay 20 are used with the addition of small amounts of colouring oxides.

Olive Celadon
White granite 40
Cornish stone 40
AT ball clay 10
Limestone 10

Pale Green Celadon
White granite 30
Cornish stone 30
China clay 20
Quartz 10
Limestone 10

Temmoku
White granite 30
Cornish stone 1.5
China clay 20
Quartz 35
Black iron oxide 5

Khaki Overglaze 2
Penmaenmawr granite 20
Potash feldspar 10
Limestone 2
China clay 20
Quartz 35
Black iron oxide 5
Titanium dioxide 2

Tessha (deep iron speckle) Glaze
Penmaenmawr granite 15
Feldspar 15
Dolomite 6
Whiting 2
Quartz 35
China clay 20
Black iron oxide 6
Titanium dioxide 1

Annette Fuchs

Speckled Beige-yellow Stoneware
Feldspar 33
Dolomite 33
China clay 34
Light rutile 2%

Fires to 1280°C cone 9. (Fired in an electric kiln in oxidised firing.)

Tony Gant

Glazes

Straw Orton Cone 9
FFF feldspar 50
Whiting..3
China clay 10
Calcined china clay (superfine molochite) 12
Dolomite 21
Flint 4
+ Red iron oxide 0.75%

Slate (Blue-grey) Orton Cone 9
Same base as straw but with:-
Red iron oxide 0.5%
Black cobalt oxide 1%

Jade Orton Cone 9
FFF feldspar 50
Whiting..2
China clay 10
Calcined china clay (superior molochite)..10
Dolomite 20
Flint 8
+ Turquoise green (B115) 2%
+ Turquoise Blue (B116) 2%
Glaze stains from WG Ball Ltd, Stoke on Trent

We use the above glazes on our domestic ware and though not glossy, they are durable.

Grey-White Orton Cone 9
FFF feldspar ....3 parts (50%)
China clay ....1 part (16.66%)
Dolomite ....1 part (16.66%)
Flint ....1 part (16.66%)

This is a useful, durable, shiny glaze.

Glaze is applied at a pint-weight of approx. 30oz on to biscuit fired to about 966°C. We fire in a gas kiln, taking 12 hours to 1080°C, followed by 5 hours reduction to shut down at Orton cone 9.

Ray Gardiner

Matt White Orton Cone 9 Reduction
Dolomite 22
Potash feldspar 60
China clay 15
SMD ball clay 30
Quartz 9

A versatile and reliable glaze. It is adapted for raw glazing but can be used on biscuit equally well. Should be applied thickly: on a red stoneware body gives a grey matt opaque, particularly good over iron slips. Also good on a white body and porcelain. It can be trailed or poured over temmoku, without loss of definition.

Celadon Orton Cone 9 Reduction
Magnesium carbonate 10
Cornish stone 75
TWVD ball clay 20
Washed ash 20
Quartz 2
Iron oxide as required

A celadon for porcelain. Opaque satin to clear shiny, depending on position in the kiln. A little Zircon can be added, a trace of cobalt is pleasant. Good surface for brushwork.

Margaret Gebhard

A Temmoku Glaze for Once-firing 1240°C Oxidised
Potash feldspar 800
Nepheline syenite 300
Whiting 200
Red clay 700
Red iron oxide 50 (2.5%)
Iron spangles 20 (1%)

I have found red clays, both local types and commercial bodies, very useful for once-firing glazes. This is best used fairly thickly, on leatherhard clay. I usually soak at 1240°C for 25 minutes.

John Glick CR 111
(work illustrated)

Clay Body
Hawthorne fireclay 78.75lb
APG fireclay 78.75lb
Kentucky stone 78.75lb
Gold art 78.75lb
OM-4 ball 78.75lb
Nepheline syenite (must pre-sift) 42lb
#295 Silica 63lb
Grog 30lb
Iron oxide (sifted 30# seive) 1189gm (0.5%)

Memphis Mashiko Glaze (Pete Sohngen)
Bone ash (synthetic) 7.2
Talc 85
Wollastonite 113.4
Kona F-4 feldspar 751.6
Calcined red art 782.4
Raw red art 82.2
Flint 178.2
Red iron oxide 72.2
Macaloid 5gm
Darvan 0.25tsp
Epsom salts 0.5gm

    60 mesh sieve only. Needs more Epsom salts to stay in suspension at times. I use this a lot in trailing over other glazes and love it over shinos which have wax resist decorations. Rich and wonderfully giving in relation to all my glazes. One of my favourite contrast glazes.

C7 (10) Celadon
Soda feldspar 280
Whiting 20
Gerstley borate (calcium borate frit) 40
Flint 60
Bone ash 20
Zinc oxide 20

    Milky white, highly melted 'Celadon' type base. Used plain or coloured. Very reactive to oxide washes over the glaze or slip under.

    These are some of my recipes. I do use a total of about 16 glazes, each mixed in a plain (uncoloured) version and often carried out with at least one, if not two, colour variations beyond the plain version. Typically I overlap two or four glazes to achieve richer effects. All are poured or dipped quickly on pure bisqued pots. I spray only when the size of the pots prevents simpler methods.

    I usually fire in a longish, heavily reduced atmosphere using the oxygen analyser as a guide. My readings from 1600°F on up to cone 10 are typically in the .60 - .68 on the reduction side of the oxygen analyser scale readings. A firing begins at about 4p.m. to start on pilot lights and very slowly increases up to 10p.m. for final overnight setting at modest burner settings. 6a.m. temperature is about at body reduction time (about 1600°F) and then reduction begins and is largely held throughout remainder of firing which will usually end about 8.30p.m. on day number two.

    Presently I fire in three kilns. The main kiln is a 70 cu.ft. capacity car kiln with propane. The secondary kiln is a 27 cu.ft. car kiln fired about five times a year and the third is my 30 cu.ft. salt/soda kiln, about 6-8 times a year.

Glazes I use but by other potters:

S-2 Shino
Soda ash 120
F-4 soda feldspar 600
Nepheline syenite 2000
Spodumene 520
EPK kaolin 120
O M No.4 ball clay 640

    Likes rich reduction. Always apply first before any other glazes to be used with it – otherwise bubbling happens. Often used with wax resist technique as a base glaze for succeeding layers.

PB-1

F-4 soda feldspar	430
Bone ash	20
O M No.4 ball clay	96
Talc	85
Whiting	100
Flint	330
Bentonite	2% of batch weight (add to dry batch)

Glossy base glaze. Suitable uncoloured or lovely with iron oxide 1% and cobalt carbonate 0.5%. Good for other colours. For nice celadon add 1% red iron oxide.

David Green

Alkaline 1280°C

Cornish stone	50
Potash feldspar	20
Flint	15
Whiting	15

Alkaline Earth (Lime) 1280°C

Potash feldspar	41.8
Whiting	17.5
China clay	13
Flint	27

Alkaline Earth (Barium) 1280°C

Potash feldspar	40
Whiting	9.6
Barium carbonate	14.2
China clay	14.1
Flint	21.6

Alkaline Earth (Magnesium) 1280°C

Potash feldspar	35
Dolomite	16
China clay	9
Flint	34

Zinc Oxide 1280°C

Potash feldspar	60.1
Whiting	6.8
Zinc oxide	7.7
China clay	13.9
Flint	10.9

Ian Gregory CR 172

Stoneware Body 1 Reduction

Dobles fireclay	40
Pikes AT ball clay	60

Stoneware Body 2

Dobles fireclay 50
Pikes AT ball clay 30
SM ball clay 20

    Both good for paperclay mix. Add up to 25% paper pulp by volume, mix as slip then dry out.

Raw Glaze Green-grey Speckle 1280°C Reduction

Potash feldspar 50
AT ball clay 25
Talc 10
Whiting 10
Bentonite 3
Quartz 5
Manganese dioxide 5
This lowers fluxing temperature to 1260°C

    Good in saltglaze, but crazed.

Greenish Ash Looking Glaze 1260-1280°C Moderate Reduction

Ball clay 36
Whiting 28
Potash feldspar 8
Quartz 18
Red iron oxide 4
Talc 3

Shino 1260°C Orange in Moderate Reduction

Nepheline syenite 33
Feldspar 33
AT ball clay 33

    Petalite instead of nepheline syenite lowers temperature.

Satin Gloss Yellow

Feldspar 24
Whiting 18
AT ball clay 30
Flint 30
Red iron oxide 13

    For porcelain in salt or stoneware.

Engobe Recipe for Slip Decoration or for Salt 1280°C

China clay 25
White ball clay 25
Feldspar 25
Flint 25
Add:
Green
Rutile 1-6%
Cobalt 1-3%
Dark blue
Cobalt 1-3%
Blue-green
Chrome oxide 1-5%
Cobalt 1-3%

Matt White Reduction 1260-1280°C
Barium carbonate 50%
China clay 50%
> Heavy speckle over iron clay like St Thomas. White in oxidation, grey white in reduction. Remains matt in salt firing.

Celadon (light) 1280°C Reduction
Talc 12
Potash feldspar 31
Whiting...14
China clay 7
Quartz..33
Red iron oxide 3

Michael Guassardo   CR 165, 178

GB56 Base Cone 7-13 Oxidation/Reduction
Potash feldspar 47.3
Silica..29
Whiting...10
Dolomite 6.2
Zinc..5.8
Bentonite/Wyoming 1.7

Base Glaze A3 Orton Cone 12 Reduction
Cornish stone 73
Talc 5.5
Whiting...9.5
Kaolin 10.5
Bone ash 1.5

R5
Potash feldspar 40
Silica..20
Bentonite 2
Wollastonite 10
Frit (G142)..28
+ Copper carbonate 1%
+ Tin oxide 2%
> Flambé with plum/purple tones – fairly stable.

J28
Kaolin 12.9
Potash feldspar 36.5
Whiting...11.7
Silica..28.9
Frit (G142)..10
+ Copper carbonate 1%
+ Tin oxide 1%
> Transparent pink – stable.

R2D
Frit (G142) 26
Potash feldspar 18
Soda feldspar 15
Wollastonite 16
Calcined kaolin 20
Silica...8
+ Copper carbonate 0.6%
+ Tin oxide 1%
    Bright blood red transparent – very fluid.

R1
Potash feldspar 79
Frit (G142) 9
Whiting 12
+ Copper carbonate 0.58%
+ Tin oxide 1%
    Dark transparent red.

Factors Influencing Reds
Although our copper reds are all used as over-decorators, the following points are also pertinent if you wish to apply the glaze directly on to the biscuited pot. Obviously a fine, low iron clay body is preferable.

Guidelines: Dark Transparent Red
Low copper e.g. 0.25-0.5% copper carbonate
High boron 5-8%
High alkali ....8% (up to)
Low alumina 8-10%
Tin oxide...1% approx.
No magnesia

Guidelines: Opaque Pink/Red
High copper e.g. 1-2% copper carbonate
Low or no boron
Low alkali 5%
High alumina 13-14%
Tin oxide...1% approx.

    Copper red glazes need to be well matured to develop the red which poses another problem as the most brilliant red develop in a fluid low alumina glaze. We have found that a deep rich red when stiffened by increasing the silica and alumina but keeping the ratio of all oxides the same, did not run at all but fired to an uninteresting pinky red.

Babs Haenen CR 160

Glaze 1240-1260°C Reduction
Barium carbonate 59.1
Whiting 30
Zinc oxide..8.1
Nepheline syenite 133.8
Quartz 24.6
    An addition of 2.5% or 5% tin oxide makes different colours. Babs Haenan plays around

with this glaze: instead of using nepheline syenite she uses potash feldspar, which gives a different surface.

Susan Halls CR 146, 177
(work illustrated)

Paperclay
Wood pulp is simply paper-pulp. My source is egg-boxes of the crudest quality. There is a little size in them and so they are easier to break down. Also the hairy quality gives extra strength in making. Glossy magazines have proved unsatisfactory and newspapers, with all their ink, leave unpleasant residues in the clay.
Method: Tear up paper. Soak for 0.5-1 hour. Mix in a liquidiser, blender or hand whisk – the latter takes muck longer. Add the pulp to the clay slops and treat as reclaim.
Thanks to Colin Pearson, **Cellulose Fibre for Paperclay** is now available in this country and is sold by Potterycrafts, Stoke-on-Trent.

A Very Reliable Slip-glaze Cone 9 Reduction
Ball clay (HVAR) 10
China clay...45
Whiting...45
Red iron oxide 2

An excellent sculptural glaze. Rusty where thin and mustardy coloured where thick. Brighter yellow on porcelain. Apply less thickly than a regular glaze.

Frank Hamer CR 133

Matt to Shiny Semi-Transparent Glaze Reduction or Oxidation 1250-1280°C
Potash feldspar 43
China clay...14
Flint 9
Whiting...14
Dolomite 7
Low expansion frit 6
Zirconium silicate 7

This glaze has a good colour response to slips. The mattness occurs most at the lower temperature range and with very slow cooling.

Matt White Semi-opaque Glaze Reduction or Oxidation 1250-1280°C
Potash feldspar 41
China clay...21
Flint 5
Whiting...16
Talc 7
Dolomite 4
Standard borax frit 3
Zirconium silicate 3

This glaze is ideal for brushwork decoration painted on the unfired glaze surface because it is very stable. Being semi-opaque it is also useful over coloured slips. Mattness depends upon speed of cooling. It is complementary to the glaze above.

Cone 6 Whiting Glaze 1200°C Oxidation
Potash feldspar 44
China clay 13
Flint 16
Whiting 20
Standard borax frit 7

This is the equivalent of Leach's cone 8 limestone glaze but for 1200°C instead of Leach's 1250°C. On most stoneware clays this glaze is a shiny transparent when thin but a frosted matt when thick. The opacity is from the suspended bubbles which also enlivens the colour from slips and oxides painted underneath.

Temmoku Glaze 1200-1250°C Oxidation or Reduction
Potash feldspar 35
China clay 8
Flint 19
Whiting 15
Borax frit (P2246) 10
Natural red iron oxide 13

This is an excellent recipe upon which to try variations. The amounts of clay and frit can be rebalanced to obtain stiffer glazes (more clay) or more fluid glazes (more frit). Also other clays and frits will give differing results. The iron oxide can also be varied between 10 and 20 to achieve the 'break' required, remembering that the type of body itself is an equally important factor here.

John Harlow

Green Glaze Seger Cone 8 Oxidation
Mixed wood ash unwashed 25
Triscombe stone 42.5
Hymod AT ball clay 10
Nepheline syenite 10
Standard borax frit 10
Zircon silicate 1
Titanium dioxide 1
Cobalt oxide 0.5

Cream Glod Opaque Seger Cone 8 Oxidation
Triscombe stone 50
Standard borax frit 20
Titanium dioxide 5
Zircon silicate 5
Talc 10
Hymod AT ball clay 5
Limestone 5

Matt Yellow Brown Seger Cone 8 Oxidation

Triscombe stone 46
Limestone local 18
China clay...27
Iron oxide 9

Roger Harris CR 180

Clay Body
Hymod AT 25kg
Hyplas 67 ....25kg
Feldspar 1kg
Sand 8kg
Red iron oxide 200gm

This makes a superb throwing body for pots, from small cream jugs up to large cider jars.

Glazes

Temmoku 1
Potash feldspar 70
Calcium borate frit 10
Limestone (whiting) 10
China clay...10
Red iron oxide 10

Firing range cone 8-10, oxidation or reduction, medium thickness, ideal temperature 1280°C with a 45 minute soak. Any stoneware clay.

Temmoku 1 is particularly good for giving a lush shiny black which breaks bright orange-rust on thin sections such as rims and edges of handles. This is because I have included a 'colour enhancer' in the recipe, in this case calcium borate frit, which brightens colour considerably. An alternative enhancer would be colemanite if you have no CBF, but this is a less reliable material.

Temmoku 2
Potash feldspar 65
Silica (quartz or flint) 15
Limestone (whiting) 12
China clay...8
Red iron oxide 8

Firing details are as for the Temmoku 1.

Temmoku 2 is a good standard temmoku glaze, which comes out shiny black with red rust on thin edges. Very nearly all temmoku glazes work at their very best at 1280°C or higher, due to the melting characteristics of iron oxides. Many potters claim that reduction is necessary, but this is due to the fluxing action which reduction has on iron oxide. If you try a temmoku glaze in an electric kiln and it comes out a brown treacle colour, this can often be corrected by increasing the iron in the recipe by half as much again e.g. from 8-12%.

Harrow Glazes

Harrow Dolomite and Tin Cone 8-10 Oxidation
Potash feldspar 52
Dolomite 23.5

China clay 21
Whiting 3.5
Tin oxide 8

Harrow Cone 9 Oxidation
Soda feldspar 25
Dolomite 15
China clay 25
Bone ash 10
Quartz 25
Iron oxide 10

Temmoku Cone 9-10 Oxidation
Cone 9 Reduction
Potash feldspar 88
Whiting 12
Iron oxide 8
Colemanite or calcium borate frit 4

Talc Cone 9 Reduction
Soda feldspar 50
Talc 20
Flint 15
Borax 1
China clay 5
Zirconium oxide 2
Ash (mixed) 8

Makoto Hatori   CR 141

UK Glaze 1270°C Electric Kiln
Cornish stone 16.2
Lead bisilicate frit 33.5
Whiting 4.3
China clay 20
Tin oxide 5.9
Dolomite 17.2
Flint 2.7

Father Bernard Hedge

Stoneware Body 1280-1300°C Reduction
W.B.B. HVAR 70
W.B.B. china clay 10
Curtis silica sand 15
Red iron oxide 1

Ewen Henderson CR 98
(work illustrated)

Glaze 1260°C Electric Kiln
Whiting 100
Soda feldspar 100
China clay 70
Lithium carbonate 10
Tin oxide 10
Vanadium pentoxide 10

David Hewitt CR 186

Brown-black Cone 8 Oxidation
Cornish stone 50
China clay 22
Dolomite 23
Whiting 6
Talc 10
Black iron oxide 6%

Kathleen Higgott

White Satin Matt 1250°C Oxidation
Cornish stone 6
Dolomite 2
China clay 2

Andrew Holden

Stoneware Body 1280-1300°C Heavy Reduction
W.B.B. HVAR ball clay 25
W.B.B. BBV ball clay 12.5
W.B.B. china clay Airflow S 12.5
Dobles sand 5
Red iron oxide 1.2

Raw Glazes 1250-1300°C
Potash feldspar 50
Ball clay 30
Whiting 10
Talc 10

    Fired to about 1270°C this glaze has a buttery texture.

1250-1280°C
Ball clay 36
Whiting 28
Potash feldspar 8
Quartz/flint 25

Talc 3

A very high lime glaze which can produce some unusual colours with the addition of varying amounts of iron.

Glaze 1250-1300°C
Potash feldspar 45
Whiting..25
Ball clay 20
Quartz..10
Talc 2
Bone ash 3
Bentonite 3

This glaze is adjusted to work raw by substituting the china clay with ball clay and adding 3% bentonite. This did not change the fired quality of the glaze appreciably. Adding a small amount of bentonite can be useful – it gives plasticity to the glaze out of all proportion to the amount added but the maximum limit is about 5%.

Yellow Base Glaze 1270-1300°C Reduction
Red earthenware clay..................................30
Ball clay 30
Whiting..30
Talc 10

The red clay contributes about 3% iron to the recipe.

With additions of 2% to 8% of red iron oxide this glaze fires yellow-green to various ochre-browns. This is a low silica glaze and it is the type that produces the cleanest yellows.

Harry Horlock Stringer

Taggs Yard Stoneware Matt Speckle Glaze 1260°C Electric Kiln Oxidation
Dolomite 22
Whiting..4
Cornish stone 49
China clay...25
Bentonite 2

This works well over a pyrites body, but speckles can be introduced with the addition of 1oz of magnetic iron added to a 2 gallon bucketful of the glaze.

Joanna Howells CR 183
(work illustrated)

Crackle Glaze 1280°C Reduction
Flint 16.8
Feldspar 32
China clay...16
Wood ash 32
(Different ashes give different results)
Whiting..3.2

Clear Glaze 1280°C Reduction
From Mo Jupp, a well fitting glaze

Flint 16
China clay..11.9
Dolomite 5.3
Wollastonite 17.6
Cornish stone 63.2
Bentonite 2

> Calcium chloride is used to suspend the glaze. I ball mill for two hours. My kiln is 18 cu.ft. downdraft. Reduce heavily for 950-1220°C then approach neutral, to 1300°C, and soak for one hour.

Sylvia Hyman

Deep Green Celadon (Best for Porcelain) 1260°C Reduction
Potash feldspar 50
Dolomite 6
Ball clay 12
Whiting..10
Zinc oxide...2
Flint 20
+ Red iron oxide 1.5%

Glaze On Glaze (Best on Stoneware) 1260-1280°C Reduction

Basic Glaze (Dip or Pour)
Soda feldspar 26.1
Dolomite 31.9
Kaolin 26.1
Whiting..8.7
Flint 7.2

Top Glaze (Spray)
Potash feldspar 65.46
Dolomite 30.12
Whiting...4.42
+ Rutile 9.5%
+ Yellow ochre..6.5%

Combo Blue 1260-1300°C Oxidation or Reduction
Potash feldspar 17.6
F4 soda feldspar 20.2
Kaolin 16.35
Dolomite 10.05
Whiting...6.55
Talc 9.60
Flint 19.65
+
Cobalt oxide 1.50
Rutile 0.55
Iron oxide 0.50

> This is a good deep blue-purple, reliable glaze which combines well when applied side-by-side or overlapping Basic Glaze, or sprayed on top of Basic Glaze (above) or as a glaze by itself.

To all glazes add:
Bentonite 2%
Few drops of CMC
Epsom salts .... 1 tsp per 100gm

John Jelfs   CR 184
(work illustrated)

Fine White Clay Body
Hyplas 71 .... 55 kg
China clay .... 6 kg
Quartz (120 mesh) .... 5 kg
Molochite (120 mesh) .... 4 kg
FFF feldspar .... 1 kg

Ideal for smaller pots, very strong. Dough mixed, pugged and left for one month at least.

Leach Standard Red Slip
Local red clay
+ Red iron oxide 25%
Sieved through 80's mesh.

Temmoku 1290°C Reduction
Potash feldspar 72.5
Whiting 8.5
Flint 4.6
Iron oxide 7.0
Ball clay 7.4

White Glaze
Cornish stone 49
China clay 16.50
Whiting 10.25
Talc 10.25
Flint 14

Basic Ash
Ash (Beech/Ash/Elm) 45
Potash feldspar 45
Local black iron bearing clay 7.5
Flint 7.5

This glaze varies widely according to the source of the ash. Adjustments can be made with the flint content. Usually good over iron bearing slip.

Dry Ochre Ash
FFF feldspar 35
China clay 30
Limestone 23
Mixed ash 12
+ Iron ochre 5%

This glaze varies widely with thickness, but is always interesting. A wide variety of stains can be added to the basic glaze.

These three glazes benefit from a long gentle reduction (8 hours).

All pots are biscuit fired to 1000°C and then reduction fired to cone 10 in a 30 cu.ft. natural gas kiln.

Caitlin Jenkins CR 177

Silk Glaze 1280°C Reduction/Oxidation
Potash feldspar 35
Dolomite 5
Whiting 20
Flint 15
China clay 25

Chris Jenkins

Semi Shiny White Ash 1270°C Oxidation
Wood ash 18
Cornish stone 18
Feldspar 18
Whiting 9
Ball clay 9
Flint 19
Zirconium silicate 10
Tin oxide 3

Jean Jones CR 177

Stoneware Body
Clay body is white stoneware from Ceradel of Limoges KPCL 87 700. Firing in electric kiln to 1650°C over 12 hours.

Shiny Green Glaze (Copper Underglaze)
Ash 500
Silica 250
China clay 250
Black copper oxide 25

WM Top Glaze
Feldspar 600
Ash 500
Silica 400

The only commercial glaze I use is David Frith's deep iron, for which I thank him.

Malcolm Jones

Broken Brown – Electric Kiln 1260°C
Feldspar 80
Flint 20

Ball clay 15
China clay..20
Barium carbonate...40
Manganese dioxide 5
Vanadium pentoxide 10

    Expensive glaze but gives pleasant rust colour and spectacular results over other glazes.

Stephanie Kalan

Copper Red Glazes 1160°C Reduction

From 0.5-1% Copper oxide and from 1-2% Tin oxide should be added to the following 4 glazes to produce reds.

Lead bisilicate 10
Feldspar 16
Soda ash 10
Whiting...10
Zinc oxide..5
China clay..3
Calcined borax 23
Flint 23

    Produces iridescent blue deep red, golden sheen when reduced on cooling.

1160°C

Lead bisilicate 23
Feldspar 31
Calcined borax 19
Whiting..3
Barium carbonate...3
Boric acid 1
China clay..3
Flint 17

    Results as above. Both glazes are pale blue when oxidised.

Porcelain Glazes 1300°C

Feldspar 31
Whiting...11
Barium carbonate...22
China clay..13
Flint 28

    Alright on siliceous porcelain. Might craze on stoneware.

Feldspar 20
Whiting...13
Barium carbonate...14
China clay..20
Flint 33

    Both porcelain glazes produce very good sang de beouf.

Calcium Matt Glaze 1160°C

Feldspar 40
Dolomite 14

Whiting 7
China clay 11
Boric acid 4
Flint 24

Alumina Matt Glazes

1250°C
Feldspar 33
Dolomite 5
Whiting 18
Boric acid 2
China clay 26
Flint 16

1300°C
Feldspar 31
Dolomite 5
Whiting 22
China clay 27
Flint 13

Barium Matt Glazes

1230°C
Feldspar 37
Whiting 14
Barium carbonate 27
China clay 13
Flint 9

1160°C
Lead bisilicate 12
Feldspar 10
Whiting 13
Barium sulphate 36
China clay 13
Flint 16

Walter Keeler CR 113, 152, 179
(work illustrated)

Body
Body is fireclay and handbuilding clay. Biscuit 1000°C, glaze 1280°C with various degrees of reduction – some with reduction through cooling cycle.

Big Pots Base Glaze 1280°C Reduction
China clay 50
Feldspar 25
Whiting 25

with additions of iron oxide and cobalt/copper oxide combinations.

Chris Keenan CR 186
(work illustrated)

Geoffrey Whiting's Temmoku Orton Cone 9 Reduction
Cornish stone 85
Whiting...15
China clay..10
Quartz..20
Red iron oxide 10
    Reduction after 1000°C.

Deep Celadon Orton Cone 9 Reduction
Quartz..21
China clay..27
Potash feldspar...19
Wollastonite 33
Red iron oxide 0.5
    Reduction after 1000°C.

Christy Keeney CR 178
(work illustrated)

Stoneware Body
The early heads are modelled from a crank body and painted with porcelain slip, coloured stains and rutile light. They were fired to a final temperature of 1280°C.
The flattened heads and figures are all made from a raku crank body covered with a white earthenware slip and given the first layer of underglaze stains then fired to 1040°C. Manganese dioxide mixed with copper oxide 50/50 and vanadium are rubbed in, the final coat of underglaze stain is added then fired to 1140°C.

Gouri Khosla CR 73

Orange with Black and White Speckles 1285°C Reduction

First Glaze
Feldspar 25
Whiting...12
Ball clay 25
Quartz..25
Red iron oxide 13

Second Glaze
Feldspar 48
Whiting...20
China clay..22
Flint or quartz 10
Titanium dioxide 8

On its own the first glaze is a rich red. I used the second glaze over the first glaze to produce a beautiful orange with streaks of white with black spots in a gas kiln. The thinner the second glaze, the more rust. But it is better when both glazes are fairly thickly applied. I have fired this in an oxidised kiln but the result is not half as good.

Iron Glaze 1260-1280°C Oxidation or Reduction

Feldspar 50
Whiting..10
China clay...15
Quartz...10
Borax..5
Red iron oxide 9

A reliable glaze for utility ware. In India (where I have my pottery) we don't get any borax frits so I have used ordinary borax crystals ground down with hot water (it is quicker with hot water) in a pestle and mortar, then added to the glaze and sieved.

Brick Orange Glaze 1260-1280°C Oxidation or Reduction

Feldspar 70
Whiting..10
China clay...18
Quartz...10
Dolomite 23
Borax..13
Tin oxide..8
Bone ash 3
Red iron oxide 8

A very reliable glaze (one of my favourites). Different strength of the brick orange colour depending on the temperature. Rise of temperature should be slow from 1050°C onwards, with 25-30 minutes soak. Double dip with the same glaze gives good result.

Wollastonite Glaze 1260°C Oxidation

Wollastonite 30
China clay...40
Feldspar 15
Talc 10
Tin oxide..5

This glaze has a wide firing range from 1250-1280°C. It's a smooth matt white glaze, breaking to orange white, where thinly applied, particularly on a stoneware body. Usual firing schedule with a soak of 25-30 minutes after cone bends. Have not yet tried in reduction kiln. Could try with part ball clay.

Zinc, Barium and Nickel Glazes 1260°C Oxidation
E.C.1

Feldspar 49
China clay..5
Quartz..5
Barium carbonate 21
Zinc oxide...15
Nickel oxide 3

Smooth matt turquoise blue, very flat colour, no texture. Thin areas are mauve-brown.

E.C.1a

Feldspar 49
China clay 5
Quartz 5
Barium carbonate 26
Zinc oxide 15
Nickel oxide 1

Matt midnight blue with bright pink where thick. Quite sensational.

E.C.1b

Feldspar 48
Whiting 6
Quartz 6
Barium carbonate 25
Zinc oxide 15
Nickel oxide 2

Dark mauve-purple with pale blue specks on thin areas and magenta spots in thickly applied areas. Smooth, matt.

E.C.1d

Feldspar 35
China clay 2
Quartz 10
Barium carbonate 30
Zinc oxide 10
Nickel oxide 2

Speckly ash grey with pink spots in thick areas. Smooth matt.

E.C.3a

Feldspar 45
Whiting 8
China clay 5
Quartz 5
Barium carbonate 20
Lithium carbonate 5
Zinc oxide 2
Nickel oxide 3

The first test was beautiful. Speckled dark grey and white, like a river stone, smooth matt. But I must have made a mistake somewhere while weighing, because I've never got that first result back again.

E.C.4a

Feldspar 49
Whiting 4
Zinc oxide 2
Titanium dioxide 9
Dolomite 23
Nickel oxide 3

Glaze has pooled in a bright green with round crystals. Sides are a lustrous pearly pale green with brown specks.

E.C.4b

Feldspar 40

Whiting......4
Zinc oxide......2
Titanium dioxide......9
Dolomite......25
Nickel oxide......3
   Similar to E.C.4a but better.

E.C.4c
Feldspar......40
Whiting......15
Quartz......5
Lithium carbonate......2
Zinc oxide......5
Magnesium carbonate......10
Nickel oxide......3
   Speckled light and dark green pooling. Thin glaze on sides a beautiful textured, lustrous grey-brown-gold.

E.C.6a
Feldspar......36
Whiting......12
Quartz......5
Barium carbonate......35
Zinc oxide......12
Nickel oxide......2
   Speckled brown and off white sides where glaze is thin. Pooling in the centre is pink with purple spots.

Crystal Glaze
Feldspar......36
Whiting......13
China clay......5
Quartz......22
Zinc oxide......24
Copper carbonate......0.5
Nickel oxide......0.5
Titanium dioxide......2
Red iron oxide......0.5
   Bright turquoise crystal flowers on pale lime green base. Very beautiful.

Peter Lane CR 161

Silky Matt Porcelain Glaze 1260-1280°C Oxidation
Nepheline syenite......50
Barium carbonate......15
Zinc oxide......20
Flint......15
   Silky matt surface with small crystals where not too thickly applied. Interesting variegated colour from additions of up to 4% rutile together with up to 2% copper carbonate or up to 1% cobalt carbonate. (Titanium may be used in place of rutile with slightly different results.)

Shiny Porcelain Glaze 1260-1280°C Oxidation
Nepheline syenite 70
Whiting...9
Zinc oxide...9
Flint 10
Lithium carbonate 2

> Shiny glaze studded with tiny crystals. Inclined to run at 1280°C if applied too thickly. Addition of 2% rutile and 2% copper gives fascinating results but it is worth experimenting with other oxides with the rutile.

Dry Ochre Glaze 1280-1300°C Oxidation
Mixed ash 50
China clay...50
Yellow ochre..5

> Fascinating texture when thickly applied. Additional colour and surface variation come from the selective use of temmoku glaze brushed on the bisque before spraying the ash glaze.

1280°C Oxidation or Reduction
Mixed wood ash 50
China clay...50
Cobalt carbonate 0.5%
(also try with other colouring oxides)

> Reduction firing 1280°C is recommended but also attractive when oxidised. Very dark brown when thinly applied but selective over-glazing of some areas (using pouring, painting or resist techniques) with a light glaze such as the clear glaze below reveals the content and rich contrasts of colour and texture can be achieved.

Clear
Cornish stone 85
Whiting..15

Bernard Leach CR 134, 168

Porcelain Body
China clay..45
Feldspar 25
Ball clay 8.33
Flint 13.33
Bentonite 5.5

David Leach CR 125, 126, 149
(work illustrated)

Porcelain Body 1260-1300°C
ECC Standard porcelain china clay............53
Potash feldspar (Potterycrafts or ECC) 25
Water ground or fine ground quartz(ECC) 17
Quest white bentonite 3

> ECC Standard porcelain china clay is more plastic than Grolleg so I have reduced the usual amount of bentonite from 5% to 3%. Quest white bentonite from Colin Stewart, Wharton Lodge Works, Winsford, Cheshire.

Stoneware Body 1280-1320°C Reduction

Hyplas 71 ball clay (ECC) 224
CY ball clay (ECC) 112
Local sand 30's mesh 60
 396lb dry weight
Water 10 gallons 100
 496lb plastic body

> Dry mix for quarter of an hour. Add water slowly. Wet mix for further half hour. The clay is then taken from the mixer in a throwable state but needs ageing in a densely packed bin for about three weeks or it will throw 'short'. This then makes a very throwable plastic textured body. The tooth or texture largely depends on the sand particle size and shape.

Alternative Stoneware Body Reduced 1280-1320°C

BBV ball clay (Watts, Blake & Bearne) 56
TA ball clay (Watts, Blake & Bearne)..........16
Hymod AT ball clay (ECC).........................20
30's mesh sand 16

Y Ching Celadon (Chinese sky after rain)

Average china clay 25
Potash feldspar 25
Whiting...25
Quartz (at least 200's mesh) 25
Natural red iron oxide 0.5

> Liable to craze on some porcelain bodies

Yellow Celadon 1300-1320°C (Orton)

Talc 12
Potash feldspar 31
Whiting...14
China clay...7
Quartz...33
Red iron oxide 3

> This recipe tends to give a mustardy yellow glaze which is dependent on the thickness of application and temperature; it can crystallise.

Orange to Red Glaze 1260-1300°C Reduction (Orton)

Nepheline syenite 50
Old CY ball clay 50
(or certain red clays)

> This glaze has a wide range, producing tomato red at around 1260°C going to orange at 1300°C. Needs reduction. Has to be applied thickly. I use it chiefly for decoration from a slip trailer over other glazes. The clay should be lightly calcined to a temperature of about 600°C to remove plasticity or over contraction; if not will tend to crawl on top of other glazes. It can be applied thickly enough to be used uncalcined on raw bodies as a slip glaze. It may be necessary to experiment with a variety of iron bearing earths on clays to get the red you want.

Grey Korean Celadon 1280°C Reduction (Orton)

Barium carbonate 2
HP Stone (if obtainable, feldspar if not) 60
Whiting...7
China clay...5
Quartz...24

Black iron oxide 1.5
Bentonite 1

    The glaze should be lawned as fine as possible, say 200's mesh, to disperse the bentonite. If applied thickly this glaze gives a very pleasant characteristic crackle.

Gun Metal Glaze 1260-1280°C Reduction
China clay..25
Potash feldspar...26
Whiting..25
Quartz...25
Cobalt oxide 1
Red iron oxide 8
Manganese dioxide 3

    Tends to be matt at cone 9 but breaks to shiny black at cone 10+.

Gilles Le Corre
(work illustrated)

Stoneware Throwing Body 1280-1295°C
Potclays Reduction St Thomas (1104) 50
Potclays stoneware throwing body (1110) 50

    This is pugged twice and left one or two weeks to settle before throwing.

Stoneware Glazes to Orton Cone 9-10 Reduction

White Glaze Base for Decoration
Potash feldspar...20
Quartz...27
China clay..21
Dolomite...12
Talc...20

Decorating Glazes for Brush and Trailer on White Glaze
Green Glaze
Potash feldspar...62
Whiting...7
China clay...5
Quartz...24
Cobalt carbonate 0.5
Chrome oxide...1

Blue to Purple Glaze Orton Cone 9-10 Reduction
Potash feldspar...40
Quartz...36
Whiting..19
Cobalt oxide 2
Tin oxide..2

Golden Brown Orton Cone 9-10 Reduction
Potash feldspar...60
Whiting..24
China clay..15

Red iron oxide 8
Titanium dioxide 4
Rutile 5

Dick Lehman CR 138

Glaze Recipes
All glazes Orton cone 9-10, Kaolin (China clay) = EPK, Ball clay = OM-4, Flint = 325 mesh

Gloss White
Whiting.....................................2180
Custer feldspar 4000
Kaolin 1270
Flint 2550
Zircopax 910

    A consistent glossy white.

Glick C-7
Custer feldspar 5600
Whiting.....................................800
Kaolin 800
Gerstley borate 800
Flint 800

    For all my 'stains' I mix dry ingredients as per recipe provided and then add this clear glaze to bring the mix to a brushable consistency.

Lehman White
Dolomite...................................1432
Kaolin 1498
Flint 955
Talc 955
F-4 spar (soda) 3822
Zircopax 1338
Spodumene 700

    A creamy satin matt white (on the yellow side of white). Responds nicely to brushwork of other glazes over the top. Very forgiving of small runs or unevenness in glaze application.

2-D Blue
Custer feldspar 4900
Ball clay 2500
Dolomite...................................2300
Whiting.....................................400
Rutile 400
Cobalt carbonate 50

    A variation of the Rhodes glaze base. Satin green when thin. Glossy blue-green when thick. Reveals alterations and throwing rings nicely.

Lehman Red
Nepheline syenite 3700
Flint 3500
Dolomite...................................1200

Whiting..800
Strontium carbonate 600
Kaolin 200
Tin oxide...300
Copper carbonate 50

    Cantankerous and widely varying – but when it is nice it is so lovely – enough so that I keep using it.

Mark's Special
Nepheline syenite 3700
Flint 3500
Dolomite..1200
Whiting..800
Strontium carbonate 600
Kaolin 200
Rutile 500
Copper carbonate 200

    A fine 'sea-foam' (or so our customers call it). Green glossy.

Rhodes 32 with Rutile
Custer feldspar....................................4704
Ball clay 2400
Dolomite...2160
Whiting...336
Rutile 768

    We still use this gold matt glaze after 20 years.

Landshark Blue
Albany slip...4210
Nepheline syenite 526
Cobalt carbonate 264

    Almost black-blue, so strong that I only use it to decorate with or over the top of other glazes.

Breakfast Special
Nepheline syenite 3700
Flint 3488
Dolomite...1194
Whiting...804
Strontium carbonate 636
Kaolin 207
Red iron oxide 258
Rutile 502
Cobalt carbonate 30

    A rutile blue.

Temmoku
Custer feldspar....................................2378
Flint 2883
Whiting...1225
Kaolin 721
Iron oxide 793

    Nice metallic flashing on a dark, rich brown-black glow.

Will Levi Marshall CR 173, 179

Clay Body
Will's Wonderful White Stoneware (Revised)
Grolleg china clay 40
Hyplas 71 ball clay 40
Potash feldspar 15
Silica...5
+ Molochite 80's ....10 parts
+ Molochite 120's ....15 parts
+ Bentonite ....1 part

Glaze Recipes
All cone 10 except where stated.

Caramel Yellow
Petalite 46
Nepheline syenite 36
Titanium dioxide 12
Dolomite 9
Plastic kaolin 9
    Oxidation or reduction. Semi-gloss/opaque.

Will's Scarlet Fever
Cornish stone 27
Calcium carbonate 8
Dolomite 5
Gerstley borate 13
Plastic kaolin 10
Silica...27
+ Potclays high temp. red stain ....10 parts
+ Bentonite ....2 parts
    Oxidation gloss/transparent.

'Dictionary' Chrome Tin Pink
Cornish stone 48
Plastic kaolin 14
Silica...5
Calcium carbonate 28
Tin oxide..5
Chrome oxide 0.1
    Oxidation. Gloss/semi transparent.

BaO Turquoise
(DANGER: outside of functional pots only)
Barium oxide 32
Silica 8
Plastic kaolin 8
Soda feldspar 44
Dolomite 4
Bentonite 1.5
Copper 2.5
    Oxidation. Satin.

Will's Clouded Sky Blue Cone 9-10
Nepheline syenite 36
Calcium carbonate 14
Talc 9
Tin oxide 9
Grolleg (china clay) 14
Silica 9
Soda ash 15
+ Copper carbonate .... 1 part
    Oxidation or reduction. Satin/opaque.

ZnO Base Cone 9-10
(With slow cooling can crystallize)
Potash feldspar 40
Gerstley borate 12
Dolomite 7
Zinc oxide 15
Ball clay 5
Silica 20
Bentonite 2
+ colourant
Pale green-blue
Copper carbonate .... 1 part
Lavender
Tin oxide .... 2 parts
Cobalt .... 0.25 parts

Will's Oribe (Deep Green)
Potash feldspar 50
Calcium carbonate 15
Plastic kaolin 5
Silica 30
+ Copper carbonate .... 5 parts
+ Bentonite .... 3 parts
    Oxidation. Shiny/transparent.

Cobalt Green Cone 9-10
Deep green breaking into black where thin
Nepheline syenite 70
Calcium carbonate 5
Gerstley borate 2
Petalite 15

Ball clay 8
+ Cobalt carbonate ....1 part
+ Rutile ....2 parts
    Oxidation or reduction. Semi-matt.

Teal Blue
Potash feldspar 33
Calcium carbonate 27
Silica 27
Ball clay 11
Gerstley borate 2
+ Cobalt carbonate ....1 part
+ Chrome oxide ....1 part
    Oxidation or reduction. Satin/opaque.

Will's BaO Chartreuse
(DANGER: outside functional pots only)
Nepheline syenite 24
Lithium carbonate 13
Calcium carbonate 3
Barium carbonate 23
Ball clay 3
Bentonite 3
Silica 31
+ Chrome ....0.5 part
    Oxidation. Shiny/transparent, runny.

VC Black Satin Matt
Soda feldspar 20
Potash feldspar 20
Dolomite 15
Talc 13
Calcium carbonate 2
Ball clay 10
Silica 20
+ colourant
Chrome oxide ....1 part
Red iron oxide ....3 parts
Manganese dioxide ....2 parts
Cobalt oxide ....3 parts
    Oxidation or reduction. Satin.

MgO (White) Cone 9-10
Potash feldspar 41
Gerstley borate 12
Dolomite 7
Talc 15
Ball clay 5
Silica 20
Bentonite 2
Tin oxide..2
    Oxidation. Opaque butter/satin.

+ colourants:
Pastel yellow
Zirconium yellow stain W.G. Ball 100 ......10 parts
Flasher pink
High temperature red stain ....5 parts
Orange
Mandarin stain ....10 parts
Purple-black
Black cobalt ....2 parts

Will's High CaO Glaze (Steel Blue) Cone 9-10
(DANGER: outside of functional pots only)
Potash feldspar 14
Dolomite 9
Barium carbonate 9
Calcium carbonate 29
Ball clay 17
Silica 18
+ Cobalt oxide ....0.5 parts
+ Red iron oxide ....2 parts
    Oxidation or reduction. Gloss/matt/runny.

VCDI
Nepheline syenite 45
Calcium carbonate 15
Talc 10
Tin oxide..10
Silica 10
Grolleg (china clay) 10
+ Chrome oxide ....0.2 part
    Oxidation or reduction. Opaque/satin. Only just pink-lavender.

Nickel/BaO Pink
(DANGER: outside functional pots only)
Potash feldspar 33
Barium carbonate 39
Zinc oxide..16
Grolleg (china clay) 3
Silica 6
+ Nickel ....0.5-1.5 parts
+ Bentonite ....2 parts
    Oxidation. Matt/semi-opaque, runny.

A.1 Turquoise Cone 9/10
Barium carbonate 31.99
Flint 7.99
Grolleg 7.99
Soda feldspar 43.98
Dolomite 4
+ Copper oxide 2.5%
+ Bentonite 1.5%
    Colour: Semi-opaque blue
    Surface: Semi-matt or satin

A.2 Turquoise Cone 9/10
Strontium carbonate 31.99
Flint 8
Grolleg 8
Soda feldspar 43.99
Dolomite..4
+ Copper oxide 2.5%
+ Bentonite 1.5%
    Colour: Semi-opaque blue
    Surface: Semi-matt or satin

A.3 Turquoise Cone 9/10
Soda feldspar 68.8
Dolomite..4.4
Grolleg 3.1
Flint 3.7
Strontium carbonate 21.9
+ Bentonite 2%
+ Copper carbonate......................................2.5%
    Colour: translucent blue
    Surface: semi-matt or satin

B.1 Chartreuse Cone 6/10
Nepheline syenite 23.99
Lithium carbonate 12.99
Whiting...3
Barium carbonate..22.99
Flint 30.99
Ball clay 3
+ Chrome oxide...0.52%
+ Bentonite 3.09%
    Colour: Transparent blue-green
    Surface: Shiny or glossy

B.2 Chartreuse Cone 6/10
Nepheline syenite 24.74
Lithium carbonate 13.4
Whiting...3.09
Strontium carbonate 23.71
Flint 31.96
Ball clay 3.09
+ Chrome oxide...0.54%
+ Bentonite 3.19%
    Colour: Transparent blue-green
    Surface: Shiny or glossy

B.3 Chartreuse Cone 6/10
Nepheline syenite 30.5
Lithium carbonate 12.3
Whiting...3.6
Strontium carbonate 15.2
Flint 36.1
Ball clay 6.6

+ Chrome oxide 0.5%
+ Bentonite 3%
    Colour: Transparent blue-green
    Surface: Shiny or glossy

Nickel Pink Cone 9/10
Potash feldspar 33
Barium carbonate 39
Zinc oxide..16
Grolleg 5
Flint 6
+ Nickel oxide 0.5%
+ for red increase 1.5%
+ Bentonite 2.0%
    Colour: Opaque purple-opaque red
    Surface: Semi-matt or satin

C.2 Nickel Pink Cone 9/10
Colour: Opaque purple-opaque red
Surface: Semi-matt or satin
Potash feldspar 33
Strontium carbonate 39
Zinc oxide..16
Grolleg 5
Flint 6
+ Nickel oxide 0.5%
+ for red increase 1.5%
+ Bentonite 2%

C.3 Nickel Pink Cone 9/10
Colour: Opaque purple-opaque red
Surface: Matt
Potash feldspar 43.1
Strontium carbonate 28.8
Zinc oxide..16.6
Grolleg 3.4
Flint 5
+ Nickel oxide 0.5%
+ for red increase 1.5%
+ Bentonite 2%

Eileen Lewenstein   CR 169
(work illustrated)

Stoneware Body for Handbuilding 1250°C Oxidation
Hymod SMD ball clay 4
China clay...1
Molochite 30-80 1
    Useful when a strong whitish body is required. A finer mesh Molochite (such as 80's dust) could be substituted for throwing.

Shiny Brown 1250°C Oxidation
Mixed wood ash 31
Red clay 40
Feldspar 4
Flint 18
Dolomite 7

Semi-matt, Yellowish Brown 1250°C Oxidation
Mixed wood ash 40
Red clay 40
Feldspar 20

These work with my present supply of wood ash. The red clay is from Sussex Weald.

Ash Glaze 1245°C
Feldspar 21
Mixed wood ash 35
David Leach Porcelain Body 33
Flint 11
Responds well to the addition of small percentages of oxides for colouring such as:
Grey-green
Red iron oxide 0.5
Copper carbonate 0.5
Cobalt carbonate 0.1

Chris Lewis CR 162

Clay Body
Hyplas 71 ....2 bags (50kg)
Hymod AT ....1 bag (25kg)

Plus addition of 25% Molochite 80's to 0.0180's mixed with silver sand for garden pots (slightly more Molochite than sand) or 25% Molochite with sand dug from Selmeston, East Sussex, for other wares. Clay is mixed in pit dug in ground and then pugged.

White Glaze Reduction
Cornish stone 14
China clay 8
Flint 3
Whiting 3
Zircon 3

Used over white slip: 50/50 Harry Fraser porcelain body and Hyplas 71 ball clay.

Grey Glaze
Cornish stone 20
Whiting 1
Hyplas 71 81
China clay 2
Wood ash 5
Talc 2

Used over iron bearing slip: red clay 65, iron 35.

Martin Lewis CR 146

Stoneware Glazes 1200-1240°C Electric Kiln

No.1
Ash 50
China clay...50

No.2
Porcelain...65
Barium carbonate..25
Lithium..10
Barium carbonate..50

No.3
Nepheline syenite 50
Plus various amounts of oxides.

Roger Lewis CR 179
(work illustrated)

Clay Bodies
Stoneware V9A (Valentines), White Stoneware (Potclays 1145) and Harry Fraser Porcelain (Potclays 1149). V9A is used for most of the earthenware but with a high biscuit it seems to be satisfactory for this decorative, rather than functional, work. White stoneware and porcelain are used at the higher temperature. Porcelain slip is sometimes applied to larger white stoneware pieces at the leather stage for a porcelain-like appearance.

Semi-gloss 1270°C
Potash feldspar 36.3
Whiting..15.5
China clay...13
Quartz...11
Barium carbonate......................................10.4
Nepheline syenite 7.75
Talc 5.2
Bone ash 1
Inside:
+ Copper carbonate.................................1.5%
+ Cobalt carbonate 0.15%
Outside:
+ Copper carbonate.................................1%
Lid:
+ Yellow stain 7%
+ Coral stain 2%

Stoneware and porcelain are biscuit fired to 1100°C (but this could be fired lower) and glaze fired to 1270°C with a 30-minute soak.

Adrian Lewis-Evans

Stoneware Body 1280-1300°C Medium Reduction
Pike's PK (Excelsior) 50
Pike's SM 40
Fireclay 10
Sand 8

Dark 'Horticultural' Body 1200-1280°C Medium Reduction
Pike's PK (Excelsior) 20
Pike's SM 15
Blaney's K 40
Fireclay 60
Sand 45

The first body can be made with endless variations in that the fireclay (in my case containing fireclay grog) can be replaced with two or three times its amount of Pike's AT or Fayle's Blue and the sand and grog increased up to porosity if for flower vases etc. Testing for this should be with unturned feet and with unglazed interiors. If for drinking, the glazed vessels should be able to withstand the boiling and then cold water test three times. A kindly 'annealing' fill first with 'off the boil' water is to be favoured. The PK to SM ratio should be near to 60:40.

The 'Horticultural' body can be made as listed or the last three items separately, then wedge or pug in 25% of the first stoneware body to improve throwing.

Blaney's local clay is a high firing 'ball' clay with about 10% iron. It can be substituted with rather less earthenware clay and iron added for colour.

Both bodies can be made in slip or doughmixer but always it is essential that SM ball is kibbled or rolled to at least 0.5" down and poured into ample water separately and left to soak for at least an hour before mixing and then adding other clays.

The Dorset ball clays, known to potters as Pike's and Fayle's are obtainable from John Keay House, St. Austell, Cornwall, Tel: +44 1726 74482. They may also arrange for collection at Wareham.

Pike and Fayle, clay cutters for 250 years, merged to become Pike Bros, Fayle and Co., later absorbed into English China Clays. As ECC International, they became part of the French mineral company Imetal and, in turn, the present French company Imerys, though still trading as ECCI.

Two of my much used glazes from the 1950s, reduced at 1280-1300°C:

SC3 Celadon
Potash feldspar 49
China clay...8.5
Whiting..18
Flint 24.5
+ Red iron oxide 2%

This is calculated from Hermann Seger's obsolete cone 3 (1190°C) percentage formula, complete even to its iron content and gives a fine celadon, very close to Nigel Wood's 'technically perfect' Lime-Alkali glaze in 'Ceramic Review' No. 59.

KC1 Temmoku
Potash feldspar 63
Whiting...7

China clay 5
Flint 25
+ Red iron oxide 10%
>This glaze is simply 10% red iron oxide replacing the 1.5% in Kawai's Celadon from Bernard Leach's 'A Potter's Book'. Follow the usual temmoku firing procedures, especially including re-oxidising at the end of the firing.

J Glaze
A chun type glaze giving blue clouds over fireclay or iron slip.
Cypress ash 1
(Macrocarpa or Lawson's, unwashed)
Feldspar 1
Flint 1
+ Yellow ochre (and bentonite) 2%

David Lloyd Jones CR 157

Stoneware Body 1210-1300°C Reduction
Leeds fireclay 35
Hymod SMD ball clay 22
(or W.B.B. HVAR ball clay)
Hymod AT ball clay 22
Potclays red earthenware 9
Nepheline syenite 5
White sand 7
>A warm pale brown. Dry materials are mixed thoroughly in dough mixer (10 minutes), then water is added and mixed for a further 20 minutes. The clay is then pugged (some drying out may be necessary before this) and allowed to mature for at least one month before use.

Matt Blue/Dark Brown Where Thin Cone 9 Reduction
Cornish stone 32
Whiting 23
Flint 9
China clay 36
Manganese dioxide 2
Cupric oxide 1
Cobalt oxide 1
>Try other oxide combinations for different colours.

Tin Glaze
Potash feldspar 48
Flint 30
Whiting 10
Dolomite 6
China clay 2
Tin oxide 4

Good Shiny Celadon Cone 8 1280°C Reduction
Potash feldspar 46.25
Whiting 18
Flint 28

China clay 7.75
Iron oxide 1.5-3%
>Can be opacified with tin oxide 4%.

Temmoku
Cornish stone 60
Flint 15
Whiting 10
China clay 8
Red iron oxide 7

Cone 8 1280°C Reduction
Potash feldspar 10.25
Nepheline syenite 30.75
Dolomite 17
China clay 23.75
Flint 10.75
Whiting 7.5
Iron oxide 5
>Warm cream breaking to red brown, where thinner, over iron bearing body. Do not overfire. Good for iron decoration. Can be opacified with tin oxide 4.

John Lomas

Stoneware Cone 9 Reduction
SMD ball clay (E.C.C.) ....56 lb
AT ball clay (E.C.C) ....28 lb
Joseph Arnold 81 Sand ....15 lb
Cornish stone ....5 lb
Quartz ....5 lb
Red iron oxide ....0.75 lb
>Mixed in a dough mixer, pugged and stored for as long as possible. Cone 9+. Good general purpose reduction body for large and small pots.

Oatmeal Cone 9 Reduction
Cornish stone 42
Dolomite 23
Whiting 3.5
China clay 25
Flint 6.5
>Apply thinly.

Green Speckle Cone 9 Reduction
Potash feldspar 56
Whiting 13
Flint 21
Magnesium carbonate 10
Cobalt carbonate 0.2
Chrome oxide 0.4
>Apply thickly.

Textured Yellow Cone 9 Reduction
Mixed wood ash 55
China clay 45
Rutile 2
Coarse Ilmenite 2
   Apply thinly.

Gillian Lowndes   CR 103, 181
(work illustrated)

Casting Slip 1260°C Oxidised
The casting slip in which she dips fibreglass matting is an American recipe given by Scott Chamberlain.
Grolleg china clay 660
Feldspar 300
Flint 240
Sodium silicate 2
Dispex 1
Water ....1 pint

Stains

Khaki
Chrome oxide 4%
Nickel oxide 4%
Grey
Manganese dioxide 4%
Copper oxide 4%
Pale Grey
Cobalt oxide 1%
Manganese dioxide 4%

Semi-matt Yellowish Ash Stoneware Glaze 1260-1280°C Oxidised
Ash (unsieved Elm) 40
Feldspar 40
Whiting 20
China clay 20
+ Cobalt oxide 2%
+ Nickel oxide 3%
to give blue-grey

Andrew McGarva   CR 145, 166
(work illustrated)

Smooth White Glaze Cone 11 Reduction
Potash feldspar 6
Whiting 1
SMD (or similar ball clay) 4
Talc 1
Zirconium silicate 2

Anne and Laurie McMichael

An Engobe
Kaolin 25
Ball clay 25
Feldspar 20
Quartz 20

For Colours

Blue-Grey
Cobalt 2%
Red iron oxide 1
Manganese dioxide 4

Turquoise
Copper oxide 10%
Cobalt oxide 0.5%

Red
Red iron oxide 25%

> Over these engobes we mostly use our vine ash glaze, poured or sprayed or our clear stain glaze.

Vine Ash Glaze
Vine ash (50's) 31.4
Soda feldspar 32.3
Kaolin 20
Quartz 5
Whiting 9
Bentonite 4

Clear Satin Glaze
Potash feldspar 40
Whiting 25
Kaolin 10
Quartz 25
Bentonite 5

White Glaze
Nepheline syenite 42
Talc 11.6
Kaolin 14
Whiting 19.7
Quartz 7
Ball clay 5.8
Bentonite 5

Ash Slip
Vine ash (50's) 40
Kaolin 50

Colours

Maganese dioxide ....6% Brown-black
Cobalt ....1% Blue
Yellow ochre ....5% Rust yellow
Nickel oxide ....2% Brown to pink

We spray these slips one over the other.

Our only other glaze

Soda spar 21
Chalk..28
Kaolin 45
Colemanite 6
Bentonite 3

This fires ochre or white depending on thickness. On to this we spray oxides – the same glaze plus iron chromate 4, cobalt 8, for a deep blue-black. Or yellow ochre 5% or cobalt 1% one over the other and sometimes washed down with an ordinary hand spray (for house plants) and water, giving fascinating runs and textures. There are endless combinations of these oxides and others and we are always trying them out. The result here is a very dry matt glaze and separate colours.

White Glaze Orton Cone 9 Reduction

Feldspar potash 36
Talc 10
Kaolin 21
Whiting.......................................16.6
Quartz 10
Ball clay 5.5
Bentonite 3

Temmoku Orton Cone 9 Reduction

Feldspar potash 71
Ball clay 8.5
Quartz 8.5
Whiting......................................12.5
Bentonite 3
Red iron oxide (synthetic) 8

Temmoku 1250-1280°C Reduction

Feldspar 68
Whiting..12
Red iron oxide 10
Flint 8
Ball clay 8
Bentonite 3

Light reduction with oxidising conditions during cooling.

Stoneware Body Orton Cone 9 Reduction

Workshop Body

French clay (SAPEC G13).............3
St Thomas white 1
+ Chamotte (40's to dust) 3%

All our work is now raw glazed, and fired in a gas kiln to Orton cone 9 over about 13 hours with light reduction from cone 5 to cone 8 only. The present clay body is mixed roughly by hand and then passed once through a small pug mill. This fires beige.

Carol McNicoll CR 117

Engobe (Daniel Rhodes)

Slip

China clay 5
Ball clay 15
Molochite 20
Leadless frit 5
Nepheline syenite 5
Feldspar 20
Flint 20
Zirconium silicate 5

Jane Maddison CR 182
(work illustrated)

Dolomite Glaze 1260°C

Dolomite 20
Cornish stone 50
China clay 25
Whiting 40
Bentonite 10

Apply as a fine spray over oxides, firing to 1260°C.

Carol Magos

Stoneware Body 1260-1280°C Reduction

Schoolware Clay Body

Potash feldspar 15.7
Powdered Grey's red clay 20
TWVD ball clay 15.5
China clay 14
Powdered Leeds fireclay 13.3
(passed through 60s mesh after weighing)
SM ball clay 5.2
Flint 16.3

The plasticity of this body improved greatly with blunging.

Smooth White Semi-Matt Base Glaze 1270°C Reduction

Potash feldspar 55
Whiting 2
Talc 15
CY ball clay 15
Flint 5
Zircon 8

Coloured Glaze 'Paints'

Black Brown
Potash feldspar 60
Whiting 7
China clay 5
Flint 24
Red iron oxide 8

Red Brown
Potash feldspar 40
Whiting 13.5
TWVD ball clay 20
China clay 2.5
Flint 22
Red iron oxide 8
Titanium dioxide 2.5

Dark Blue
Potash feldspar 32.5
Nepheline syenite 41.25
Ash 7.5
Wrecclesham clay 8.75
TWVD ball clay 2.75
Flint 7.5
Bentonite 5
Copper oxide 4
Cobalt oxide 1

Buff Yellow
Potash feldspar 21.25
Nepheline syenite 20.625
Whiting 10
TWVD ball clay 21.375
Wrecclesham clay 4.375
Flint 10
Bentonite 2.5
Titanium dioxide 2.5
Red iron oxide 1.5
Cobalt oxide 0.5

Turquoise
Potash feldspar 40
Ash 30
Flint 30
Copper oxide 4

Jim Malone CR 161
(work illustrated)

White Slip
Hyplas 71 60
China clay..25
Cornish stone 15

Strong Red Slip
Red clay 75
Iron oxide 25

Ash Celadon Orton Cone 8-10 Reduction
Hornfels 6
Pink granite 26
Hyplas 71 26
Quartz..6
Elm ash...32

This glaze will mature at Orton cone 8 and is good up to cone 10. Good results can be obtained over 'strong red slip' at the upper end of the temperature spectrum.

Pink granite is simply what it says it is, i.e. a pink felspathic granite. Hornfels is a high iron becoming metamorphic rock, its igneous cousin is mudstone or shale. Use any iron bearing stone available in place of the Hornfels if necessary and the pink granite can be replaced by potash feldspar or Cornish stone. However, the result will not be as interesting with refined materials.

Cobalt Pigment
Cobalt carbonate 20
Tin oxide..20
Manganese dioxide 10
Talc 10
Red clay 15
China clay..20
Red iron oxide 5

Quality of pigment is dependent on thorough grinding with a pestle and mortar.

John Maltby CR 29, 78, 102, 122, 137, 166
(work illustrated)

Temmoku 1260-1280°C Reduction
Cornish stone 85
Whiting..15
China clay..10
Quartz..20
Iron oxide 10

Clear Feldspathic Glaze 1260-1280°C Reduction
Feldspar 35
Quartz 20
China clay 20
Dolomite 20
Whiting 5

Victor Margrie

Porcelain Glazes Seger Cone 8 Light Reduction

Semi-Matt Barium Glaze
Potash feldspar 178.2
Barium carbonate 67
Whiting 34
Alumina hydrate 12.5
Tin oxide 15

Shiny Feldspathic Glaze
Potash feldspar 440
China clay 54.2
Flint 16.8
Whiting 21

Semi-Matt Zinc Glaze
Potash feldspar 66.8
Whiting 47
Alumina hydrate 40.6
Flint 46.8
Magnesium carbonate 9.2
Zinc oxide 26.7

Shiny Talc Crackle Glaze
Potash feldspar 131.4
Whiting 29
Flint 48
Magnesium carbonate 42.8

> Biscuit firing (cone 07). Glost kiln is reduced from cone 06-cone 07 and matured at cone 8. I aim at fast firing with light but consistent reduction – too much reduction sullies the glaze.

Bill and Clare Marno

Stoneware Body Orton 10 Heavy Reduction
HVAR ball clay 100
+ sand 10
Feldspar 5
Red iron oxide 1
and grog for large ware.
> Clay in powder form from Watts, Blake & Bearne.

Green 1280°C Reduction
Potash feldspar 53
Flint 20
Talc 10
Whiting..10
China clay...5
Bentonite 2
+ Purple iron oxide 3%
    Good texture, very reliable. Brown if too thin.

Temmoku 1280°C Reduction
Cornish stone 30
Potash feldspar 27
Flint 19
Whiting..8.5
Hardwood ash 5
China clay...4
Iron oxide 8.5

Pearly White 1280°C Reduction
Nepheline syenite 80
Talc 10
BBV ball clay 5
Bentonite 5
    Crazes. Excellent response to colour.
    All glaze materials now bought from 'Craftline' 222 Uttoxeter Road, By the Bridge, Stoke on Trent.

John Mathieson   CR 169

Stoneware Clay
For both domestic ware and individual pieces I use DSS from W J Doble. It toasts well in reduction (to Orton cone 10 down), takes a cone 9 firing in oxidation, and survives raku firing.

Stoneware Glazes

Mt. St. Helen's Volcanic Ash Glaze
I experimented with a sample of Mt. St. Helen's volcanic ash which my Canadian brother sent me, and from tests it appears to make a perfect glaze. Fired in an electic kiln to Orton cone 8, the ash gave an attractive retrained glass brown and black glaze which did not run; in reduction at cone 8 it gave predominantly brown.

Raw Glazes for Oxidation and Reduction
(adapted from Andrew Holden's recipes)

Orton Cone 9
Potash feldspar 60
Red clay 30
Talc 20
Whiting..10

Fired to Orton cone 9, this gives a restrained gloss honey glaze in oxidation, and a celadon in reduction. With the addition of 5 parts iron oxide a rich dark green-brown hare's fur glaze can be obtained in oxidation; this tends to be predominantly brown in reduction.

Orton Cone 8
Red clay 36
Whiting..20-25
Flint 25
Potash feldspar 8
Talc 3

Fired to Orton cone 8 (though cone 7 should be satisfactory) this shiny glaze gives a honey colour in oxidation, and an attractive celadon in reduction. The addition of 5 parts iron oxide gives a dark treacle. As Andrew Holden states, the glazes tends to run, reducing the amount of whiting can help correct this. The above glazes are equally suitable for applying to biscuit ware. Michael Casson's Magnesium Glaze works well in an oxidising atmosphere, especially with the addition of 5 parts iron oxide, when it gives an attractive blue-black at Orton cone 9. Gordon Baldwin's Dolomite Glaze, with the addition of 5 parts iron oxide, gives sand-beige, breaking to iron red where thin, grey-green where thicker, when fired to Orton cone 7-9. Use thinly at the higher temperatures.

Eric James Mellon CR 65, 114, 172, 183
(work illustrated)

Elm Ash Glaze 1280-1290°C
Elm ash 4
Potash feldspar 4
Ball clay 0.5
China clay..2.5
Flint 1

Philadelphus Ash Glaze 1280°-1305°C
Philadelphus ash 4
Mixed feldspar 4
Ball clay 0.5
China clay..2.5
Flint 2.25

Escalonia Ash Glaze 1250°-1300°C
Escalonia ash 4
Nepheline syenite 4
Ball clay 0.5
China clay..2.5
Flint 5

In reduction firing s additions of 10% of flint can be an advantage (tests always advised). Lower temperature required on bodies containing some red clays. Higher temperatures possible on other white clay bodies (e.g. Potclays 1120 or 1147). These glaze recipes require ash passed through a 60/80 mesh sieve. Careful burning is required to obtain the fine ash. Similar types of tree/shrub grown in other areas may require adjustment of recipe and/or different clay bodies, e.g. St. Thomas body is not symathetic with all glaze recipes. Each batch of glaze needs testing.

Ashes Producing Kinetic Glazes (Unstable)

No.1
Apple ash 4
Nepheline syenite 4
Whiting...2
Ball clay 3.5
China clay...0.25
Flint 2

No.2
Pear ash...4
Potash feldspar 4
Whiting...2
Ball clay 3.5
China clay...0.25

Colouring oxide must only be applied to the top quarter of the ceramic or collapse of glaze can stick piece to kiln shelf.

Reg Mills

Stoneware Body 1270°C Light Reduction
W.B.B. HVAR ball clay 56
W.B.B. TA ball clay..7
Stoke red..7
Silver sand 14
Fireclay 14
Bentonite 2

Koheiji Miura CR 155

Daniel Smith Celadon Glaze 1250-1300°C Reduction
Cornish stone 60
China clay..11
Wollastonite 17
Dolomite 6
Flint 6
Red iron oxide 0.5

The amount of red iron oxide can be increased to 2% for various depths of blue-green.

Firing
1. Pieces are first biscuit fired in an electric kiln to between 800°C and 950°C
2. They are then glazed and re-fired to between 1250° and 1300°C (again in an electric kiln).
3. At approximately 950°C, Miura introduces thin strips of red pine into the firing through an opening in the doorway of the kiln which changes the atmosphere from oxidation to reduction.
4. Red pine is added continuously until very heavy reduction of the glaze is achieved and it is this process that gives the celadons their characteristic blue-green appearance (the effect of 1 to 2% iron oxide in the glaze recipe). Great care should be taken when inserting wood into an electric kiln to

ensure that it falls free of the elements. Fumes and smoke given off should be well ventilated from the kiln room.

David and Avril Morris

Casting Slip Orton Cone 8
Ball clay (1102W) 3480
China clay (1112W) 3480
Flint (1122W) 1720
Cornish stone (P3314)
or feldspar (P3316)................................2240
140°TW Sodium silicate
in 8 parts hot water 38.4
    Add powder to water + sodium silicate, mix and sieve.

David Morris

Dark Brown Glaze 1250-1260°C Oxidation
Feldspar 46
China clay...25
Dolomite 15
Whiting...6
Alkaline frit 20
Bentonite 2
Iron oxide 5
Manganese dioxide 3

Broken Green 1250-1260°C Oxidation
Feldspar 40
Whiting...28
China clay...14
Flint 18
Soft alkaline frit 10
Iron oxide 10
Cobalt oxide 0.5

White Gloss Orton Cone 8 Oxidation
Dolomite 8
Calcium borate frit ....6 to 12
Talc 14
Feldspar 47
China clay..5
Flint 15
Zircon silicate 5
    The dolomite or the talc can be omitted for different surface qualities.

Blue Underglaze Colour
Feldspar ....108 gm
Whiting..136 gm
China clay...32 gm
Bentonite ....40 gm

Nepheline syenite ....40 gm
Cobalt carbonate ....35 gm
Wax resist ....2.5 tablespoons.

Brown Colouring Slip
Red clay ....40 gm
Crocus martis ....20 gm
Nepheline syenite ....10 gm
Rutile ....3.3 gm
Whiting..10 gm
Bone ash ....10 gm
Wax emulsion resist......................................2 tsps

Beaston Stoneware Shiny White Orton Cone 8 Oxidation
Feldspar (1117W) 25
Cornish stone (P3314) 25
Whiting..12
Flint 0.8
Calcium borax frit (P2244 not P3316)........10
Calcined bone ash 5
Zirconium silicate (1027W)..........................4

   Add 2% tin oxide if not white enough. Add bentonite 2% if the glaze tends to settle out too quickly.

Tom Morrissey

Extruding Clay Body Cone 8-10
Cedar Heights..150
Cedar Heights Redart 150
Lincoln fireclay 300
Sand 50
Vermiculite 10

Ivo Mosley CR 86, 94
(work illustrated)

1260°C Reduction

Transparent Clear
Feldspar 30
Kaolin 10
Wollastonite 25
B.K.S. 20
Lepidolite 10
Bentone EW 5

Transparent Frosted
Cornish stone 80
Kaolin 20
Wollastonite 5
Bentone EW 8

White
Feldspar	23
Wollastonite	8
Lepidolite	11
Bone ash	3
Zircon	23
Bentonite EW	4
B.K.S.	28

Blue
Feldspar	35
Wollastonite	20
B.K.S.	30
Cobalt oxide	1
White bentonite	3

Red
Feldspar	30
Wollastonite	20
Kaolin	10
B.K.S.	20
Silica	10
Zircon	3
Potterycrafts P4126 'Coral Red'	20
Bentonite EW	5

Transparent Blueish
B.K.S.	20
Soda feldspar	70
Wollastonite	10
White bentonite	3
Bentone EW	5

Yellow
Cornish stone	25
Silica	10
Wollastonite	25
B.K.S.	20
Kaolin	10
Bentone EW	5
Zr/Pr Yellow	45

Yellow 2
D3202 'Cream'	20
Zircon	10
Cornish stone	25
B.K.S.	40
Wollastonite	20
Bentone EW	5

Green
Cornish stone	40
B.K.S.	20

Wollastonite 10
Chromium oxide 3
Zircon 10
Bentone EW 5

Black
Feldspar 25
Lepidolite 15
Wollastonite 20
B.K.S. 35
Uranium oxide 20
Bentone EW 5

Two Slips
Cornish stone 37
Flint 15
DBG (Watts Blake Bearne) ball clay 20
Whiting..25
White bentonite 3

Cornish stone 85
Flint 5
DBG (Watts Blake Bearne) ball clay 15
Whiting..20
White bentonite 3

Pigments that work well in slip under a transparent glaze using oxides and prepared colours.

Black
Uranium oxide ....+25%
White
Zircon ....+ 20%
Red
Zr-Cd High Temperature Red
from Potterycrafts....................................+ 60%
Pinks
Mn-Al Stain ....+ 15%
Silica..+ 10%
    Some Cr-Al stains survive at stoneware, it depends on the batch.
Yellows
Zr-PrSi stain
(e.g. Lemon Yellow) ....+ 80%
Sn-V 'Deancraft' D ....+ 10%
Orange
Zr-Cd (Mandarin Yellow)
from Potterycrafts....................................+ 60%
Blues
Add 3% CoO for strong dark blue. There are many cobalt based stains on the market giving different shades of dark blue, and for pastel shades Zircon-Vanadium based stains survive firing well, many different shades becoming available.
Greens
Many green stains become unstable at high temperatures, or bleed into the

glaze as does chrome oxide. These ones work:
Grass green
Zr-V-Si Deancraft 3111............................+ 15%
Dark green
Co-Cr ....+ 12%
  3% the same gives paler sea-green
Turquoise green
Pr-V Potterycrafts P4011 ....+ 15%
Deep sea-green
Potterycrafts Grey P4012 ....+ 10%

Greys
The cheapest and best is to make your own stain by calcining 10% MoO_3 (Molydbenum oxide) with 90% alumina oxide Al_2O_3 to temperature then powdering it with a pestle and mortar. This is quite easy. Add 10% of this slip along with 10% silica and 10% zircon.

Browns
Most commercial brown stains lose their colour and bleed green into the glaze. An iron brown can be made from 50% red clay 50% WBB.

White Glaze for Base Layer
Soda feldspar 55
Whiting...16
China clay..7
Flint 10
Zircon 18
White bentonite 2

Overglazes

Red
Cornish stone 75
Whiting..12.5
China clay..3
Potterycrafts High Temperature Red 20
Flint 6

Black
Cornish stone 70
Whiting...10
China clay..4
Flint 5
Uranium oxide 9
Bismuth oxide 5

Browns
Cornish stone 25
Flint 30
Whiting...25
China clay...20
Nickel oxide 1
  A transparent brown. Or additions of 5-50% of iron chromate to Cornish stone 85, whiting 5, flint 10, china clay 3.

Yellow
Cornish stone 85
Whiting...20
Zr/Pr yellow stain...45
Zircon 5
China clay..3

Orange
Same glaze as for yellow, substitute Potterycrafts Mandarin High temperature stain.

Blues
Many blue stains survive at stoneware temperature, as in slips. A good cobalt blue for glaze-on-glaze is:

Feldspar 35
Whiting...22
Flint 20
Calcined china clay 14.5
China clay..3
Cobalt oxide 1.7

Chrome green
Cornish stone 80
Whiting...15
Chrome oxide 6
China clay..3

Many Vanadium-based stains give good greens. In feldspar 60, whiting 12, Zircon 5, china clay 3, plus some green stains 20% give brilliant greens.

Grey
Use the stain described under grey slip. 5% in the recipe Cornish stone 80, Whiting 10, China clay 3. Commercial greys vanish or go green.

Louis Mulcahy CR 133
(work illustrated)

Shiny White Reduction 1300°C
Potash feldspar 29.5
Whiting...12.25
China clay..7.2
Flint 14.4
Zirconium silicate 9

Copper Red Reduction 1300°C
Potash feldspar 17
China clay..4.5
Whiting...2.4
Copper carbonate 0.48

Blue Reduction 1300°C
Potash feldspar 20
Whiting 11
Flint 9.47
Nepheline syenite 7.5
Cobalt carbonate 1

Green Reduction 1300°C
Potash feldspar 27.5
Whiting 11
Lead bisilicate 2
Flint 9.5
Copper carbonate 1.25

Temmoku Reduction 1300°C
Potash feldspar 12
China clay 4
Whiting 5.8
Flint 15
Red iron oxide 4

Bryan and Julia Newman

Stoneware 1260-1300°C Reduction

Body No. 1
SMD ball clay 12
AT ball clay 3
Dobles fireclay 5

> Good throwing body for weights up to about 6lb. Off white fairly smooth texture. Good for domestic ware. Fired in reduction 1260-1300°C approx. Dough mixed. (The fireclay is sieved wet through 20 mesh.) This usually adds enough water to wet the ball clay. Kept approximately six weeks before using.

Body No. 2
SMD ball clay 12
AT ball clay 3
Dobles fireclay 5
Diamond Clay Co. saggar clay 10

> Made for slab building (low warpage and crackage) but also makes a good body for throwing big pots. Pale grey. Dough mixed. Fireclay sieved wet 20 mesh. Ball clay added dry. Saggar clay added plastic. Fired in reduction 1260-1300°C approx. Kept about six weeks before using.

Dry Feldspathic 1260-1300°C Reduction
Potash feldspar 20
Whiting 40
China clay 80
Colemanite 4%
Ochre 5%

Dry Ash
Ash 50
China clay 50

White Dolomite
Cornish stone 50
China clay 25
Dolomite 20
Quartz 10
Whiting 5

Tony O'Donovan

Brown-Green Glaze 1250-1260°C Oxidation
Earthenware clay 40
Feldspar 25
Lime 30
Flint 10
Chrome oxide 0.5

> This gives a rich chocolate brown glaze, but a double application (or a thicker one) gives a fresh cucumber (?) green with brown breaking through. Glossy.
>
> The same recipe with iron chromate 0.5 instead of chrome oxide 0.5 yields a pleasant light brown.
>
> Both glazes give a strong pink under a tin-bearing glaze.

White
China clay 1
Whiting 2
Flint 3
Feldspar 4

Cream
Feldspar 6
China clay 2
Dolomite 2

Raw Glaze 1255°C
Clay (as dug) ....6 or 7 parts (according to sand content)
Wood ash ....2 parts
Feldspar ....1 part
Whiting ....1 part

> This I put through an 80 mesh sieve, and fire at a nominal 1255°C. It will fire higher, but does not like soaking. (Parts by weight)

Jeff Oestreich   CR 166

White Crackle Slip
Kaolin 15
Ball clay 15

Calcined kaolin 20
Custer feldspar 20
Flint 20
Zircopax 5
Borax...........5

    Applied to bisqueware; the heavier it is applied the more it crackles.

Amber Glaze Cone 8-10 Reduction
Ball clay 454
Whiting...........908
Flint 1362
Custer feldspar 1816
Iron oxide 316
Bentonite 135

    I usually apply this glaze over the crackle slip. It is somewhat transparent and allows the texture of the slip to show through. It should be applied thinly.

Carbon Trap Shino Glaze Cone 8-10 Reduction
Nepheline syenite 45
F-4 feldspar...........10.8
Spodumene 15.2
Ball clay 15
EPK China clay...........10
Soda ash 4

    This glaze is especially good in wood firings. The fly ash fluxes into the glaze for interesting variations. It is applied thickly.

Temmoku Cone 9-10 Reduction
Custer feldspar 48.38
Whiting...........11.64
Barium carbonate 2.24
EPK China clay...........5.37
Flint 20.14
Zinc oxide...........2.24
Iron oxide 8.05
Bentonite 1.93

Matthias Ostermann CR 123
(work illustrated)

Basic Slip Cone 8 1263°C
Feldspar 30
Flint 15
Ball clay 55

Additions
Blue-grey:
Iron chromate...........2%
Cobalt carbonate 1.5%
Green:
Copper carbonate 3%
Cobalt carbonate 1%

Stoneware Glazes

Red Ash Orton Cone 8 1263°C Electric Kiln
Mixed hardwood ash 30-40
Soda feldspar 30
Albany clay 20-25
Ball clay 10-15
Red iron oxide 10-20

> Test with different ashes and varying quantities of red iron. I do not sieve or decant. Can come up to a tomato red breaking into gold. Likes lots of heat.

Transparent Glaze Orton Cone 8 1263°C Electric Kiln
Soda feldspar 40
Flint 30
Whiting..20
Kaolin 10

> Glaze is transparent with fine, regular crazing. Best on a light stoneware, porcelain body or over a white slip.

Additions
Cream:
Rutile 2%
Mauve:
Tin oxide..4%
Iron chromate..2%
Cobalt carbonate 0.25%
Dark pink:
Tin oxide..4%
Iron chromate..2%
Manganese dioxide 1%
Royal blue:
Cobalt carbonate 1%
Green:
Copper carbonate 3%
Bright yellow:
Rutile 4%
Yellow stain (High-fire) 4%

> Additional glassiness occurring through additions of colourants can be toned down with 5-10% addition of kaolin or ball clay.

Paul Ottaway

Wordsmith Lesson Plastic Bone China Paste
Natural bone ash 47.6
Feldspar (potash 200#) 28.6
Super standard porcelain china clay 23.8
White bentonite (Bentolite H ECC) 5

> It is whiter, more translucent and always achieves greater plastic interpretation on the potters wheel than any other thrown porcelain of roughly comparable quality.
> A feldspathic glaze (No.309 in Emmanuel Cooper's 'The Potter's Book of Glaze Recipes') is applied to the soft biscuited body and then both the body and glaze mature at 1305°C in electric kiln.

Inlay Slip

Feldspar (potash 200#) 75
Super standard porcelain china clay 50
Silica 200# 25
Cobalt carbonate 1.5

Richard Parkinson

U16 Porcelain Body 1300-1380°C Reduction

E.C.C. JM China clay 51
E.C.C. BB Pulverised ball clay 7
Potash feldspar 18
Quartz (passing 300's sieve) 24

Dennis Parks

All-purpose Buff Stoneware Body

Lincoln fireclay 100
Kentucky ball clay 50
Feldspar 15
Silica 10
Sand (30/60) 25
Plus a volume of mica equal to the sand

White Stoneware

Lincoln fireclay 50
Kentucky ball clay 50
Feldspar 50
Silica 50
Sand (30/60) 50
Plus mica

Porcelain Body

Kaolin 50
Kentucky ball clay 50
Feldspar 50
Silica 50
Sand (30/60) 50
plus mica

B.P.W. Best Possible (Parks) White Gloss Orton Cone 10

Kaolin E.P.K. 1
Kentucky ball clay 1
Nepheline syenite 5
Silica 1
Gerstley borate (calcium borate frit) 1
Talc 1
Zinc oxide..0.15

This glaze evolved after using the porcelain body as an engobe in salt firings.

B.P.W Matt Orton Cone 10
Kaolin 1
Kentucky ball clay 1
Nepheline syenite 5
Silica 1
Gerstley borate (calcium borate frit) 1
Whiting 2

Colin Pearson CR 108

Oxidised Electric Kiln

Matt Glaze Orton Cone 8 Stoneware
Lithium carbonate 6.8
Whiting 13.8
Nepheline syenite 63.4
China clay 16

Matt Glaze Orton Cone 7 or 8 Stoneware and Porcelain
Barium carbonate 11.1
Lithium carbonate 8.3
Whiting 2.8
Nepheline syenite 77.8
add Bentonite 2

Reserved Gloss Orton Cone 7 or 8 Stoneware and Porcelain
Nepheline syenite 36.1
Lithium carbonate 3.9
Whiting 7.8
Quartz 52.2
add Bentonite 2

Restrained Gloss to Semi Matt Orton Cone 7 Porcelain
Potash feldspar 49.1
Talc 6.7
Whiting 8.8
Barium carbonate 10.4
Zinc oxide 4.3
Quartz 10.9
Lithium carbonate 1.3
China clay 8.8

With copper carbonate (1%) added, all these glazes will give green effects.

Standard Glazes 1260-1280°C Reduction

Butter White
Potash feldspar 35.7
Talc 8
Whiting 9.4
China clay 14.5
ECC Hymod SMD ball clay 20.3
Dolomite 11

Orange White
Petalite 38
(reduces thermal expansion and crazing)
Nepheline syenite 38
ECC CY ball clay 9
ECC Hymod SMD ball clay 16

Brown Black
Potash feldspar..35.6
ECC Hymod SMD ball clay 19.7
Whiting..16.3
Quartz...13.5
China clay...8.2
Red iron oxide 6.7

    Recipes balanced for raw glazing but are suitable for biscuit ware.

Bronze Pigment 1180-1260°C
Manganese dioxide 10
Copper oxide 1
China clay..1
+ Glaze binder SMC 1%

    Ball mill if possible. Apply by spray or painting.

Matt Black 1200-1260°C
Feldspar 25
China clay..25
Manganese dioxide 25
Copper oxide 25

    Use alone or over or under bronze.

Henry Pim   CR 142

Base Engobe Recipe
Fireclay 50
Flint 20
Feldspar 10
Fine grog...10
Zirconium oxide...10

Two glaze recipes arrived at by doing a quadriaxial test:

No.1
Feldspar (soda) 45
Feldspar (potassium) 10
Barium carbonate......................................15
China clay..10
Whiting..10
Flint 10

    This produces a matt, slightly blistered surface when oxidised at 1260°C.

No.2
Feldspar (soda) 47.5
Feldspar (potassium) 10

Barium carbonate 17.5
China clay 10
Whiting 20
Flint 20

A shiny glaze which has a slight craze. I also make use of Emmanuel Cooper and Derek Royle's beautiful turquoise glaze which is on page 164 of 'Glazes for the Studio Potter' (Batsford).

Matt Glaze 1260°C Electric Kiln
China clay 90
Whiting 39
Nepheline syenite 45
Zirconium silicate 63
Nickel oxide 9

Cracks like dried mud when applied very thickly. This glaze is white without nickel and is reasonably colour responsive. I have done some tests adding silicon carbide which makes it a bit more frothy.

Ian Pirie

White Talc Body 1150°C
Ball clay (Hyplas 71) 40
Uncalcined china clay 40
Talc 20
+ Fine molochite 18%

This body can be used for throwing and hand-building, and is also suitable for raku firing.

White Stoneware Body 1260-1320°C
Ball clay (Hyplas 71) 40
Uncalcined china clay 40
Cornish stone 20
+ Fine molochite 18%

The Cornish stone should be slaked in water and sieved through a 60 mesh lawn; it is usually added to the dry mix in solution. This clay provides an all-round white stoneware body and is proving to be an excellent saltglaze body.

The addition of vinegar to either of these clays during mixing will shorten the souring and ageing process of the day.

White Talc Body 1150°C
Ball clay (Hyplas 71) 50
China clay (un-calcined) 15
Talc 20
Flint 10
FFF feldspar potash 5

This body can be used for throwing and handbuilding, and is also suitable for Raku firing.

White Stoneware Body 1260°-1320°C
Ball clay (Hyplas 71) 50
China clay (un-calcined) 25
Flint 15
FFF feldspar potash 10

This clay provides an all round white stoneware body in either oxidation or reduction atmospheres.

Both the above recipes have been provided in their smooth form without the addition of grog. They can be altered to suit personal preference by replacing some or all of the china clay with varying grades of molochite. 100s-80s for throwing through to 60s-40s for handbuilding or raku. Any loss of plasticity can be recovered by adding 3%-5% of a white bentonite to the recipe.

Velvet Black Glaze 1260°C Oxidation
Nepheline syenite 44
Whiting..15
Zinc oxide..6
Ball clay (Hyplas 71) 35
China clay..6
+
Nickel oxide 2%
Iron oxide 2%
Cobalt carbonate 3%
Manganese dioxide 1%

This glaze was developed primarily for porcelain, although it can be successfully used on suitable stoneware bodies. To the above recipe, as is standard with all my glazes, I add 1% bentonite (which must be mixed through the DRY powder before adding water) and a tablespoonful of saturated solution of calcium chloride per five kilos. This helps to keep the glaze in suspension when not in use and also facilitates glazing by prolonging the immediate drying time, thus allowing possible streaks to even out.

Underglaze Colour for Airbrushing and Painting 1260°C Oxidation
Commercial underglaze colour 30
Feldspar 65
China clay..5

(Some colours will also withstand reduction.) The above recipe can be left unglazed then polished, or be glazed in the conventional manner. The introduction of feldspar causes a degree of vitrification at the stated firing temperature and intensifies the colour, rather than weakening it, hence reducing the costs involved in using commercial underglazes. This recipe is normally mixed with water, with a little underglaze binding medium, and should be passed through a 200 mesh sieve for airbrushing.

Joining Slip/Paste
The following process is used extensively in industry to produce virtually a liquid glue for joining clay together. In many cases, such as applying handles and spouts, there is no need to score the adjoining surfaces first. It has been tested with a number of clay bodies and has readily adapted to studio processes.

Dry clay body 1000gm
Feldspar 20gm
Bentonite 20gm
Gum arabic..20gm

Mix the dry ingredients together to disperse the bentonite. Measure out 500ccs of water and add 5ccs of Dispex. Slowly add the dry mixture to the water, whilst stirring, until a pouring slip consistency is reached. You may not require the full amount of dry mix. When ready for use, the deflocculated slip MUST be reflocculated by adding small quantities of magnesium sulphate (Epsom salts) in solution.

This action of first defloccuation and then reflocculation is important and should not be omitted.

Katharine Pleydell-Bouverie

Box Ash Glaze 1350°C Reduction

Box ash (shrub 'Box') 4
Potash feldspar 4
China clay 1
White ball clay 1

Colour from olive to dark grey green, texture almost silky.

Basic Formula 1260°C

Feldspar 40
Ash 40
Clay 20

If too matt or undefined, quartz 10 may correct this. 2-5% boro-calcite lowers the fluxing temperature without altering the quality. Up to 10% of good colourless frit can do the same.

Ash Glazes 1270-1300°C Reduction

Matt Glaze

Ash 4
Potash feldspar 4
China clay 1
Ball clay 1

Usually matt, and matures between 1270°-1300°C according to ash.

Less Matt Ash Glaze 1240-1270°C Reduction

Ash 4
Potash feldspar 4
China clay 1
Ball clay 1
Quartz 1

Usually less matt, matures between 1240°-1270°C and may 'spread' better.

Raw Ash Glaze

Ash 5
Potash feldspar 5
Ball clay 4
Quartz 4

For stoneware brushed on bone dry raw body pots. Usually fits a raw pot best because the ball clay alone shrinks the glaze better than the mixtures of china clay and ball clay.

Sara Radstone CR 100
(work illustrated)

Typical Base Glaze Cone 7 Electric kiln
China clay...30
Whiting..30
Lithium carbonate 10
Potash feldspar..10

> Oxides are added in small amounts (1%-5%) and various combinations, or zirconium silicate to whiten, opacify, and produce a smooth 'bubbly' surface.

Lucie Rie CR 134, 150
(work illustrated)

Stoneware 1250°C Oxidation
Body 1
T-material 75
Chesterfield clay 25
+ Grolleg China clay 10

Body 2
T-material 100
Red clay 25
+ Grolleg China clay 12.5

Porcelain (after Bernard Leach)
China clay...45
Feldspar 25
Ball clay 8.33
Flint 13.33
Bentonite 5.50

> Either soda or potash feldspar is used. The soda porcelain gives brighter colours while the potash body tends to distort less and keep its shape.

Slip Number 1
Porcelain body 100
Whiting..50

Slip Number 2 Blue
Porcelain clay..100
Cobalt oxide 5

Slip Number 3 Terracotta
Porcelain clay..100
Iron oxide 10

Whiting Glaze 1250°C Oxidation
Feldspar 64
Whiting..26
China clay...12
+5-7% tin oxide for a tin opaque

Dolomite Glaze 1250°C Oxidation
Feldspar 64
Dolomite 13
Whiting 13
China clay 12
+5-7% tin oxide for a tin opaque

Zinc Glaze
Feldspar 58
Whiting 8
China clay 14
Flint 8
Zinc oxide 10
+ Tin oxide for white opaque

Leo 4 (Turquoise)
Feldspar 30
Nepheline syenite 35
Barium carbonate 22
Flint 8
+ copper oxide 2%

Leo
Feldspar 30
Nepheline syenite 40
Barium carbonate 25
Flint 5
+ Copper oxide 2%

Deborah Roberts

Barium Matt 1250-1260°C Electric and Reduction
Nepheline syenite 55
China clay 10
Flint 20
Dolomite 5
Barium carbonate 20
Bone ash 3

A matt fairly smooth glaze.

Clear Matt 1250-1260°C Oxidation and Reduction
Feldspar 50
China clay 20
Whiting 20
Flint 10

A semi clear matt glaze which gives a dense attractive surface. Good for decorative rather than practical pieces.

Temmoku 1250-1280°C Oxidation and Reduction
Flint 73
Feldspar 60
Whiting 30

China clay 15
Red iron oxide 22

> A good dark black temmoku which breaks to a sharp bright orange on edges and rims. Do not apply too thinly. In electric kilns needs a soak or a higher temperature.

Ann Robertson

Toronto Rosey Red Orton Cone 6-9 Electric Kiln
Flint 29.7
EPK (China clay) 4.95
Soda feldspar 19.8
Talc 13.86
Gerstley borate (Calcium borate frit) 31.68
+ Red iron oxide 15

> I tried this without the iron and added tin and it worked well at cone 7. I also tried substituting cobalt carbonate 0.1 and copper carbonate 0.5 for the 15 red iron oxide and found it attractive.

Jim Robison CR 122. 155
(work illustrated)

White Slip
China clay 35
Pale ball clay 35
Feldspar 15
Quartz 15

Red Slip
Red earthenware clay 70
Alumina 30

> Slips are often applied to dry ware.

Base Ash Glaze Orton Cone 8
Wood ash 40
China clay 40
Whiting 10
Potash feldspar 10

> A cream to yellow colour.

Additions to Base Glaze
Milk white orange:
Disperzon 12%
Greenish yellow-black:
Copper oxide 6%
Blue green olive-blue black:
Cobalt carbonate 1.5%
Copper oxide 3%
Red metallic-dark rust:
Yellow ochre 6%
Pale brown-dark chocolate:
Manganese dioxide 9%

Dry Glaze

Potash feldspar 20
Whiting...35
China clay..35
Ball clay 10

Additions are similar to those with the Basic Ash Glaze, but the colour response varies and is sometimes brighter. This Pale Dry Glaze is often mixed with Ash Base (in liquid form) for lightened colour, usually in a ratio of 3 Dry Glaze: 1 Ash Glaze.

Speckled Plum Smooth Matt Glaze Orton Cone 8

Potash feldspar 55
Barium carbonate 20
Flint 10
Dolomite 5
China clay..10
Additions
Tin oxide..4
Manganese dioxide 4
Granular Ilmenite..1
(add post sieving)

Turquoise Matt Glaze

Potash feldspar 51
Whiting..9
Zinc oxide..8
Barium carbonate 20
Ball clay 10
Titanium dioxide 2
Additions
Copper carbonate 3
Cobalt carbonate 0.5

White Satin Glaze

Potash feldspar 29.5
Nepheline syenite 29.5
China clay...11.0
Whiting..13.5
Dolomite 3.0
Zinc oxide...3.0
Disperzon 5.0
Tin oxide...5.0

This white glaze when over sprayed with either turquoise or the ash blue-green (copper cobalt) mixture will result in a range of copper red to plum purple colours in reduction. Colour variations depend on thickness of application. Base Ash and Dry Glazes are used on sculptural pieces and for contrasting surface of functional work. Most large pieces are made from a crank clay (Clay pots or Earthstone varieties), although increasing numbers are made from grogged white bodies, for brighter colours. Fragile pieces are bisque fired to 950°C. while larger, more robust works are glazed when dry and raw fired.

Porcelain and red clay slips along with stains are often applied to clay during the making process to created patterns and colour variations under translucent glazes.

Base Ash Glaze uses Elm or mixed ash as available. This glaze and the Dry Base Glaze are mixed with oxides and colourants for a muted range of colours.

Several coloured versions of these glazes, as well as the base mixtures are then applied in thin layers by using a spray gun. Great variations in colour occur when used thick and thin. The White Satin Glaze is often used over white slips, along with a variety of coloured glazes to increase areas of lighter colour and contrast.

Up to six glazes may be applied, sprayed from thin to thick with the aid of stencils. Pieces are allowed to dry briefly between coats. Overwetting dry pieces may cause raw slips to lift from the clay body.

Pieces are fired to Orton cone 8 (1260 to 1280°C) in a gas kiln and kept in moderate reduction from 1080°C onwards. Choice of clay and slips will influence final colours and reduction atmosphere will induce considerable body iron speckling in many cases.

Traditional Shino recipe
Nepheline syenite 1
Potash feldspar 1
A.T. Ball clay 1
Brushed on mixtures of oxides and water give additional colour.

Mary Rogers

Barium Matt Glaze 1260°C approx.
Barium carbonate...30
Flint 10
Ball clay 10
Feldspar 55
Dolomite 5

Ash Glaze
China clay..12.5
Elm ash..50
Ball clay 12.5
China stone 7.5
Feldspar 10
Whiting...7.5

Ash Glaze (Elm)
Elm ash..50
Feldspar 25
China clay..25
Colour variations
Good red-brown:
Red iron 5%
Good blue:
Cobalt 1-5%
Ochre:
Yellow iron ....1-5 %

Phil Rogers CR 151

Stoneware Body for Reduction
Hyplas 71 ball clay ....1.5 bags
AT ball clay ....1 bag
Dobles sand 4.5kg

Dobles fireclay ....4 kg
White silica sand ....2.5 kg
Whitfields 202 fireclay ....5 kg
Feldspar ....1 kg
Red iron oxide 350gm

> A dark version of this clay is used in both the stoneware kiln and the salt kiln particularly in conjunction with hakame decoration.
>
> Dark version: as above but with 850gm. red iron oxide.

Glazes

No.1 Standard Ash Formula
Ash 2200
Cornish stone 700
Feldspar 700
China clay 250
Whiting...200
Quartz..300
Hyplas 71 100
Optional extra:
Red iron oxide 200gm

> This recipe works with many different varieties of ash and varies in colour from a deep bottle green from Pine ash, to a cool blue-green with most of the hard woods.

No.2 Nuka
Cornish stone 50
Wood ash 60
Flint 35

> A stoney white matt to a smooth, creamy off white depending on temperature and body clay.

No.3 Iron Ash
Cornish stone 1770
Ash 2400
Hyplas 71 ball clay 828
Whiting......................................660
Feldspar 960
Flint 208
China clay 200
Bone ash 240
Red iron oxide 300

> A long and rather complicated recipe that has developed and grown over the years. This glaze is similar to the Japanese Ame and benefits from being over the white Molochite slip.

Temmoku
Cornish stone 85
Whiting..15
China clay..8
Red iron oxide ....6-8 (Depending on batch of iron)

> Apply thickly and fire hot (cone 11 or 12). This glaze is also very good in the salt kiln where it fires a textured light green.

A Smooth, Shino-like Celadon
Ash 1000
Feldspar 1700
SMD ball clay.......................................200
Quartz..250
Iron oxide 25

Good over slips and under kaki. Particularly good over hakame.

Good Satin White 1280°C Reduction
Potash feldspar......................................64
Quartz..28
China clay...16
Bone ash...16
Talc..16
Ball clay 3
Bentonite 2

Use over slips or oxide brush work. My ash glazes are formulated to take account of around 30% of the original weight to be thrown away as grit after sieving into the batch. I do not dry sieve the ash, but weigh it and sieve it separately to the other ingredients. This saves having to wash and then dry the ash before use. The batch weight is weighed two or three days before required and washed four or five times before final sieving and combining with the other materials. Potters using pre-washed and seived ash can reduce the ash content by approx. 30%.

Coll Minogue & Robert Sanderson CR 181
(work illustrated)

Clay Body
Orton Cone 11-12 Reduction or Oxidation
ECC/Hyplas 71 ....50kg (2 bags)
ECC/Hymod AT ....25kg (1 bag)
+ Stoddard's/90's silica sand ....10% to 15%

Original slow method: the dry powdered clay and silica sand are blended as a slip in a dough mixture then decanted into a large water tank to settle; the excess water evaporates. The slip is then dolloped out onto a drying rack lined with cheap nylon material (usually used to make underskirts for wedding dresses).
Approximately 12% shrinkage from plastic to fired (cone 11). Suitable for wood-firing.
Once stiffened the clay is foot wedged before being bagged and stored.
Quick Lazy Method: In the autumn mix up materials in dough-mixer as a clay body, and bag by the 25kg. Store covered outside over winter. Wedge and use as required in the spring.

White Slip Orton Cone 9-11 Reduction or Oxidation.
China clay.....................................50
Ball clay 50

Both the thickness, type of application and clay body will effect the fired result. Produces a variety of surface and colour effects when wood-fired. For best results experiment with various types of clays and firing temperatures and atmospheres.

Clear Glaze Orton Cone 9-11

Hyplas 71 40
Potash feldspar 20
Whiting...20
Flint 20

For high iron glaze add 10% Fe_2O_3. Likes to be wood-fired.

May be fired in either reduction or oxidation. Best protected from too much fly-ash when used in wood-firing.

This is a raw glaze designed to be applied to greenware, however it may also be applied to biscuit-fired work in the normal manner. When raw glazing apply to the interior surface of work when complete but still leatherhard. Allow the work to completely dry out before applying glaze to exterior surfaces.

For a 5kg mix of dry materials use 4.5 to 5 litres of water. Add materials to water in the order they are listed for easy mixing. Sieve to 80's mesh, and leave to settle overnight or longer if possible. Draw off excess water before stirring up to remove any scum which may have formed on the surface, then add sufficient fresh water for desired thickness of application. Both the thickness, type of application and clay body will effect the fired result.

Alan Sidney

Green and Pink Semi-Matt Orton Cone 9-10 Oxidation

Nepheline syenite 40
Whiting...10
Barium carbonate..20
Flint 5
China clay...5
Soda feldspar 27.5
Dolomite 2.5
Titanium dioxide 3
Chromiun dioxide 0.4
Copper oxide 1
Bentonite 1
(Mixed and passed through 120 mesh)

Best when dipped and used on white bodies such as Potclays 1146.

White Speckled Semi-matt Alumina Glaze Orton Cone 9-10 Oxidation

Soda feldspar 48
China clay..26
Dolomite 22
Whiting...4
Tin oxide..6
Bentonite 1
(Mixed and passed through 120 mesh)

This glaze, which should not be applied too thinly, has a soft, waxy-white texture where thick and shows light reddish patches and speckles where it is thinner when used on white bodies on white bodies such as Potclays 1146 also St. Thomas's. Best dipped.

Off-white Semi-matt Orton Cone 01 High Fired Earthenware

Lead bisilicate 100
China clay...50
Whiting..25

Tin oxide..........5
Dolomite..........5
Vanadium pentoxide 2
Bentonite 1

> To this can be added copper oxide and cobalt oxide. I use this glaze over Potclays 1129 St Paul's Clay, with which body the iron breaks through on edges. The glaze also works well with underglaze colours.

Peter Simpson CR 121

Stoneware Cones 8-9 Oxidation

Body 1
Kaolin 40
Bentonite 4
Flint 20
Nepheline syenite 30

Body 2
Kaolin 45
Bentonite 4
Flint 20
Feldspar 30

Body 3 Off-white 1230-1260°C
Ball clay (any) ....50 kg
Kaolin ....25 kg
Flint ....7.5 kg
Quartz ....7.5 kg
Molochite (25-85) ....20 kg
Sand ....10 kg

> Soaking plays a very important part in the firing cycle. Preferable at least two or three hours at the top end, firing with two cones soaking at cone 8 and holding at 1250°C until cone 9 falls.

1250-1280°C Oxidation or Reduction
Nepheline syenite 80
Whiting 10
China clay 10
Bone ash 2

1240-1260°C
Nepheline syenite 74
Whiting 13
China clay 7
Flint 8
Bone ash 2
Barium carbonate 8

1260-1280°C
Nepheline syenite 50
Whiting 3.5

Dolomite 23
China clay 25

1240-1260°C
Nepheline syenite 40
Whiting 7
Dolomite 20
China clay 20
Flint 20
Bone ash 2
Barium carbonate 6
Zinc oxide...6

> All glazes can be coloured by the additions of oxides. Most glazes are white, off-white, semi-transparent, matt, semi-matt.

Mildred Slatter

Stoneware 1260-1280°C Reduction

Standard Workshop Body
Hymod SMD ball clay 85
Leighton Buzzard sand 10
Quartz 4
Bentonite 1
Red iron oxide 0.5

> The quartz is mixed into a slop before mixing with the rest in a dough mixer. The body is then dried a little, pugged twice and stored. It works well for throwing, slabbing, coiling and raku. Add more sand for large garden pots.

Red Brown Semi-Clear Glaze with Gold Flecks 1250-1260°C Reduction
Feldspar potash 20
Flint 13
China clay 2
Whiting..6
Colemanite 3
Barium carbonate 4
Magnesium carbonate 2
Red iron oxide 4

Peter Smith CR 96

Temmoku 1260-1280°C Oxidation
Fremington earthenware clay 2
Dorset ball clay 1
Ochre 0.2
Cornish stone 2
Limestone 1.5
Flint 1
Haematite iron ore 0.08
+ 10% by weight reducing material (charcoal, coal dust ,etc.)

Khaki 1260-1280°C Oxidation
Fremington clay 2
Cornish stone 2
Limestone 1.5
Flint 0.7
Haematite iron ore 0.05
+10% reducing material (charcoal, coal dust, etc.)

Iron Red 1260-1280°C Oxidation
Fremington clay 1
Feldspar 1.4
Nepheline syenite 2
Iron oxide 0.02
+10% reducing material (charcoal, coal dust, etc.)

Thickly applied gives oil spot glaze which is a 'glass in glass' separation. Very small lime additions (about 2%) produce a buttery glaze illustrating how lime can act opposite to a flux.

Coal Ash Glaze Runny Green

Celadon 1260-1280°C Oxidation
Coal ash 4.7
Devon ball clay..1.8
Limestone 4.9
Feldspar 7.2
Red clay 0.7
Ochre 0.4
Flint 3.5

Carbon in the ashes is sufficient to cause reduction.

Coal ash can be regarded as a clay of approx 42% SiO_2 24% Al_2O_3 with impurities such as iron oxide, fluxes, etc. and of course carbon.

A chun glaze can be obtained by the addition of dicalcium silicate. Steel works slag often contains proportion of this material + phosphate 1.0 can be added to celadon formulae.

Celadon 1260-1280°C Oxidation
Fremington earthenware clay 2
Devon ball clay..1.5
Ochre 0.1
Cornish stone 2
Limestone 1.5
Flint 0.5
+10% by weight reducing material (charcoal, coal dust, etc.)

Julian Stair CR 163

Semi-matt 1280°C (Oxidation only)
China clay..15.5
Ball clay 2.3
Soda feldspar 9.6
Quartz..13.8
Whiting..23.1
Zinc oxide..9.6
Potash feldspar 26.2

Gary Standige

Bottle Green Celadon Orton Cone 8-9 Reduction
Potash feldspar 42
Quartz 28
Whiting 16.5
China clay 11.3
Red iron oxide 2.2
    Needs good reduction. Pools nicely in sgraffito.

Cornish Stone Glaze Orton Cone 9 Reduction
Cornish stone 85
Whiting 15
    Opaque white on porcelain.

Northern Celadon Orton Cone 8-9 Reduction
Cornish stone 26
Ball clay (HVAR) 15
China clay 15
Whiting 25
Flint 17
Red iron oxide 2
    Needs a good reduction. Olive-green celadon.

Charles Stileman CR 187
(work illustrated)

Black Slip Standard
Red earthenware clay 87
Flint 4.3
Cobalt oxide 1.7
Red iron oxide 2.6
Manganese dioxide 4.3

Black Slip Variation 1
Red earthenware clay 87
Flint 4.3
Cobalt oxide 1.7
Red iron oxide 2.6
Manganese dioxide 4.3
Calcium borate frit 5

Black Slip Variation 2
Red earthenware clay 87
Flint 4.3
Cobalt oxide 1.7
Red iron oxide 2.6

Black Slip Variation 3
Red earthenware clay 87
Flint 4.3

Cobalt oxide 1.7

These slips were used in trials with four different batche so of wood ash to trace the cause of unattractive colour response. The trials showed that the wood ash was responsible and that slip composition had only marginal effects. Only one batch of wood ash gave good response with black slip and this was equally satisfactory with green slip.

Green Slip Standard
Hymod AT ball clay 50
Potash feldspar 20
China clay..20
Flint 10
Black copper oxide..3
Chromium oxide 1

Green Slip Variation
Hymod AT ball clay 50
Potash feldspar 20
China clay..20
Flint 10
Black copper oxide..5
Chromium oxide 1

Slips containing 3% and 5% copper tried origininally with dolomite glazes gave 'celadon' greens. The paler 3% copper was adopted as standard. When used with wood ash glaze gave richer colours from green to aquamarine.

Dolomite Glaze Cones 8-9 Electric Kiln
Dolomite 18.0
Flint/Quartz 8.5
Zircosil 9.0
Nepheline syenite 54.0
Hymod SM 8.5
Bentonite 2.0

I use this glaze over a black (cobalt containing) slip to obtain greys or blue/greys which sometimes have an attractive reticulation effect revealing patches of the underlying slip. Over green slip (containing 3% copper) the glaze can give pale 'celadon' type greens.

Wood Ash Glaze Cone 9 Electric Kiln
Flint/Quartz 33.3
Nepheline syenite 33.3
Wood ash 33.3
Bentonite 2.0

Over black (cobalt containing) slip I have obtained rich and varied blues. Reticulation can occur revealing small patches of the underlying slip (Dolomite glaze over the same slip gave greys and grey/blues).
Over green slip (containing 3% copper) the glaze has given beautiful greens and aquamarines. (Dolomite glaze over this slip gives a pale 'celadon' type green).
Over dark clay bodies alone the glaze can give blue 'chun' effects.
To be effective wood ash glazes need to be applied thickly (in order of the 1520gm per litre) and behaviour varies considerably according to type of ash.

Peter Stoodley

Stoneware Body Cone 6-8 Oxidation
Potclays Etruria red marl, dry
powder 1271 ....15lb 4oz
Potclays Fireclay, dry powder
1273/2 ....15lb 4oz
Potash feldspar 6lb 4oz
Haematite (natural red iron
oxide) 2lb 5oz
Coarse grog (+20's) 3lb 2oz
Finer grog (20's to dust) 4lb 0oz

The dry clays and the feldspar and haematite, but exclusive of the grog, are mixed together in approximately 4 gallons of water and blunged for several hours (in my case using a rapid mixer). The weights given will fill a 5 gallon bucket. The grogs, having previously been washed repeatedly to remove any floating sediment or soluble salts, are then added. Since the red clay powder may contain a defloculent as part of its preparation by the supplier, this process may now be reversed by the addition of a flocculent before any water is extracted. The flocculent used is calcium chloride (Epsom salts) 2ozs dissolved in 0.25 pint hot water. This will turn the milky mixture into a thick creamy consistency, considerably assist the drying and make about 56lb of plastic clay. The body produces a dark brown vitrified stoneware at cone 8 (1250°C), but is probably better at cone 6 (1200°C) when the colour is warmer without any appreciable increase in porosity. Highly burnished surfaces will tend to blister slightly above this temperature. This refers to firing in an electric kiln. Its coarseness makes it unsuitable for glazing without extreme pinholing.

Vitreous Slips
White
Potash feldspar ....13 parts by weight
Kaolin (Grolleg) ....3.5 parts by weight
Ball clay (Hymod SMD) ....3.5 parts by weight

Black
Red clay body (less grog) ....10 parts by weight
Manganese dioxide ....1 part by weight
Flint ....1.5 parts by weight

Pauline Storie and John Dix

Ash Glaze Orton Cones 7 or 8 Once Fired Oxidation
Ash (mostly pine, burnt pallets
washed 60 sieve) 50
White earthenware clay 50

Add 15 fluid ounces water to 1lb of glaze approx.

This is a simple recipe that usually makes a good oatmeal or light grey/green glaze with a reserved mottle. It responds well to additions of colouring oxides and I add calcium borate frit (up to 10%) if the glaze is too dry. It can be applied to biscuit if more water is added – it will crawl if applied thickly.

Additions
Zircon ....5 to 10%
(often needs similar quantity of colemanite)
Brown-green mottle, blue where thick:
Copper oxide 2%
Light rutile 6%
Brown to greenish brown:
Iron oxide 4%
Manganese oxide 4%
Mottled blue-turquoise:
Cobalt oxide 1%

Geoffrey Swindell CR 186
(work illustrated)

Glaze Orton Cone 8 Electric Kiln
Feldspar 48
Dolomite 24
China clay...24
Whiting...4

Jonathan Switzman

Ash Glaze 1260°C Oxidation
Elm ash (washed, sieved and dried) 45
China stone 45
Ball clay 10

>The resulting glaze I call Julie's Elm Glaze after the student. It is a smooth semi-gloss, butter in colour with a hint of celadon green and varying flecks of off-white. I used an 80's mesh only to sieve this final recipe. Interesting effects with oxides brushed onto the glaze like copper where alkaline blue sometimes develop.

Andrea's Barium Matte Cone 9 Oxidation
Feldspar potash 28
China clay...20
Barium carbonate 44
Flint 8

Colour variations
Blue green:
Copper oxide 4%
Warm blue green:
Copper oxide 3%
Rutile 3%
Warm green:
Copper oxide 3%
Titanium dioxide 4%
Green tan:
Copper oxide 3%
Red iron oxide 2%

Warm bright green:
Copper oxide 3%
Vanadium pentoxide 4%

> Surface texture: satin matt. Colour luminous barium blue green
> Possible Health Hazards: Barium carbonate: Highly toxic if ingested–avoid ingestion. Do not use in glazes intended for use with food. Harmful by absorption.

Blue Pink Volcanic Cone 8-9 Oxidation
Potash feldspar 35
Barium carbonate 40
Zinc oxide..15
China clay..5
Flint 5
+ Nickel oxide 1.5

> Blue-pink, semi-opaque matt surface.
> Possible Health Hazards. Barium carbonate: Highly toxic if ingested – avoid ingestion. Do not use in glazes intended for use with food; harmful by absorption. Nickel oxide: can cause allergic skin reactions; possible carcinogen if inhaled.

Vellum Matt Blue Cones 8-9 Oxidation
Potash feldspar 33.33
Dolomite 33.33
China clay...33.33
Rutile 2.02
Cobalt oxide 0.3

Oxidised Celadon Cone 8-9
Potash feldspar 40
Flint 30
Whiting...20
China clay...6
Bentonite 4
+ Turquoise stain..4
+ Red iron oxide 1.25

Felicity's Green Vellum Matt Cone 8-9 Oxidation
Barium carbonate...17.4
Flint 26.5
Dolomite 13.6
Magnesium carbonate 1.2
Lithium carbonate 3.3
China clay...38
+ Copper carbonate 2%

> Semi opaque green. Pastel colours with glaze stains.
> Possible Health Hazards. Barium carbonate: highly toxic if ingested – avoid ingestion; do not use in glazes intended for use with food; harmful by absorption.
> Lithium carbonate: irritant.

George's Nepheline Green Matt Cone 9 Oxidation
Nepheline syenite 63.4
Whiting...13.8

China clay..16
Lithium carbonate 6.8
+ Copper carbonate......................................2
> Over tin oxide with 2% copper; broken light green to mottled black. Translucent if thin.
> Possible Health Hazards: Lithium carbonate: irritant

Helen Swain's Barium Matt Blue Cone 9 Oxidation or Reduction
Potash feldspar..45
Barium carbonate...45
China clay..10
+ Copper carbonate......................................1.5
> Semi-opaque blue green.

JS Barium Matt Turquoise Cone 9 Firing Oxidation or Reduction
Potash feldspar..58
Barium carbonate...22
Whiting...11
China clay Grolleg 4.25
Tin oxide..4.75
+ Copper oxide 4
+ Illmenite, coarse..2
+ Silicon carbide 3
> Satin matt jade green or mottled metallic black if thick. Eggshell muted red brown with green mottle in reduction. Good on white slip/porcelain.
> Possible Health Hazards: Barium carbonate: highly toxic if ingested-avoid ingestion.; do not use in glazes intended for use with food; harmful by absorption.

JS Medway Yellow Cone 9
Whiting...42.06
China clay Grolleg 42.06
Hymod red ball clay 9.35
Borax frit P2959 ....6.54
> Best in reduction, but can be oxidised. Pale lemon yellow to dark tan yellow oxidised, yellow ochre/brown to pale mint green if reduction fired on Casson Body in reduction.

Judy's Medway Gold Cone 9
Whiting...42.06
China clay Grolleg 42.06
Ball clay SMD..9.35
P2959 High temperature frit 6.54
+ Red iron oxide 0.93
+ Yellow ochre oxide....................................4.67
+ Vanadium pentoxide 0.93
> Best in reduction, but can be oxidised. Gold/brown/pink satin matt/stone matt firing.

Jenny's Ochre Yellow Medway Slip Glaze Cone 9
Whiting...42.06
China clay Grolleg 42.06
Ball clay SMD..9.35
P2959 Borax frit high temperature 6.54
+ Red iron oxide 9.35
+ Yellow ochre..4.67
+ Vanadium pentoxide 0.93

Oxidation or reduction. For Straw Yellow version add red iron oxide 3.3%, yellow ochre 1.6%, Vanadium pentoxide 0.3%

Possible Health Hazards: vanadium pentoxide is TOXIC – avoid ingestion or inhalation.

GS No.6 Temmoku Cone 8-10 Reduction

Cornish stone 88.00
Whiting..12.00
+ Red iron oxide 8.00

A deceptively simple recipe. A rich rust brown breaking to black where thick – must be fired in reduction on a dark body for richest results. Likes a long reduction cycle.

Sandy's Red Cone 9 Oxidation or Reduction

Soda feldspar 31.11
Quartz..26.67
Whiting..8.89
Dolomite 8.89
China clay Grolleg 17.78
Bone ash 6.67
Red iron oxide 13.33

Shiny rust red with golden spots/halos, darker and richer in reduction. Especially good on porcelain in reduction. Needs to be applied fairly thickly.

GS PD2 Temmoku Cone 9-10 Reduction or oxidation

Feldspar potash 38.95
Whiting..19.74
China clay Grolleg 13.94
Flint 9.96
Cornish stone 17.42
Red iron oxide 6.97
Yellow ochre oxide...6.97

Matt Purple/Brown. Plum matt brown in oxidation. Same in reduction with zones of metallic black spots and margins of ochre yellow.

Rhodes Satin Goldsmiths' Version Cone 9-10 Oxidation or Reduction

Cornish stone 48.94
Flint 6.38
China clay Grolleg 6.38
Dolomite 14.89
Talc 12.76
P2959 Borax frit 10.64
+ Tin oxide 5.32

A classic Rhodes recipe. Adapted at Goldsmiths' College for firing at the slightly lower 1280˚C temperatures used in the UK. A soft grey white semi gloss, which can be used as a high temperature majolica.

Malachite Green 1 Cone 8-9 Oxidation
Nepheline syenite 55
Barium carbonate..26
Whiting..2
China clay..6
Flint 7
Lithium carbonate 4

    A satin-matt gemstone green. Green-blue add copper carbonate 1.4 and chromium oxide 0.6. Blue-green add copper carbonate 1.4 and chromium oxide 0.2

Harrow Dolomite Cone 9 Oxidation or Reduction
Feldspar Potash 48.15
Dolomite..21.76
Whiting..3.24
China clay..19.44
Tin oxide...7.41

    Works well with a strong reduction from 1100°C upwards. Colour: semi opaque tan-cream. Sometime flashes of pink in reduction satin matt.

Janine's Satin Matt White Cone 9 Firing Oxidation or Reduction
Soda feldspar 48.00
Petalite 19.00
Dolomite..17.00
China clay..16.00
Tin oxide...8.00

Versions:
Pale Lavender Blue
Cobalt oxide .... +1%
Metallic Grey Green
Cobalt oxide ....+ 1%
Manganese dioxide ....+3%

London Slip Glaze Cone 9-10 Reduction
London clay 57
P2247 Borax Frit..43
Iron scale (rust) 3.00 3
Red iron oxide 4.00 4

    Use 7-10% iron oxide if no rust is available. Colour: opaque black-brown.
    Surface texture: glossy or shiny/satin matt.

Karen's Vellum Matt Cone 8 Oxidation
Feldspar potash 36
Wollastonite 26
Quartz...23
Calcium borate frit 7
Ball clay 5
Talc 3

    Designed to fire on porcelain without developing shine or crazing. Silky cream, satin matt.

Monica's/Eimear's Satin Matt Yellow Cone 9 Oxidation
Feldspar soda 36
Dolomite..8

Whiting 12
China clay 36
Flint 8
+ Illmenite 4.8
+ Copper oxide 1.2
Plus:
1. Lime Ash 5:1 Dry Matt
2. Lime Ash 2:1 golden yellow shiny
3. Lime Ash 1:1 broken golden yellow

    Mottled grey green turning yellow if combined with lime wood ash. Surface texture: satin.

Magnesia Matt Project Glaze Cone 8 Oxidation or Reduction
Potash feldspar 29.2
Magnesium carbonate 16.6
Ball clay 11.7
Dolomite 17.5
Flint 25

    A satin matt tile glaze. Firing – 1260-1280°C, cone 8/9 with a 20 minute soak. Develops creamy soft colours when stained. May run on vertical surfaces unless fired lower.

Zinc Project Glaze Cone Oxidation or Reduction
Feldspar potash 30.43
Zinc oxide...19.09
China clay...12.20
Dolomite 12.20
Flint 26.09

    A satin matt tile glaze. Suitable for crystal growth and bright high temperature colours. Firing – 1260-1280°C, cone 8/9 with a 20 minute soak and slow cool. Best on a white body.

Robert's Velvet Matt Turquoise Cone 9 Oxidation
Nepheline syenite 29.20
Barium carbonate..27.02
Cornish stone 24.88
China clay...6.18
Lithium carbonate 3.49
Quartz..3.39
Whiting..2.34
Zinc oxide...1.79
Bentonite 1.70
+ Copper carbonate 2-3%

    Velvet matt, light turquoise with 2% copper oxide. Can crystallise with fast fire to 1289°C and slow cool at 50°C per hour to 900°C.

    Possible Health Hazards: Barium carbonate: highly toxic if ingested, avoid ingestion. Do not use in glazes intended for use with food.

Janice Tchalenko CR 135
(work illustrated)

White (Base Glaze) 1260°C Reduction
Potash feldspar 55
China clay 15
Quartz 15
Whiting 10
Talc 5
    Best fired 1260-1265 °C.

Yellow 1260°C Reduction
Potash feldspar 45
Barium carbonate 20
Talc 10
China clay 7
Zirconium silicate 15
Iron oxide 3
Whiting 3

Green 1260°C Reduction
Alkaline frit (ferro) 44.5
China clay 19.5
Quartz 36
Chromium oxide 1
Tin oxide 5

Copper Red 1260°C Reduction
Potash feldspar 301.07
Calcium borate frit 35.02
Whiting 46.97
Copper oxide 1.47
Tin oxide 3.83

Pink 1260°C Reduction
Barium carbonate 20
Nepheline syenite 40.5
Potash feldspar 37.5
China clay 2
Copper carbonate 2

Blue 1260°C Reduction
Potash feldspar 30
Whiting 16
Talc 12
China clay 8
Ball clay 6
Quartz 6
Cobalt oxide 2
Iron oxide 3

Byron Temple CR 156, 164

Saggar Bodies
No.1 Dense Body
Scrap stoneware clays ....10lb dry wt.
Soft brick dust ....1.5lb dry wt.
> ('Stoneware Throwing Marl' will give a saggar body roughly equivalent, although its high iron content tends to bleed onto kiln shelves).

No.2 Loose Body
By volume:
Fireclay ....2 parts
Ball clay 1
Soft brick dust 1
Sawdust (damp) 2
Scrap stoneware 6
> Difficult to throw. Saggars must be high fired prior to packing with pots or sawdust.

Porcelain body
Grolleg china clay 55
Potash feldspar 22
Flint 23
Bentonite 2

Glaze
Albany slip 85
Nepheline syenite 15
> This is a reliable glaze I use as a liner for saggar-fired pots. Apply it thinly to biscuited pots and allow it to dry thoroughly before placing in saggars.

Martina Thomson CR 186
(work illustrated)

White Engobe
China clay...50
Ball clay 40
Zirconium silicate 5
Potash feldspar 5

Dry Green Glaze 1260°C
Whiting..45
China clay...35
Potash feldspar 20
Copper oxide 2

Simple Dry Glaze 1260°C
Whiting..45
China clay...45
Flint 10
> I experiment with this glaze a little. For blue I add cobalt (to 100ml. I add the tip of my teaspoon handleful) and have tried my luck with an admixture of a barium-based glaze

(e.g. Cerulean) to bring out other colours.

I rub oxides, mostly rutile, into my pots when dry, at which stage I also often draw on them using the finest brush and oxides, a favourite mixture being red iron oxide with a small amount of cobalt. My main research now is into the use of engobes as a base for the drawings.

My pots are fired to 1260°C, electric kiln. I often re-fire pieces in order to 'mature' them.

Owen Thorpe
(work illustrated)

Stoneware Glazes 1250°C All Oxidising
No.1
Feldspar (potash) 50
China clay..16
Whiting...16
Magnesium carbonate 10
Yellow ochre..2
Rutile (dark) 2
Iron spangles 1
    Buttery satin sandy colour

No.2
Cornish stone 46
China clay...18
Dolomite 18
Flint 12
Whiting...4
Red iron oxide 2
Tin oxide..2
    Semi-transparent semi-matt glaze and useful over slips

No.3
Feldspar 25
China clay...25
Whiting...25
Iron oxide 3
Borax standard 'E' frit 3
    Very dry yellow glaze: good for slip work and over glaze brush work with oxides.

No.4
Cornish stone 50
China clay...22
Whiting...6
Dolomite 23
Talc 10
Iron oxide 3
Cobalt oxide 0.5
    Satin matt textured green.

No.5
Feldspar potash 50
Flint 13

Whiting..20
China clay..10
Tin oxide..10
> Shiny white glaze bright at 1250°C, but stable enough for majolica brushwork and calligraphy to melt but not run.

Nilza Torres Calver

Temmoku Cone 10 – Reduction 1300°C
Feldspar potash 36.6
Soda ash 0.8
Dolomite 1.7
Red iron oxide 3.9
Whiting...12.1
China clay..16.1
Titanium dioxide 0.3
Flint 32.4
Tin oxide..0.6
Copper oxide 0.5
Ashes 1.0

Tom Turner CR 103

Turner Porcelain Body Cone 9
Vee Gum T 4
Talc – 10AC 2
Tile Six kaolin 75
Kaopaque 20 38
Potash feldspar 60
200 mesh silica..................................60
Ball clay 12
> Mix by first blunging the Vee Gum T into hot water, then the talc, and then the remaining materials one at a time, adding the most plastic materials first.

Turner Celadon 1280°C Reduction
Ball clay 1600
Whiting...1000
Flint 1950
F-4 feldspar...................................2500
Iron oxide 140
> Based on Bernard Leach and adjusted for my porcelain.

Medium Green
Ball clay 1600
Whiting...1000
Flint 1950
F-4 feldspar...................................2500
Iron oxide 350

Dark Green to Black
Ball clay 1600
Whiting...1000

Flint 1950
F-4 feldspar 2500
Iron oxide 560

Rick Urban CR 74

White/Rust Glaze Orton Cone 10 Reduction
Soda feldspar 47
EPK china clay 20.9
Dolomite 23.8
Whiting 3.8
'Ultrox' 4.8

Orange Spot on Red Glaze Orton Cone 10 Reduction
Soda feldspar 46.75
Whiting 19.25
Talc 13.66
China clay 22
Bone ash 2.75
Red iron oxide 3.66
Rutile 1.01
Ilmenite 0.92

Temmoku Orton Cone 10 Reduction
Potash feldspar 40.78
EPK china clay 9.71
Whiting 16.99
Flint 26.46
Black iron oxide 6.07

Wood Ash Glaze Orton Cone 10 Reduction
By volume
Albany slip .... 1 part
Whiting 2
Wood ash (washed Oak Ash) 60 mesh 3
Ball clay (OM4) 3
Flint 1

Midnight Blue/Haywood Cone 9-10 Reduction
Flint 35.9
Custer feldspar 29.52
Whiting 16.82
China clay 10.13
Cobalt carbonate 2.04
Rutile 1.93
Red iron oxide 1.93
Bentonite 1.73

Dark blue, where heavy milky blue. White glaze is good course brushed, splatter or trailed over this glaze.

Off White Cone 9-10 Reduction
Custer feldspar 20

Whiting 11
Talc 11
China clay 21
Silica 20
Superpax or Ultrex 6.5
Bone ash 5
Ball clay 6
    Semi-gloss to glossy off white with good colour responses.

Foster Blue Cone 9-10 Reduction
Nepheline Syenite 45
Flint 12
Whiting 5
Dolomite 8
Ball clay 10
Barium carbonate 20
Copper carbonate 2
Bentonite 3
    A matt turquoise, good with white glaze brushed, trailed or splattered over this glaze which goes pinkish.

Rutile Blue Cone 9-10 Reduction
Dolomite 15.8
Potash feldspar 30
Whiting 11.1
EPK China clay 16.8
Flint 26.3
Rutile 8
    A glossy sometimes runny speckled light to medium blue, good with white glaze brushed, trailed or splattered over this glaze.

Peter Venning
(work illustrated)

Ying C'hing Celadon Porcelain Reduction 1250-1280°C
Soda feldspar 35
Flint 17
China clay 15
Magnesium carbonate (precipitated
is preferred) 10
Mixed wood ash 20
Bone ash 5
Yellow ochre 2-4
    This reliable glaze was given me by Geoffrey Ideson at Richmond College when I was a very mature student some 30 years ago and has served me well ever since so I can pass it on with confidence. The glaze gives a soft satin sheen at 1250°C plus, when it will pool as a beautiful pale limpid blue in the hollows, and is particularly attractive on engraved wares. Wood ash is once washed. Some experimentation is advisable with yellow ochre as the strength is extremely variable between suppliers. The combination of materials in this recipe makes for a thick mix so the pt/wt, for dip glazing must be watched. I dip engraved porcelain at 27oz/pt.

Edmund de Waal CR 158
(work illustrated)

Basic White Cone 9 Reduction
Potash feldspar 23
Dolomite 8.5
Bone ash 1.5
China clay 11
Quartz 10.5
Talc 4.5
    A useful glaze for porcelain.

Crackle Blue-Green Cone 9 Reduction
Nepheline syenite 42
Whiting...19
China clay 16
Flint 23
Yellow ochre 1.5
    A pleasant light blue crackle glaze – a variant of a Cooper glaze.

Andrew Walford CR 183

Walford's Porcelain Mix
Kaolin 60
Feldspar 9
Bentonite 5
Silica 30
    I add milk to age it then I leave it for a year to mature. The porcelain is processed in a huge dough mixer, formerly the property of a monastery nearby.

Dark Celadon Glaze
Kaolin 35
Feldspar 48
Whiting...28
Silica 30
Ball clay 20
Iron oxide 4

White Glaze
Kaolin 50
Silica 80
Whiting...36
Feldspar 40
Talc 50
Ball clay 10

Chun
Feldspar 40
Silica 30
Whiting...8
Wood ash 6

Bone ash 4
Yellow ochre 1
Bentonite 1

James Walford CR 124

Stoneware Body 1260-1280°C Reduction
White ball clay 23
Red Devon clay 20
China clay...30
Fuller's Earth 'Surrey Powder' 7
Flint or quartz 10
Feldspar 5
Sand 5

Grey-Green Celadon of Kuan Type 1260-1280°C Reduction
Feldspar 22
Flint or Quartz 22
Limestone 16
China clay..19
White ball clay 3
Fuller's Earth 'Surrey Powder' ....11 (calcined)
Elm tree ash 4
Wenger's Frit 1455w (Potterycraft) 3

This is a glaze with a pleasing texture and on the right body, a widish crackle, which I think is nearer to the original glaze than the later Chinese imitations, (Kang-Hsi). To get the glaze of a reasonable thickness and to avoid crawling I have had to spray it on to the pots, which is rather time consuming, but in the end, well worth the effort. For use on biscuit I use half of the China clay in calcined form.

Celadon 1280°C Reduction
Feldspar 22
Quartz 25
DBG ball clay 6
Limestone 18
China Clay (calcined) 12
Fuller's Earth 'Surry Powder' (calcined) 13
Standard borax frit 2
Wood ash 2
Red iron oxide 0.4

Copper Red 1280-1300°C Reduction
Underglaze
Cornish stone 40
Limestone 20
China Clay 11
Quartz 24
Standard borax frit 5

Top Glaze
Nepheline Syenite 45
Cornish stone 11

Limestone 15
Quartz 9
DBG ball clay 3
Wood ash 4
Standard borax frit 10
Barium carbonate 2
Tin oxide 1
Red iron oxide 1
Copper oxide 0.45

For good colour the top glaze has to be well melted and is inclined to run. For this reason I use an underglaze (dipped) to stabilise and a top glaze which is sprayed on.

John Ward CR 96
(work illustrated)

Body Recipe
HVA ball clay 30
Fireclay (Potclays 1276/3) 24
Potclays buff 1120/2 20
Silver Sand 13
Molochite (30 – 80s) 13

All materials from Potclays Ltd.

Glaze Recipes All Orton Cone 7 Electric Kiln

White Semi-matt
Potash feldspar 60
China clay 24
Whiting 24
Zirconium silicate 12
Titanium dioxide 6
Zinc oxide 6

Brown Matt
Potash feldspar 55
China clay 12
Barium carbonate 22
Whiting 7
Iron oxide 3
Cobalt carbonate 1.5
Vanadium pentoxide (or Ammonium metavandate) 2

Black matt
Copper oxide 100
Manganese dioxide 100
China clay 100

Must be thinly applied.

Blue-Green Matt
Potash feldspar 67.5
China clay 10.5

Barium carbonate............22
Whiting............4
Copper carbonate............2
Rutile............4
Ammonium metavanadate............2
   Bubbles if fired to high

Blue/Brown Matt Once Firing Cone 7
Nepheline syenite............57
Barium carbonate............25
Lithium carbonate............3
Quartz............7
Bentonite............8
Cobalt carbonate............1
Rutile............4
Iron oxide............1

Robin Welch CR 136
(work illustrated)

White Matt Glaze 1260-1300°C Reduction
China clay............5
Whiting............4
Feldspar............10
Ash............2

The ash is a mixture of many woods – sycamore, elm, birch, apple, oak. Put through a 40-mesh sieve DRY and added by weight into glaze mixture. Thickness of glaze application important. Put on thick and depending on impurities picked up in the ash at 1300°C in a reducing atmosphere it will produce a variegated surface on grogged iron-barring clays pitted and speckled with iron spots. Thin applications on pure clays produce a sugary texture and will remain off white with the blue tinge in the same firing conditions.
One part (5%) of red iron oxide added to the glaze gives speckled rust-red (yellow ochre when doubled-dipped). A blue is obtained by adding 5/16ths part (1.5625%) red oxide and 3/16ths part (0.9375%) cobalt oxide. Again double dipping provides variety of colour. Less feldspar gives a drier white.

Temmoku 1250-1300°C Reduction
China clay............10
Whiting............20
Flint............40
Feldspar............40
Iron oxide............10

Thickish applications on heavy iron-bearing clays and heavy reduction at 1250-1300°C best for most satisfying results. If glaze is put through 120/160 sieve with medium thickness application on smooth iron-bearing clay will produce satin texture with a warm red-brown colour. Very hard glaze and practical on domestic stoneware.

Chun 1300°C Reduction
Feldspar............50
Flint............23
Whiting............14
Zinc oxide............11

Medium to heavy reduction at 1300°C on iron-bearing clay can produce a variety of results – a very fluxy glaze and needs testing as it tends to run at top temperatures. If possible to control will produce rolls of glaze at sides and bases of pots semi-opaque light blue when pooling inside pots – where glaze has run down can produce hare's fur effect. Will generally produce many different results in different firing conditions on various clays. Thick applications for the best results suggest small tests to ensure melting effects.

Frans Westerveld CR 53

Temmoku 1250°-1280°C Oxidation or Reduction
Feldspar 30.5
China clay...10.5
Quartz...37.5
Lime 14.5
Iron oxide 7.5

Temmoku 1250°-1280°C Oxidation or Reduction
Cornish stone 46.7
China clay...11.1
Quartz...20.2
Lime 14.5
Iron oxide 7.5

In both cases the glaze, especially when hard fired, tends to crawl away from sharp edges. I normally fire this temmoku in a reducing atmosphere, but it works quite well in oxidation, where it needs a slightly higher temperature because the fluxing action of the FeO is then absent.

John Wheeldon CR 154

Fine Translucent Porcelain Glaze Cone 7-8 Oxidised
Alkaline frit 7.5
Soda frit 24
Whiting..18
China clay...10
Flint 23
FFF feldspar 12.5
Molochite (200's) 7

Mary White

Pearl White Glaze 1250°C
Talc 23.4
Feldspar 26.2
China clay...22.2
Whiting..13.3
Quartz...22.4

This is a very smooth, fine glaze, which I was given when I started potting and have used ever since. I have always been grateful to the potter who gave me this recipe and would like to pass it on as reliable.

Soft White Matt 1250°C
Feldspar 48
Whiting..20
China clay...22
Flint 10
+ Talc 5%
    Good with colours.

Geoffrey Whiting   CR 120
(work illustrated)

High Iron I 1280°C Reduction (School Glaze)
Feldspar 21
Whiting..16
Ball clay 26
Quartz...26
Red iron oxide 12

High Iron II
Ball Clay 5
China clay...10
Whiting..10
Feldspar 40
Quartz...20
Red iron oxide 13

Standard Stoneware – Oatmeal Grey
Ball clay 23
China clay..8
Whiting...2.5
Cornish stone 52
Talc 5
Ash 12.5
Quartz..5

Standard Celadon
Ball clay 12
China clay..15 (20)
Whiting..26
Cornish stone 26
Quartz...20
Red iron oxide 2.5

Porcelain Celadon
Feldspar 40
Quartz...30
Whiting..10
China clay...10
Talc 10
Red iron oxide 1.5-2

Caroline Whyman CR 102

Glazes for Oxidation Orton Cone 8-9

Dusky Pink Grey Glaze
Potash feldspar 52
China clay 23
Dolomite 22
Whiting 4
Copper carbonate 1.5
   This glaze has tremendous variation depending on thickness

Turquoise Speckle Glaze
China clay 23
Whiting 28
Cornish stone 50
Bone ash 1.5
Rutile 1.5
Copper carbonate 1.5
   For best results it should be applied quite thickly and placed in a cooler spot.

Irene Winsby CR 153

Glaze 1280°C
Cornish stone 80
China clay 8
Whiting 15
Red iron oxide 5
Iron spangles 3
Cobalt oxide 0.5
   Blackish temmoku.

Penny Withers

Base glaze No.1 1250-1280°C
Cornish stone 50
Whiting 20
Quartz 15
China clay 15
   This is a good glaze for blending with others. It is semi-transparent and glassy. However too much colouring oxide (over 15% of glaze) will make it too runny as will its combination with high flux glazes.

Base Glaze No.2 1280°C
Feldspar 45
Whiting 17
Ball clay 8
China clay 8
Quartz 8

A more refractory base than glaze 1. With additions of 9% iron oxide, 5% maganese and 4% cobalt carbonate it makes a good black.

Basic Wood Ash Glaze 1260-1280°C
Feldspar 40
Wood ash 40
Ball clay 20

Variation:
Feldspar 25
Wood ash 50
China clay 25

Turquoise 1280°C
Lepidolite 45
Barium carbonate 20
Whiting 5
Feldspar 5
Quartz 15
Ball clay 10

This is good over underglaze painting, best over white slip.

Rutile Glaze 1250-1280°C
Feldspar 33
Dolomite 19
Whiting 8
Barium carbonate 5
Quartz 20
Bentonite 5
+ Rutile 10%

A glaze of many moods. Effects vary according to firing temperature, a good glaze for blending.

Nigel Wood

Jun Glaze 1260°C in Reduction
Potash feldspar 33
Quartz 40
Grolleg china clay 8.5
Dolomite 2.5
Whiting 15.5
Iron oxide 1
Bone ash 1

Jun glazes need to be dipped to a good thickness and look best on light coloured, rather refractory stonewares. Good reduction gives the best colours and slow cooling in the 1250-1150°C range should encourage the 'Jun' effect.

A Song Hare's-fur 1290-1310°C Oxidation
Potash feldspar 21
China clay 32
Quartz 24
Dolomite 8
Whiting 5
Iron oxide 6
Bone ash 3
Manganese dioxide 1
Titianium dioxide 0.5

Use a high-iron stoneware clay and an oxidised stoneware firing. The glaze needs to be fairly thick, but the high clay content in the glaze recipe could cause difficulties on biscuit.

Ivory White 1260°C Oxidation
Potash feldspar 42
Quartz 28
Whiting 10
Grolleg china clay 17.5
Dolomite 2.5

Takeshi Yasuda   CR 151, 180

Slip
Ball clay (Hy+ 71, Powder) 2
China clay (WBB No 50) 1

Trailing Slip
Ball Clay (Hy+ 71, Powder) 2
China clay (WBB No 50) 3

(W.B.B: Watts Blake Bearne)

Glaze Creamware
Lead bisilicate 68.0
Low expansion frit 13.6
China clay 13.6
Quartz 4.7

University of Ulster STD Earthenware Glaze Modified. Highly glossy, transparent, light yellow no crazing. Bisque fire to 980°C and glaze fire to 1100°C and soak for a half hour until Orton Mini Cone 01 goes, then cool – 25°C for one hour.

Satin Transparent Glaze (No Crazing) Porcelain Oxidation
Cornish stone 48.4
Wollastonite 38.7
China clay 6.4
Talc 3.2
Petalite 3.2

Bisque fired to 980°C and glaze fired to 1235°C and soak for an hour and a quarter until Orton Mini cone 9 goes.

Base Glaze Cone 9

Feldspar (FFF) 20
Nepheline syenite (North Cape) 15
Whiting...20
Talc (Chinese)..10
China clay (WBB No 50) 15
Quartz...20
Borax frit P2957 (Potterycrafts) 10
Bone ash 2
Manganese dioxide 0.15
Red iron oxide (synthetic) 0.8

Colour Glaze Cone 9

Feldspar (FFF) 20
Nepheline syenite (North Cape) 15
Whiting...20
Talc (Chinese)..10
China clay (WBB No 50) 15
Quartz...20
Bone ash 2
Copper carbonate ....4 for green
Manganese dioxide ....8 for brown

The colour glaze is applied thickly on top of the base for Sansai effect. Very runny.

Chris Keenan – Temmoku teapot with woven cane handle. Orton cone 9, reduction fired.
Photograph Stephen Brayne

Jane Maddison – Vase, hand built, approximate H23cm.

Opposite Page **Jim Malone** – Tall Bottle. Brushed hakeme, with cobalt pigment (cobalt carbonate 20, tin oxide 20, manganese dioxide 10, talc 10, red clay 15, china clay 20, red iron oxide 5) ground in water, fired Orton cone 9, neutral atmosphere, thinly applied transparent glaze. Photograph David Bailey

Eric James Mellon – Pot, Philadelpus ash glaze.

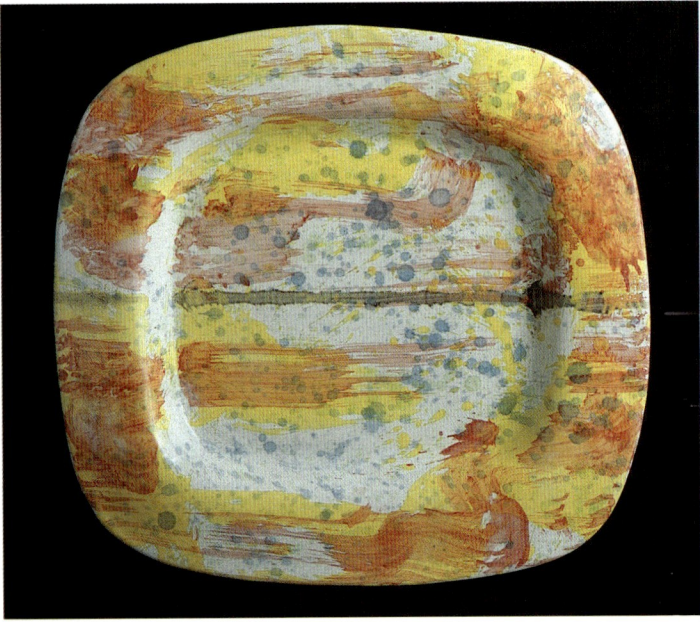

Ivo Mosley – Rectangular Dish, L35cm, coloured glazes, reduction fired.

Opposite Page **Andrew McGarva** – Two Large Dishes. Stoneware with painted decoration of owl and goat and Smooth White Glaze, reduction fired.

Louis Mulcahy – Selection of bowls, casseroles, cider jar and goblets, vase, beakers, plates, salt and pepper set, temmoku glaze.

Matthias Ostermann – Tea Bowls, 1980. Trailed green slip under rutile–coloured transparent glaze with trailed coloured glazes, off–white stoneware, Cone 8 (1263°C), electric kiln, W13cm. Photograph Paul Crouch

Jim Robison – Vase Form, H70cm. Slab built with blue, copper and white slips, sprayed glazes, reduction fired stoneware, Orton cone 8, 1260–1280°C.

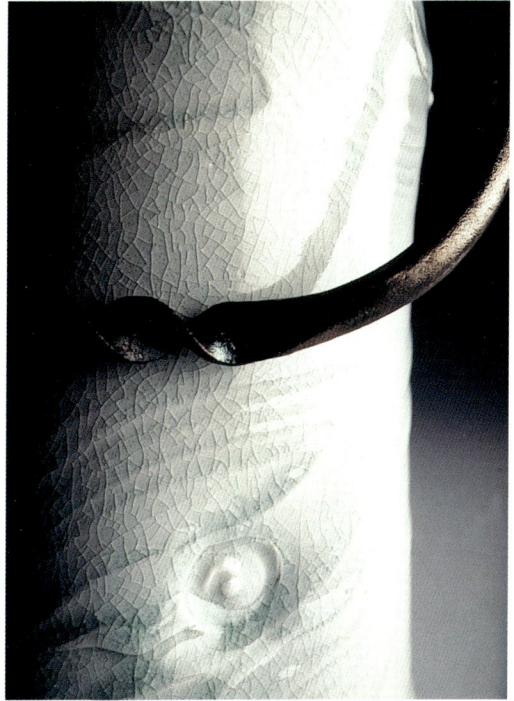

Joanna Howells – Vessel, detail. Porcelain, celadon glaze.

Robert Sanderson – Table Setting. Dinner and bread plates, cereal bowl, cup and saucer, wood-fired stoneware. Orton cone 8–11. Photograph John McKenzie

Charles Stileman – Bowl, Ø23cm. Wood ash glaze over green slip, electric kiln.

Opposite Page **Geoffrey Swindell** – Bottle. Base glaze sprayed over vanadium pentoxide and rutile, electric kiln. Approximate H9cm.

Martina Thomson – Ariadne. Dry glaze with cobalt, two firings, stoneware, electric kiln. Approximate H25cm.

John Maltby – Spade Form Pot, Church, Moon and Angel. Coloured clays plus 15% feldspathic clear glaze, black line scratched through wax filled with temmoku glaze, 1280°C (oxidised). Photograph Heather Maltby

Opposite Page **John Glick** – Plate, 1984, Ø40cm. Stoneware, multiple slip application, shino with glaze washes, reduction fired.

Owen Thorpe – Commemorative Plate, Ø26cm. Stoneware, glaze No. 5, with brushwork and calligraphy applied over raw glaze, 1250°C, electric kiln.

Peter Venning – Bowl, Ø19 cm. Porcelain with engraved decoration, Ying C'hing glaze, reduction fired, 1280°C.

Opposite Page **Lucie Rie** – Bottle, H30cm. Thrown and modelled with multipule glazes and slips, 1250°C, electric kiln.

Robin Welch – Bowl, thrown with painted decoration.

Geoffry Whiting – Bowl, thrown, with incised decoration and temmoku glaze.

Janice Tchalenko – Bowl, thrown with coloured glazes, reduction fired.

Sara Radstone – Untitled Vessel, 1998. Stoneware, hand built. Photograph Phil Sayer.

John Ward – Black and White Cut Rim Pot, H21cm. Stoneware.

Opposite Page **Edmund de Waal** – Thin Lidded Jars, 1998. Porcelain, thrown and assembled, H95cm.

Sheila Casson – Three Sauce Boats, salt glazed, orange slip (as described), fired gas kiln, 1300°C.

Opposite Page **Ruth Tudball** – Spouted Jug, H32cm. Orange slip, saltglazed.

Marcus O'Mahony – Squared Jar. Tan/chestnut slip with ash glaze, 1310°C, gas kiln.

Micki Schloessingk – Bowl, detail, saltglaze.

Opposite Page **Walter Keeler** – Tripod Bowl, detail, 2001. Saltglaze.

Lisa Hammond – Twelve Small Bowls. Tan, orange red slips, soda glaze, 1300°C gas kiln.
Photograph Artemi Kyriacon

Phil Rogers – Squared Bottle, H24cm. Iron ash glaze over brushed slip (Puraflow BLU 80, nepheline syenite 20), reduction fired cone 11.

Jane Hamlyn – Tableware. Saltglazed stoneware.

Peter Meanley – Teapot. Thrown and assembled, saltglaze.

Opposite Page **Michael Casson** – Crane Jug, H44cm. Saltglaze, blue slip, gas kiln, 1300°C.

Alan Caiger–Smith – Lustred Bowl, Ø36cm. Amber red lustre on blue.

Margery Clinton – Mary Erskin Mural.

Sutton Taylor – Vase Form, 2000. Lustre, H59cm.

Chris Carter – Vase, with textured volcanic glaze.

Aki Moriuchi – Three Grooved Bottles, H16–22cm. Thrown, weathered stone texture surface, 1260°C. Photograph Michael Harvey

Emmanuel Cooper – Highway, 2001. Bowl form, Ø30cm, with slips and glazes, multi-firing, 1260°C electric kiln. Photograph Michael Harvey

Ashley Howard – Thrown and altered bowl, copper slip and barium glaze, Ø20cm.
Photograph Stephen Brayne.

Damian Keefe – Bottle. Glaze SWNTIRC over slip No. 7, electric kiln, 1260°C.

Opposite Page **Kate Malone** – Lady Gourd, 1998. Bottle with crystalline glaze, DCE1 outside, ECAF 33 inside, stoneware, electric kiln.

Lesley McShea – Vase with Lid. Blue barium glaze, 1220°C, electric kiln.

Vapour Glazing
Bodies, Slips, Glazes

Salt or soda thrown into a reduction kiln at medium or high temperature reacts with the surface of the clay depending on its iron and silica content to form a thin layer of glaze. Some glazes work well in this atmosphere, reacting to give rich effects. Glaze is usually applied on the inside of lidded jars and tall pots, where the vapours cannot reach to give a smooth covering. As well as suitable glaze recipes, some slips are included which react well with salt and/or soda.

Lauren Berger

Dolomite Reduction Glaze
Potash feldspar 50
China clay 25
Dolomite 20
Whiting 5
  For use in salt kiln on unexposed internal areas. Goes anything from purple to mauve to white-brown to yellow-brown.

Sheila and Michael Casson   CR 58, 73, 84, 106, 126, 189
(work illustrated)

Body Recipes for Salt and Soda Glazing

Saltglaze Standard Body 1280-1300°C
HVAR ball clay (WBB) 120
AT ball clay 30
China clay 25
Leighton Buzzard sand 10
Quartz (120 mesh) 10
Grog 80's to dust 10
  The China clay brings out the reds and oranges.

Body 1
Hyplas 71 ball clay (Whitfield Minerals) .. 75
ECC porcelain powder China clay
(Whitfield Minerals) 24
Cornish stone 1
Sand and/or Molochite 200-80's mesh
as required 5-15%

Body 2
Hyplas 71 (Whitfield Minerals) 43.58
AT ball clay 21.79
ECC China clay (Whitfield Minerals) 21.79
Fireclay (Leeds) 1.56
Keuper marl red (Potclays) 2.33
Nepheline syenite 2.72
Sand (81 Arnolds Pit) 6.23

Blue Slip
Nepheline syenite 50lb
Hyplas 71 ball clay 50lb
Red iron oxide 1lb
Chrome oxide 0.12lb
Cobalt oxide 0.5lb
  Use thick or thin.

Orange Slip
ECC China clay 30

Nepheline syenite 10
Calcined China clay 5
TWVA ball clay WBB......................................25
EWVA ball clay WBB......................................25
Quartz 120 mesh 5
    Use very thinly to avoid crazing and get good colour.

Tan Slip
HVAR 50
ECC China clay 50
    Use thinly.

Jane Hamlyn   CR 74, 101, 127, 139, 155
(work illustrated)

Saltglaze Stoneware 1280°C Workshop Clay Body
Powdered SMD ball clay 25kg
(mixed to plastic consistency in doughmixer)
Plastic Moira clay........................25kg added
Sand 10% for heavier 'orange-peel' texture, then pugged.

Teapot/Mug Body
David Leach Porcelain (Potterycrafts) 25kg
Special Stoneware 1118 (Potclays) 25kg

Kiln Glaze
Potash feldspar 4lb 1oz
Whiting...8oz
China clay....................................1lb 10oz
    If painted on inside of kiln before first firing will protect bricks and should ensure good 'salting' of pots – plus right amount of salt!

Rimwash (for lids)
Calcined alumina 3
China clay....................................1 (parts by weight)

Batt Wash (for kiln shelves)
Hydrated alumina 3
Ball clay ....1 (parts by weight)
(HVAR, SMD and TWVD)

Wadding
Alumina hydrate 2lb
China clay..8oz
TWVD 4oz
Grog (80's-dust) 4oz
    Mix to a soft pastry-like consistency and roll into balls or sausages. Useful for certain lid fittings and especially for firing 'rim to rim' – these wads fire hard and come away clean.

White Slip
SMD ball clay 50
China clay 50

This is high in alumina and non-iron bearing.

Brown Slip
Any red clay, used neat. Dark rutile can be added to the wet slip for painting designs on raw or bisqued ware.

Shino Glaze Orton Cone 10
Nepheline syenite 10
AT ball clay 4

(Has iron and titanium in it. Supplied by English China Clays.)

Good for interiors and exteriors. Fires orange on stoneware, tends to pink on porcelain. Add cobalt carbonate for blue.

Lisa Hammond CR 175
(work illustrated)

Soda Glaze Orton Cone 11 Reduction

Clay Body
I use three commercially made clays which I wedge together in equal parts with 10% buff sand: Commercial Clays's Arctic White and Sandstone, and Spencroft's AWS 1 G.

Tan Slip
AT Ball clay 50
China clay 50

Orange Slip
Excelsior ball clay 50
China clay 50

Shino Slip Glaze
(used on the inside and for blue-black pots)
AT ball clay 33
Nepheline syenite 33
Soda feldspar 33

I prefer to use a white-firing clay with higher iron slips, aiming for a surface that is, at its best, a slip with a depth and a soft sheen which highlights the edges of rims and handles. I achieve this by pulling back the slip on the edges etc. The clay under the slip is more silicious than the slip on top. Brushing on the slips gives highlights. The blue-blacks are achieved by spraying over the Shino a solution of blue and black stains mixed in water: approximately one teaspoon of black to half of blue in a pint of water. I go for less soda than some, using approximately 6kg of bicarbonate of soda in total during the firing. I prefer pots to look more 'flashed' than with a uniform, all-over covering.

Walter Keeler CR 113, 152, 179
(work illustrated)

Clay Body
HVAR ball clay (Watts, Blake, Bearne) 50kg
Sand, 80's mesh (Arnolds)..........................6 kg
Mixed in a dough mixer
+ Potclays 1124 prepared body 25kg
Mixed thoroughly in a dough mixer

Engobe
Feldspar 60
China clay..40

> Can be applied to biscuit or bone dry clay. I spray mixtures of oxides and stain over this prior to saltglaze at 1280-1300°C. Alternatively, colour could be added to mixture.

Interior Glaze (Philip Wood recipe)
Cornish stone 70
Wollastonite 30
Red iron oxide 8

Lining Glaze 1280-1300°C
Feldspar (potash) 44
Flint 22
Whiting..17
China clay...12
Red iron oxide 5

> Tan to yellow-green depending on degree of exposure to salt.

Richard Launder

EB1 Clay Body for Low Temperature Saltglaze 1100-1120°C
Red earthenware (Potclays 1135) 60
St. Thomas (Potclays 1104) 40

> A warm rich brown to green, reticulates gently.

Body E3
Red earthenware (Potclays 1135) 70
HVAR white ball clay.................................30
Silica sand 5

> A warm maroon-brown, very smooth.

Body EW4
White earthenware clay (Potclays 1141)....60
St. Thomas (Potclays 1104) 40

> Pale cream going orange-brown. Good 'orange-peel' texture.

Body EW9

White earthenware clay (Potclays 1141)....70
HVAR white ball clay...................................30
Silica sand 5

Paler and smoother than EW4.

Clay Slips for Low Temperature Saltglaze 1100-1120°C

RC

Red earthenware clay................................100

Rich, smooth, red-brown.

ES5

HVAR ball clay...40
Red earthenware (Potclays 1135) 35
Borax frit...25

Smooth dark brown.

E3

HVAR ball clay...30
Red earthenware (Potclays 1135) 70

A silky dark red-brown.

R1

China clay..50
Nepheline syenite 45
Bentonite 5

Gentle cream, tan-orange, silky.

ES8

HVAR ball clay...45
China clay...15
Borax frit...40

Grey, green-yellow, matt and silky.

Harold McWhinnie

Experimental Clay Body for Saltglaze Cone 9-10

China clay...40
Ball clay 30
Flint 5
Red iron oxide 15
Manganese carbonate.................................10

This experimental clay body completely rejects the salt and fires as black as a raku clay.

Saltglaze Porcelain Body Cone 9-10

Grolleg china clay 54
Feldspar 25
Flint 25
Bentonite 5

Saltglaze White Stoneware Cone 9-10

China clay	40
Flint	15
Feldspar	2.5
Talc	12.5
Ball clay	30
Grog	15

Peter Meanley CR 130, 131, 157
(work illustrated)

Clays
Standard clay P1145 – Potterycrafts white stoneware. This stands cone 10 easily, has a high shrinkage in green stage and takes salt well. Other clays currently being included in a 3 year research project are:
Earthstone original: low iron content and similar to P1145
Earthstone reduction: mid iron giving good tans
Scarva buff: High iron. good browns
All four bodies take cone 10 and salt well.

Slips
The basis of the 'glass' in saltglaze is the ratio between the silica and alumina.
60% of silica will produce an 'orange peel'
70% of silica will produce a fluid 'orange peel'
I control my fluidity by altering the ratio between the ball clay (high in silica) and the China clay (low in silica).

My standard ball clays are:
SMD (mid silica)
Hyplas 71 (high silica)
My standard China clay is Grolleg, although Remblend is used on occasions. China clays vary very little in composition.

A good starting base for a slip is

Ball clay	2 parts
China clay	1 part

+ oxide addition

Sometimes I will go down to a 1:1 for a dry base or up to 100% Hyplas 71 for a fluid base.

Colour
The following colours take salt easily:

Iron	– tans and browns, or as a modifier of other oxides
Cobalt	– blue (+ strong)
Manganese	– weak except in large quantity (10%+) but a good modifier
Chromium	– 'dirty' on its own but produces good turquoise with cobalt (ratio 1:2)
Rutile or Titanium	– on its own, 6-10%, iridescent or with cobalt, green. Another good modifier.

Wadding

Alumina calcined	4
Wholemeal flour	4

Kyenite or fine grog dust 1
China clay...0.5

> The flour 'binds' in the prefiring stage. Wholemeal flour breaks away from the body after firing more easily than plain flour because of the larger particle size.
> Slips are normally applied on biscuit by spraying, pouring, brushing or squirting. Sometimes hot wax will be used to separate slip from slip.

Kiln Wash (walls, batts, props, everything)
Alumina hydrate 5
Molochite 130's 2.5
China clay..2.5
Silicon carbide fine 1
> Applied thinly

Rimwash (Jane Hamlyn)
Alumina hydrate 3
China clay...1
> Dampened salt in approx. 100 gram amounts continuously from cone 3 to cone 9 (approx 3-3.5kg over 1.5/2 hours.

David Miller   CR 185

Glazes for Low Temperature Saltglaze

Slip (applied to biscuit fired pots 980°C)
Boro-calcite frit ....7 parts
Flint ....20 parts
China clay .... 40 parts
> Apply thinly – milky consistency.

+ copper oxide..1-2%
> Gives attractive variations. Apply with a slip trailer or brush.

Glaze 980-1000°C
Colemanite 80
Nepheline syenite 20

> I fire my kiln for about 3 hours with a good long blue green flame winding its way through the pots and out of the chimney. The atmosphere is essentially oxidising. Above all no smoke should be seen from the chimney. When the salt, which has been packed in newspaper round the pots, appears to have volatilized, the kiln is stopped and left to cool until the following day. The salt does not actually form a glaze but serves as a catalyst to bring out the colour in the slips and the clay body, occasionally giving subtle and pleasing results.

Ole Milter Nielson

Saltglaze Body Raw Glaze Cone 9-10
RBV 73 ball clay...25
TA ball clay 7.5
Silica...5
Kalbrite 120 ....12.5

Fireclay 2
Iron oxide 0.5

Saltglaze Slip and Glazes Cone 9-10 Reduction

Blue
Ball clay 100
Zinc oxide 10
Whiting 10
Cobalt oxide 1.2
Iron oxide 2.4

Brown-green
Ball clay 60
Chrome oxide 1
Zinc oxide 1
Alumina oxide 1
Calcium phosphate 2

Yellow-Green
Turf ash 50
Feldspar 50
Whiting 15
Silica 20
Clay 10

'Seagulls' Eggs'
Feldspar 96
Barium carbonate 35
Whiting 10
China clay 30
Zinc oxide 30
Rutile 10
Nickel oxide 2

Marcus O'Mahony CR 187
(work illustrated)

Body
I use Earthstone blended with 10% reduction St Thomas's to add warmth to the body colour. I pug the clay 2 or 3 times through a Venco de-airing pugmill, an invaluable tool and very popular in Irish studios.

Slips

Light Orange
Porcelain clay 2kg
China clay 1kg
Tin oxide 300gm

A good slip to use on interiors.

Tan-Orange
AT ball clay 50
China clay 50

Tan-Chestnut
AT ball clay 50
China clay 50
Iron oxide 2%

Dry Orange
China clay 90
Nepheline syenite 10

All slips are applied thinly to bisque ware. They are often then decorated with black stain brushed on in order to highlight edges and rims etc.

Glazes

Celadon Liner Glaze
Feldspar 20
Cornish stone 50
Flint 5
China clay 10
Iron oxide 3%

PR Shino
Nepheline syenite 1
Feldspar 1
Ball clay (iron bearing) 1

Firing
At 950°C (cone 08) the kiln is reduced heavily for one hour after which the reduction is lessened and the atmosphere can move from reduction to oxidisation later in the firing. Care is taken in the last hour of the firing to ensure that the kiln is oxidising. This undoubtedly contributes to the warmth and attractive variation in tone of the tan-brown slips.

Salting takes place over a two hour period (at cone 8). Five kilos of salt are introduced to the kiln with the aid of a slate ripper. Packing volume is about 15 cubic feet and the fuel is gas. After salting the temperature is taken to cone 11 and soaked for 30 to 40 minutes, then crash cooled for 40 minutes. The complete firing schedule takes about 18 hours.

Mary Rich CR 93

Two Slip Glaze Recipes for Saltglaze Porcelain

Mottled Pink 1280°C Reduction
Parts by volume
Soda feldspar 3
Cornish stone 1
Dolomite 3
Whiting 1
Kaolin 4
Ball clay 2

Mix well with glaze mixer but do not put through the sieve. Fires a cream-yellow on bodies containing iron.

Pale Sugar Pink 1280°C Reduction
Parts by volume
Soda feldspar 4
Kaolin 2
Ball clay 1
Whiting...3

> Sieve through 120 mesh sieve. Both glazes require a light saltglaze under heavy reducing conditions to achieve their particular character.

Phil Rogers CR 108, 123, 131, 151, 173
(work illustrated)

Saltglaze Body
Hyplas 71 ball clay ....2 bags (50kg)
AT ball clay ....1 bag (25kg)
White silica sand 40's mesh (Stoddards) 5kg
Whitfields 202 Fireclay (high silica) 8kg
Fine grog..a generous handful

> Clay bodies are dough-mixed and allowed to stand for at least six weeks but the longer the better. I always add something to aid the souring process. This is usually vinegar but I have used old and undrinkable wine or yoghurt which is past its sell by date. The clay is passed through a de-airing pugmill before using.

Slips
All slips are applied by dipping or pouring after biscuit firing. The exception to this rule is the white Molochite slip which I apply as hakame or any slip which I need to draw through to incise the body as part of the decoration.

White Slip
Molochite 200 mesh....................................25
Pale ball clay 75

> I still use SMD although it is no longer available. Try Hyplas 71 or Puraflow HV.

Pale Orange to Pink
Dry and powdered porcelain clay................1kg
China clay 400gm

> A second version of this slip has 1% of iron oxide added.

Orange to Tan Slips
Combinations of different ball clays with China clay plus small additions of either nepheline syenite, feldspar or quartz, sometimes alone and sometimes two together.

For example:

Ball clay 33
China clay...33
Nepheline syenite 33

Puraflow BLU ball clay 80
Nepheline syenite 20

Ball clay 50
China clay..50
Quartz..5
Nepheline syenite 5

Excelsior ball clay 8
China clay..8
Nepheline syenite 8
Puraflow HV 4
Feldspar 2

Blue Slip
Feldspar 1200
China clay 800
Cobalt oxide 10
Red iron oxide 25
Manganese dioxide 10

Shino
Nepheline syenite 33
AT ball clay 33
Feldspar 33

Ash Glaze for the Salt Kiln
Either my standard Ash Glaze No.1, inside and outside of pots or Iron Ash No.2, insides only.

Micki Schloessingk CR 147
(work illustrated)

Stoneware Clays 1320°C Cone 12 Reducing/Neutral Atmosphere
1 Terres et Cendres du Berry. Pyrite (with pyrites). La Borne, France
2 Terre a gres de St Amand en Puisaye, France
3 Porcelaine (dure) Limoges, France
   Various combinations of the above or on their own.

Batt Wash
Alumina ....3 parts
China clay....................................1 part

Wadding
Alumina ....2 parts
Fine Molochite ....2 parts
China clay....................................1 part
+ Wallpaper paste

Slips

Shino Type Red-Orange (for insides of bowls etc.)
Nepheline syenite 50
China clay..40
AT ball clay 20

Dry Orange-Brown
Grolleg China clay 100

Green
China clay..10
HVAR ball clay 38
Potash feldspar 40
Cobalt carbonate 1
Copper carbonate 3
Titanium dioxide 8

Blue-Grey
China clay..20
TWVD ball clay 60
Potash feldspar 20
Cobalt carbonate 1
Copper carbonate 1

Anne Shattuck CR 95

I have used these successfully on porcelain to yield a wide spectrum of colours.

White Slip
China clay..18
Light ball clay..20
Flint 25
Nepheline syenite 30
Borax frit 7

Direct Brush Decoration
Stain/frit: 4/1 + water to a wash consistency
Add Mason Stains (to white slip):

Number	Name	Analysis	Amount	Colour produced
6302	Cadet Blue	Cr Co Al Si Sn	15%	Light Blue
6371	Dark Teal	Cr Co Al	20%	Dark Green
6483	Praseodymium	Pr Zr V	8%	Yellow
6003	Crimson	Cr Sn	38%	Raspberry (add frit)
6003	Crimson	Cr Sn	28% with	
6404	Vanadium	Sn V	13%	Dark Rose
6385	Pansy Purple	Cr Sn Co	15%	Lavender

Try all stains for a variety of colour results.

These are some of the slips I have used:

Pink
Nepheline syenite 75
China clay..25
6075 Manganese alumina pink stain 17

Orange*
China clay..25
Flint 25
Whiting..25
Custer spar (potash feldspar).......................25
Nepheline syenite 10
Titanium 2
Saturn orange stain 6121 (Cr FE 2n AL)....15
Vanadium stain 6404 (SnV)........................10

    A mix of equal amounts of pink and orange gives a peach slip.

    *When dark Teal Stain (Cr CO Al) in 'base glaze' is applied over the orange an intense peacock blue-green is achieved. It is a powerful colour but lovely in subtle application.

Iridescent Slip
China clay..50
Ball clay 50
Rutile 20
Nepheline syenite 30
+ Cadet blue stain mixed with frit 4/1 by eye to desired colour.

Glazes
For shiny saltglaze outside and inside with orange peel.

Base Glaze
China clay..14
Potash feldspar 16
Soda feldspar 17
Flint 31
Zinc oxide..2
Whiting..17
Dolomite 3

+ Pansy purple stain ....15% – Purple
+ Dark teal stain ....15% – Sea Green
+ Saturn orange stain ....15% – Orange-green
+ French green stain ....15% – Green

    Vary thickness for colour intensity.

Fluid Glazes for Accents (Runny)

Blue
China clay..25
Whiting..25
Flint 25
Potash feldspar 25
Nepheline syenite 15

Cobalt 1
Rutile (light milled) 7
    Apply thinly.

Yellow
Potash feldspar 42
Flint 21
Whiting...16
China clay..9
Red iron oxide 9
Zinc oxide..2
Nepheline syenite 8
    Apply thickly.

Crowell's Black
Tennessee ball clay 120
Albany clay 340
Chrome oxide...60
Cobalt carbonate 120

    For fine line brush work and blanket coverage – a beautiful rich satin black.
    I recommend that if one is seriously searching for colour variety in salt, to shift to an oxidised firing. I also suggest trying all the stains, as many of the colours that are attainable can be used even in subtle applications. As I tend to prefer the green-blue to dark spectrum for my work, I use many of the colours in a very subtle way. I also like high drama on the clay surface, the pink spectrum contrasts nicely with a dark blue or black background.

Potterycrafts Ltd suggest the following Potterycraft stains may be worth substituting:-
1 Amulet Green P4010 (Cr, Co, Zn) – as substitute for stain No. 6371
2 Canary Yellow P4017 (Pr, Zr, Si) – as substitute for stain No. 6483
3 Crimson P4004 (Cr, Sn) – as substitute for stain No. 6003. (This stain is best below 1160°C and may well not be of any use for saltglazing)
4 Rose Pink P4015 (Cr, Sn) – as substitute for stain for Nos. 6003 and 6404

Ruthanne Tudball   CR 128, 190
(work illustrated)

Clay
Hyplas 71 with some Grolleg China clay and sand.

Slip Recipes for Soda Glazing

Orange
Ball clay (approx. 1.5% iron)......................50
Grolleg china clay 50
+ Nepheline syenite ....10% if too dry

White
SMD ball clay...50
Grolleg china clay 50

Black
AT ball clay	33
Porcelain clay powder	33
Soda feldspar	33
Black stain	15%

Black Stain
Red iron oxide	55
Manganese dioxide	20
Cobalt oxide	17
Chromium oxide	8

Red Shino
AT ball clay	33
Nepheline syenite	33
Soda feldspar	33

Firing
All pots are raw fired in a 1m³ gas kiln to cone 10. Approximately 1.3kg of sodium bicarbonate is sprayed into the chamber at cone 8.

Sarah Walton   CR 104

Bodies 1300°C Cone 10

Throwing Bodies
China clay	25
Fireclay (Potter's Connection)	25
Hyplas 71 ball clay	50
Quartz 200 mesh	5
Potash feldspar	5
Local fine sand	10

This gives a pale body and is interesting with little or much reduction.

The above throwing body	50
Prepared body No. 2205	50
(Potter's Connection)	

This gives a very dark, rich body with reduction.

Birdbath Body
China clay	25
Fireclay (Potter's Connection)	25
Hyplas 71 ball clay	50
Quartz 200 mesh	5
Potash feldspar	5
Local fine sand	10
'Playpit' sand from builders' merchants	11
Fireclay grog 5's	5
Stoneware 16's	9

 35%

When evolving a body for birdbaths, Colin Pearson advanced the invaluable advice that it is the finer sands/grogs that really aerate clay. He recommended at least 10% of 80 mesh or finer. The coarser additions of sands/grogs are by comparison 'cosmetic'.

Raw Glazes 1260-1300°C

Colin Pearson's White Shino
Petalite 40.5
Nepheline syenite 40.5
CY ball clay (or AT ball clay) 7
Hyplas 71 ball clay 12

Nadine Kozdon's Red Shino
Nepheline syenite 71
CY ball clay (or AT ball clay) 29

Slips
The following recipes clearly show that it is slips composed mainly of high alumina clays (on pots placed and fired in certain ways) that give orange colourings. The orange surfaces that are semi-matt do not resist acidic juices well.

China clay..50
SMD ball clay..50

> This gives opaque oranges and yellow with a good gloss. SMD ball clay can be substituted by Hyplas 71.

Porcelain clay 80
China clay..20

> When applied 'water' thin, this gives transparent orange colourings on parts of a pot that receive little salt i.e. undersides of bowls. When applied as thick as double cream it will give a white. It will flake off any stoneware unless applied to those parts of a pot that will then receive sgraffito decoration.

China clay..95
Bentonite 5

> When applied 'water' thin this will give a thin orange matt.

Slurry
> In order to soften and 'round' a form I dip some thrown wares (i.e. jugs) in a very thick slurry made from the body itself.

Bare Body
> I leave most birdbaths unslipped. With small bowls I'll dip 1/3 in slip (inside and out) and leave the remainder bare.

Grinding After Firing
> I spend a lot of time with wet and dry carborundum paper working on all surfaces. It is by this method that the characteristic smoothness of my present work is achieved.

Lustre Glazes

Usually fired between 900-1000°C, lustre glazes rely for their effect on a very carefully controlled kiln atmosphere. A period of reduction is needed to cause the metal oxides to give the typical lustre effects.

Alan Barrett-Danes CR 36

Basic Glaze 960°C
Alkaline frit 85
China clay..10
Whiting..5

    Firing notes: Fired to 960°C and the kiln turned off. When temperature has fallen to 800°C 20-22 minutes of reduction are given, with a flame at the poker and bung 10" long as guide to gaseous content of the kiln. Metal salts used to give various lustres in reduction are added to this glaze in the following proportions:

Copper oxide 2%
Silver sulphide..2%
Cupric sulphate 2%
Silver carbonate 2%

The following combinations of metal are also recommended:

Copper oxide 2%
Silver sulphide..2%

Copper oxide 2%
Silver sulphate 5%

Copper oxide 5%
Silver sulphate 2%

Copper oxide 2%
Silver carbonate 5%

Copper oxide 5%
Silver carbonate 2%

Silver sulphide..2%
Cupric sulphate 2%

Silver sulphide..2%
Cupric sulphate 5%

Silver carbonate 2%
Cupric sulphate 2%

Silver carbonate 2%
Cupric sulphate 5%

Silver carbonate 5%
Cupric sulphate 2%

Margery Clinton CR 159
(work illustrated)

LB2 Tubeline Slip
Potash feldspar 60
Ball clay 10
Alumina hydrate 10
Lead bisilicate 20
Gum arabic 2
    To make a charcoal grey tubeline, add 2% black glaze stain.

Green Silver Lustre Glaze 1020-1080°C
Johnson Matthey no longer produce the glaze bases which I originally used. The base is 9 parts of a transparent leadless glaze and 1 part of a low sol glaze. Potclays produce the following alternative or potters can experiment with their own earthenware glazes to achieve a similar result.

Potclays 2206 90
Potclays 2204 10
Copper carbonate 1.5
Silver carbonate 0.4
Bismuth subnitrate..5
Iron oxide 0.5
Bentonite 1.5

Plum Glaze
Potclays 2206 90
Potclays 2204 10
Copper carbonate 1.5
Bismuth subnitrate..5
Cobalt carbonate 1
Bentonite 1

Pigment 5L
Copper carbonate 20
Tin oxide...25
Red clay (dried) 40
Lead bisilicate ....10 (or up to 40 parts)

I get my supplies of silver carbonate and bismuth subnitrate from:
CTM Supplies, 9 Spruce Close, Exeter EX4 9JU Tel: 01395 233077
Potclays, Brick Kiln Lane, Etruria, Stoke on Trent Tel: 01782 219816

Marie-France Conduzorgues CR 152

Metallic Green Lustre Glaze 850-950°C
Lead bisilicate frit 100
Silver nitrate...1.5
Cobalt carbonate 3
Iron oxide 3
Bismuth 4

Gold Lustre Glaze 850-950°C
Alkaline frit 85
Flint 10
Silver nitrate..3
Bismuth nitrate 3

Blue Slip Glaze 860-900°C
Ball clay 10
China clay...10
Flint 10
Alkaline frit 10-15
Tin oxide..5
Calcined china clay 20
Talc 5
Cobalt oxide 1-3
Commercial stain 5-10

Pauline Monkcom CR 190

Base Glaze 1005°C
Potterycrafts Frit P2955 33
Potterycrafts Frit P2953 33
Potterycrafts Frit P22962 33

With additions of the following:

Copper Lustre
Copper carbonate..2
(oxide works as well)
Tin oxide..4
> For a really bright, orangey red, though it does work without.

Gold/Silver Lustre
Silver carbonate 1
Cobalt sulphate 0.5
> I have used silver sulphate and carbonate, both work, though the carbonate tends to give bright gold rather than silver.

Coloured Base
Body stain or oxide 2-10
Bismuth nitrate 5
> For mattness, replace P2953 frit with more P2955 frit and add china clay 20.

Paul Spence   CR 176

Earthenware Clay
Potclays Studio White Earthenware LT25 or Cookson Matthey WB28 white earthenware, and Potclays Stoneware Throwing Clay (1110)

Pigments
Both of the following pastes give golds to reds over white glaze, or silvers over dark stains and clear glaze:

JC Paste
Calcined yellow ochre	64
Copper carbonate	20
Tin oxide	8
Red iron oxide	16
Silver nitrate	8

'Rabbit' Paste
Calcined yellow ochre	70
Red Iron oxide	10
Copper nitrate	10
Silver carbonate	8
Bismuth nitrate	2

> These pastes are not sieved, just mixed very well by hand adding boiling water and 10% sugar to help smooth and stable application.

Salts
From chemical supplier Prolabo, Diamond House, Peel Cross Road, Manchester M5 2RT (Individuals may have difficulty sourcing some of the chemicals due to Health and Safety legislations.)

Lustre Firing Cycle
> I reach 650/670°C in about 2 hours by gas, seal up the kiln and add a handful of kindling – reducing for 5 minutes; insert the burner after this period and climb back to glaze softening temperature (takes 2-3 minutes) and repeat kindling reduction for 5 minutes. This cycle of oxidation and reduction is repeated up to eight times over an hour. I sometimes draw shards from the kiln between each cycle as an indicator of lustre development. I use cones 022-018. Cones this low can be difficult to get hold of but Potclays can usually deliver given plenty of notice.

BZ Glaze 1050°C
Softening point for the lustre firing approximately 650°C

Calcium borate frit	45
Lead bisilicate	40
China clay	10
Flint	7
Whiting	5
Zinc oxide	5
Bentonite	1

JC Glaze 1070°C
Softening point for the lustre firing approximately 665°C

Lead bisilicate	65

Standard borax frit 15
Potash feldspar 10
China clay 3
Flint 7
Barium carbonate 1
Bentonite 1

> Up to 10% tin oxide can be added for the classic opaque white base glaze, increasing the maturing temperature by 5/10°C and the corresponding softening point for the lustre firing.

Sutton Taylor   CR 159
(work illustrated)

A fairly reliable glaze for 1120°C
Lead bisilicate 33
Calcium borate frit 18
Quartz 14
Potash feldspar 25
Body clay 8
Zinc oxide 2
+ Tin oxide 5-12% depending upon the opacity required

Lustre Pigments

Reds
Copper carbonate 25
Kaolin 75
+ Gum arabic 2

Copper carbonate 50
Kaolin 50
+ Gum arabic 2

> Varying the proportion of copper between 25-50% should make a range of reds from strong cadmium to iridescent copper.

Golds and Silvers

Bright Gold
Copper carbonate 40
Bismuth oxide 20
Kaolin 40
+ Gum arabic 2

Bright Iridescent Silver
Silver nitrate 30
Bismuth oxide 30
Kaolin 40
+ Gum arabic 2

Metallic Silver
Silver nitrate 40
Kaolin 60

+ Gum arabic 2

Blues to Greens

Silver carbonate 5
Bismuth oxide 15
Kaolin 80
+ Gum arabic 2

> The kaolin content may equally well be replaced by body clay or one of the ochres or any earth pigment with slightly differing results. Additions of the metals such as chrome, titanium, iron, cobalt, nickel, and manganese will also vary the iridescence. The constituents should be mixed with sufficient water to make a paste with convenient handling qualities, and ground in a mortar. Varying thicknesses of application will cause varying results. The pastes are painted onto the fired glaze surface, and allowed to dry and fired to 735°C under oxidation with 30 minutes strong reduction at 735°C and then cooled under reduction to 630°C.

Egyptian Paste

Self-glazing clay bodies contain soluble salts that are deposited on the surface of the object or pots as they dry. The first of such bodies were used in Ancient Egypt, hence the name Egyptian paste. Such bodies are compounds of materials which need careful handling – a measured amount of water should be used and the pieces should be handled as little as possible.

Alicia Felberbaun CR 40

Egyptian Paste 970°C
Feldspar 34
Quartz 34
China clay 5
Copper 3
Sodium carbonate 5
Sodium bicarbonate 5
Bentonite 4
Copper oxide gives greener colour, copper carbonate a darker colour.

Other colours:
Mauve-purple – manganese 3
Apple green – chrome 3
Salmon pink – red iron – 3

Sylvia Hyman

Nepheline syenite 39
Soda ash 6
Bicarbonate of soda 6
China clay 6
Ball clay 6
Flint 37
Bentonite 2
Fired to Orton cone 012, whether or not it is rakued.

Colouring:
Turquoise – copper carbonate 2%
Blue – cobalt carbonate or oxide 0.25-1%
Green – chromium oxide 0.5-1%
Yellow – uranium oxide 2-6%
Orange – uranium oxide 10-20%
Grey violet – manganese dioxide 0.5-2%
Commercially prepared stains may be added in same quantities as one would use in glazes.
IMPORTANT – 2 tablespoons of water are mixed with each 100gm. The water is combined with the dry ingredients in the plastic bag by pinching and squeezing the bag. It is essential to get just the right amount of water to make the mixture form a ball. This rarely takes more than 2 tablespoons and sometimes less. Start with less and add extra drops.

Variation of Recipe for a More Stone-like Quality
Orton Cone 012 to 010
Soda feldspar (or nepheline syenite) 39
Soda ash 4
Lithium carbonate 4
Bicarbonate of soda 4
China clay 6
Ball clay 6
Flint 37

Bentonite 2
Copper carbonate .... 2 (for turquoise)
    Same additions as top glaze for other colours.

Gillian Lowndes   CR 103, 181

Egyptian Paste
Based on a recipe given to her by John Forde
Soda feldspar 37
Quartz 23
China clay 10
Ball clay 12
Colemanite 9
Soda ash 9

    At 1000°C it retains its form, but when fired up to 1260°C it must be buried in sand in order to contain it.

This is a recipe for ceramic mortar used to coat mild steel pieces and to fix various components together
Molochite 9
Flint 8
Potash feldspar 1
Borax T frit 1
Sodium silicate 3

    The sodium silicate is mixed with hot water and then combined with the other ingredients.

Bernadette Pratt   CR 177

Egyptian Paste 4 (John Forde) 960-1000°C
Soda feldspar 36
Quartz 16
China clay 5
Ball clay 16
Colemanite (calcium borate frit) 4
Talc 4
Soda ash 9

Firing
Cycle for Egyptian paste:
50-60°C per hour, at 250°C a 5 minute soak, then 100°C per hour to top temperature. At 1249°C a ten minute soak.

Texture, Crystal and Colour
Bodies, Slips, Glazes

The judicious use of slips and specially formulated glazes can result in a rich variety of glazes and surface finishes. It is an area in which constant experiment is required and results depend on thickness of application and precise firing temperature. Many potters have found that the results can vary greatly from firing to firing. Test with care.

Chris Carter CR 163
(work illustrated)

Matt White 1250-1270°C
Whiting 20
China clay 20
Potash feldspar 45
Colemanite 8
Talc 5
Titanium dioxide 1
Silicon carbide 2

    This glaze has a tendency to crawl when used on its own and to run when layered with other glazes. I particularly like it over a matt black slip glaze.

Porcelain Glaze 1250-1280°C
Potash feldspar 25
Wollastonite 27
China clay 12.5
Hyplas 71 .... 12.5
Flint 20
Talc 3

    This porcelain glaze is from Nigel Wood's book 'Oriental Glazes' and works best for me when used in combination with matt glazes containing silicon carbide and/or iron oxide washes.

Emmanuel Cooper CR 136, 160
(work illustrated)

Rich Deep Red 1260°C Electric Kiln
Soda feldspar 52
Calcium borate frit/gerstley borate 10
Whiting 15
China clay 5
Flint 18
+ Copper carbonate 0.5%
    Tin oxide 1%
    Silicon carbide (fine) 0.5%

Muted Pink Grey
Feldspar 37
Calcium borate frit/gerstley borate 6
Whiting 20
Talc 5
Flint 30
China clay 5
+ Silicon carbide 0.5%
    Copper carbonate 1%

Nickel Pink
Feldspar 33
Barium carbonate 39

Zinc oxide..16
China clay..5
Flint 6
+ Nickel oxide 1.5%

    A bright nickel pink, more blue when thin. Not suitable for domestic ware.

Reactive Slips

V Slip
Nepheline syenite 20
Feldspar 50
Local clay* 15
Crocus martis 8
Red synthetic iron oxide 12
* I use London clay

YS Slip
Nepheline syenite 19
Feldspar 52
Yellow ochre..19
Ball clay 10
+ Crocus martis 8

VS Slip
Fremington clay 50
Chesterfield clay* 40
Calcium borate frit 10
+ Red iron oxide (synthetic) 10
* From Chesterfield, Derbyshire

Y Slip
Nepheline syenite 20
Feldspar 50
Local clay 20
Crocus martis 8
Red iron oxide (synthetic) 5
Cobalt oxide 2
* I use London clay

Black-Blue Slip
Ball clay (Hymod) 100
+ Red iron oxide (synthetic) 13
+ Manganese dioxide 10
+ Cobalt carbonate 3

    This slip varies according to the clay used. China clay gives a drier result. The addition of 3% fine silicon carbide gives dramatic volcanic textures under some glazes. Red local earthenware clay can be substituted for the ball clay.

Reactive Glazes
All fire to 1250-1260°C

Smooth White (M72)
Feldspar 48
Zinc oxide...7
Whiting...7
Calcium borate frit 6
China clay 16
Flint 5

Semi-opaque (M133)
Feldspar 50
Whiting..20
Bone ash 4
Alkaline frit 4
Talc 4
China clay 18

Smooth Semi-opaque White (M189)
Feldspar 50
Dolomite 10
Calcium borate frit 10
Whiting...10
China clay 20

Smooth Semi-opaque White (M15) 1220°C
Lepidolite 38
Flint 25
Whiting..22
China clay 15

Smooth Semi-opaque White (M34)
Petalite 38
Flint 32
Whiting..19
China clay 11

Smooth Matt (S47)
Nepheline syenite 65
Whiting..10
Bone ash 3
China clay 7
Flint 15

Mimi Dann CR 81, 128

Mini Crystalline Glaze Base Cone 10 Oxidation
Potash feldspar 31.5
Gerstley borate (calcium borate frit) 3
Ball clay 3
Whiting...8

Barium carbonate 6
Flint 29.5
Calcined zinc oxide 19
Additions:
+ Copper carbonate (robin's egg blue) 1%
+ Manganese dioxide (mauve) 2%
    Mix medium thickness. For bowls, spray evenly all over, then additionally inside and upper portion of outside. For plates, spray heavily in centre. Never use on outside of bowl with macrocrystalline glaze inside or piece will shatter.

Macrocrystalline Glaze Base Cone 9-10 Oxidation
Ferro frit 3110..............................48
Calcined zinc oxide 25
Calcined kaolin 1
Flint 18
Titanium dioxide 8

Peridot
Add:
Copper carbonate 1%
Silicon carbide 1%
    Pale yellow-green crystals on pinkish ground with dark green pools.

Aqua-green
Add:
Cobalt carbonate 2%
Copper carbonate 3.75%
    Blue-green crystals on greenish-beige ground.

Lichen
Add:
Black nickel oxide 1%
Copper carbonate 3.5%
    Blue-grey-green cloud crystals. Fire to cone 9.

Blue/Yellow
Add:
Black nickel 1%
Cobalt carbonate 0.5%
    Blue fan shaped or cloud crystals on mustard ground. Fire to cone 9.

Monochromatic Macrocrystalline Glaze Base Cone 9 Oxidation
Ferro frit 3110..............................52.48
Calcined zinc oxide 26.4
Calcined kaolin 1.65
Flint 19.47

Midnight Blue
Add:
Copper carbonate 3%
Cobalt carbonate 1%
    Blue ground with very dark pools.

Mystery Teal Blue
Teal crystals with lighter ground and deep teal pools

Clear Glossy Glaze Cone 10 (= SG-280 from Chappelle)
Cornwall stone 47.1
Silica 19
Kaolin 15.6
Whiting...12
Dolomite 1
   This glaze should be mixed relatively thin.

Base Glaze I Cone 8 Oxidation
Cornwall stone 40
Flint 17
China clay..12
Whiting...12
Magnesium carbonate 12
Cryolite 12
   I fire in an electric kiln

For colour:-
Yellow-green – Copper carbonate 3%
               – Vanadium stain..................6%
Gold   – Red iron oxide 3%
Pumpkin pink – Rutile...............................20%
Warm brown – Red iron oxide 5%
               – Powdered ilmenite 2%
               – Rutile...................................5%
Stony blue   – Copper carbonate 2%
               – Cobalt carbonate..............25%

For a richer surface, in some areas I spray over the matt glazes the following glossy cream glaze:

Base Glaze II Cone 8 Oxidation
Potash feldspar 50
Flint 15
China clay..10
Whiting...10
Magnesium carbonate 10
Gerstley borate 10
Soda ash 2%

For colours:
White glossy   – Tin oxide 5%
Cream glossy   – Red iron oxide 1%
Gold glossy   – Red iron oxide 3%
Peach satin matt* – Rutile 25%
* especially nice on porcelain.

   These glazes are good single or overlapped, on stoneware or porcelain, and may be applied by dipping, pouring or spraying. A rich effect is achieved by applying a thin coat of base glaze II (white, cream or gold) over Base Glaze I. Another interesting result is effected by spraying Glaze II gold thinly toward the base of a stoneware pot and thickly toward the rim; the thin areas are terracotta and the thick pale gold. On plate forms, Glaze II, Glaze II white or cream poured over Glaze I (any colour) gives a nice alligator mottled effect.

My suppliers are:
1 House of Ceramics, 1011 N. Hollywood St Memphis, Tn. 38108 USA
2 Columbus Clay Co. 1049 W Fifth Ave. Columbus, Ohio 43212 USA
3 L & R Specialities. PO Box 309. Nixa, Missouri 65714 USA

Brian Gartside CR 157

Crawl Glazes

Basic Glaze
Any stoneware glaze could be the one I have used for the past 15 years – reliable, good natured from 1200°C upwards.
In volumes
Ferro frit 3134 (or equivalent) 4
Grolleg China clay ....4 (can be increased)
Silica 2
Potash feldspar 2
Talc 1
Whiting 1
   Remember to use very thickly.

Glazes fire between 1200°C and 1300°C and are applied thickly. Amounts in volumes – spoons, buckets, jugs or handfuls.

Zinc oxide..50
Nepheline syenite 50

Ball clay 50
Wood ash 50

Titanium oxide (or Rutile) 50
Any stoneware glaze 50

Grolleg 50
Any stoneware glaze 50

Tin oxide...50
Any earthenware glaze 50

Magnesium carbonate (light).....................66
Any stoneware glaze 33

Magnesium carbonate (light).....................66
Nepheline syenite 33
   Piling up dry feldspar-like materials on flat surfaces often produced crawling around 1260°C. Adding oxides and stains yields endless variations.

Frank Hamer CR 133

Underglaze Colours
For use on stoneware up to 1280°C. Be aware that some commercial stains, especially yellow, orange and red, lose their colour in medium and heavy reduction.

Own-made Lively Blue Underglaze
Cobalt carbonate 17
Titanium dioxide 9
China clay..18
Potash feldspar 41
Potterycrafts borax frit P2955 15

Bleeding Black Underglaze
Cobalt carbonate 32
Iron chromate......................................3
Crocus martis 14
Manganese dioxide 7
Rutile 20
China clay..4
Potash feldspar 20
    Spreads into the surrounding areas with character.

Stable Black Underglaze
Cobalt carbonate 10
Iron chromate......................................30
Red iron oxide 10
China clay..10
Potash feldspar 25
Borax frit P2055 15

I use glaze and body stains by mixing them with a base glaze to attenuate the colour strength and to integrate the stain which otherwise tends to be a refractory powder resisting the fusion of the glaze above it. Mostly I paint these mixtures on raw clay which is biscuited before glazing. The glaze takes sufficiently over the underglaze although the underglaze appears fused. (These mixtures are also good used in maiolica fashion painted on to the unfired glaze surface. But that is another story.)

The recipe is:
Stain ....10 to 20
Base glaze ....90 to 80
For the base glaze I use:
Borax frit P2955 30
Potash feldspar 50
China clay..20

Ashley Howard CR 166
(work illustrated)

Dry Glazes

Matt Blue Slip
HVAR ball clay 100
Copper oxide 5

Glaze
Barium carbonate 4
Potash feldspar 1
Nepheline syenite 3

> Apply slip to ware before biscuit firing to 900°C. Apply glaze quite thinly and fire to Orton cone 6.

Damian Keefe CR 156
(work illustrated)

Reactive Slips

Slip 7 Stoneware Electric Kiln 1230-1280°C
Blue ball clay 300
Nepheline syenite 350
Crocus martis 200
Whiting 150
Bone ash 100
Titanium dioxide 35
Barium carbonate 50

> Similar to Tagg's Yard Reactive Slip, giving purples, reds and oranges.

Slip 18 Stoneware Electric Kiln 1230-1260°C
Orange-Yellow
Blue ball clay 30
Soda feldspar 35
Crocus martis 20
Whiting 15
Bone ash 10
Titanium dioxide 8
Calcium borate frit 10

Glaze RMN12 Stoneware Electric Kiln 1200-1280°C
Soda feldspar 140
China clay 60
Quartz 100
Dolomite 60
Bone ash 40
Talc 40

> Clear. Good over slips. Add 4% titanium dioxide for an opalescent blue.

Glaze SWNTIRC Stoneware 1260-1280°C

Dolomite 25
Potash feldspar 20
Red clay 25
Flint 25

Temmoku when applied over Slip 7 and given a good high temperature soak

Gouri Koshla

Crystal Glaze

Feldspar 36
Whiting 13
China clay 5
Quartz 22
Zinc oxide 24
Copper carbonate 0.5
Nickel oxide 0.5
Titanium dioxide 2
Red iron oxide 0.5

Bright turquoise crystal flowers on pale lime green base. Very beautiful.

James Lovera

Crater Glaze Cone 10

American ingredients:
China clay 42
Silica 43
Potash feldspar 159
Calcium carbonate 78
Titanium dioxide 36
Silicon carbide 21

This glaze has both a carbonaceous material in the glaze as well as reducing period in the firing. The reduction period is from cone 010 to about 3 or 4, and the oxidation period is from cone 4-10.

Screen the glaze before adding the silicon. Use a heavy application for a good crater effect. Over a black slip on a ceramic piece, this glaze creates a variety of colours and effects. Colourants may also be added to this glaze.

Michael Machtey

Porcelain Body for Crystalline Glazes

Grolleg English China Clay ....2 parts
Soda feldspar ....1 part
Flint ....1 part

The method of preparing the clay body does not seem to have any effect on the crystalline glazes, although of course it does have some effect on the working qualities of the clay.

Kate Malone CR 164
(work illustrated)

Clay Body
T-material 50
White St Thomas 50
    Bisque 1180°C, glaze fire 1080°C.

Coloured Earthenware Base Glaze Recipes 1060°-1080°C

Green 221

	a	b	c
Potterycrafts P2019 glaze	90	91	92
Chrome oxide	2	3	4
Vanadium pentoxide	8	6	4

Pearly White
Potterycrafts P2019 glaze 95
Manganese dioxide 1
Vanadium pentoxide 4
    A pearly white with purple areas.

Blue Green 205

	a	b	c
Potterycrafts P2019 glaze	95	92	90
Cobalt carbonate	1	1	2
Vanadium pentoxide	4	6	8

Pearly Green 020
Potterycrafts P2019 glaze 90
Copper carbonate 4
Vanadium pentoxide 6

Mottled Blue 213
Potterycrafts P2019 glaze 90
Cobalt carbonate 2
Rutile light 8

Mottled Blue Broken 211
Potterycrafts P2019 glaze 95
Cobalt carbonate 1
Rutile light 4

207
Potterycrafts P2019 glaze 90
Cobalt carbonate 2
Vanadium pentoxide 8

Speckled Rusty Brown 134T
Potterycrafts P2019 glaze 90
Red iron oxide 5
Tin oxide...5

Lustrous Green 039
Potterycrafts P2019 glaze 89
Copper carbonate 9
Manganese carbonate 1
Vanadium pentoxide 1

Mattish Brown 190
Potterycrafts P2019 glaze 96.5
Manganese dioxide 3
Nickel oxide 0.5

Warm Reddish Brown 258
Potterycrafts P2019 glaze 90
Rutile light 5
Rosso orange glaze stain 5

The use of a metal oxide with a glaze stain gives a warmth to the colour of the stain.

The ECAF Base 1260°C
High alkaline frit 58
Zinc oxide 23
Flint 17
Bentonite 2

The first test I ever mixed, a honey glaze with electric turquoise crystals was ECAF2: Base ECAF mentioned above plus 1.5% nickel oxide black.

Others that are essentially the ECAF clear tinted glaze that grows crystals of the same colour:

ECAF1	Base plus 2% copper carbonate. Turquoise
ECAF12	Base plus 3.2% copper carbonate. Green
ECAF33	Base plus 6% red iron oxide. Golden honey
ECAF22	Base plus 2% copper carbonate and 0.4%. cobalt carbonate
ECAF37	Base plus 3% red iron oxide and 4% copper carbonate. Honey green
ECAF61	Base plus 0.4% cobalt carbonate. Soft blue.

The DCE Base
Ferro frit 3110 44
Zinc oxide 26.4
Flint 20.4
Titanium dioxide 7.6
China clay 1.2

This is a blanket crystal glaze, very different when thin or thick.

A sample of additional base glazes are:

DCE5	Base plus 2% copper carbonate. Soft green
DCE6	Base plus 3% red iron oxide. Golden honey crystals
DCE1	Base plus 0.4% cobalt carbonate, 1.2% manganese dioxide. Soft grey blue
DCE50	Base plus 2% cobalt carbonate, 2% manganese dioxide. Stronger blue
DCE51	Base plus 2% cobalt carbonate, 6% manganese dioxide. Mystery glaze
DCE91	Base plus 3.2% vanadium pentoxide, 1.2% nickel oxide. Black

DCE148   Base plus 2% Ceramatech High Firing Colour CT 4380. Whitish yellow

These glazes run a lot at top temperatures and care should be taken to protect kiln shelves with biscuits of clay.

Supplier of T-material and frits for crystalline glaze:
Ceramatech Ltd, Units 16 and 17, Frontierworks, 33 Queen Street, London, N17 8JA Phone 020 8885 4492 Fax 020 8365 1563

Lesley McShea CR 145
(work illustrated)

Slips for Texture up to 1300°C Electric Kiln

White Slip
Ball clay 45
China clay 45
Borax or alkaline frit 10

Black Slip
Red clay 100
Red iron oxide 4
Manganese dioxide 3
Cobalt carbonate 1

Yellow Slip
Ball clay 45
China clay 45
Borax or alkaline frit 10
Lemon yellow Universal stain 10

Pink Slip
Ball clay 45
China clay 45
Borax or alkaline frit 10
Deep pink Universal stain 15

Blue Slip
Ball clay 45
China clay 45
Borax or alkaline frit 10
Deep blue Universal stain 10

I also use Amoco Velvet underglazes, all colours are very reliable firing up to 1200°C (electric kiln).

Dry Stone-like Textured Glazes

Dry Blue Barium Electric Kiln 1200-1300°C
Barium carbonate 34
Nepheline syenite 50

China clay 16
Copper carbonate 3%

> Best applied on white body/slip for brightest colours. This is a very versatile glaze which varies intensely with subtle changes in thickness and temperature. From deep vibrant purple where thick to pale sky blue where thin, it turns to a mottled deep green when fired to 1300°C.

Dry Green Barium Electric Kiln 1260-1280°C

Potash feldspar 50
Barium carbonate 25
China clay 25
Copper carbonate 2-5%

> Another good, dry barium glaze, excellent on textured surfaces. Both are fairly simple, but effective recipes.

Dry Blue-Brown Electric Kiln 1260°-1280°C

Potash feldspar 14
Whiting 29
China clay 57
Bentonite 3
Red iron oxide 1
Cobalt carbonate 1

> This is a good alternative to barium glazes, having the same characteristics but without the barium. It is particularly good over textures as it breaks to a rich brown. The colour range – pale to rich blue-green to brown – is worthy of note.

Smooth Matt Black Electric Kiln 1260-1280°C

Nepheline syenite 70
Whiting 10
China clay 20
+ Black copper oxide 3%

> A smoother matt glaze for insides of bowls. Another simple but effective recipe. Varies from a beige brown where thin to a good smooth black.

Pink-grey Texture Electric Kiln 1260-1280°C

Potash feldspar 51
Dolomite 21
Whiting 3
China clay 25
Silicon carbide 2

> The presence of a small percentage of silicon carbide gives a frothy, almost bubbly volcanic texture. as little as 2% will achieve this, any more will change the colour of the glaze. Silicon carbide is known to create artificial copper reds in larger quantities. This glaze has an added bonus in that any coloured slip applied underneath will colour the glaze accordingly, varying the colour range considerably.

Aki Moriuchi CR 148
(work illustrated)

Base Glaze for the Weathered Texture 1260°C
Nepheline syenite 60
China clay...10
Quartz..10
Zircon silicate 10
Dolomite 5

Add various materials, such as zinc oxide, tin oxide, rutile, cryolite (usually 5-10%); silicon carbide (2-3%) for pitted texture; copper oxide and chromium oxide for various greens (2-3%).

Base Glaze for the Dry Organic Texture
Potash feldspar..20
China clay...40
Whiting...40

Again add various materials. Good with colouring oxides, such as iron, manganese, copper, cobalt etc. Both glazes are more reactive with slips, which are applied before the biscuit-firing.

Glazes are applied in multiple layers by brushing, pouring, sponging, splashing etc. so that all the ingredients react to each other in the firing. Therefore the result is always different depending on the thickness of glazes and method of application.

Base Slip
Ball clay 60
China clay...40
Add:
1 – Vanadium pentoxide 10%
2 – Silicon carbide 2-5%

Sally Bowen Prange

Matt Crystalline Glaze Orton Cone 10 Reduction
China clay...30
Feldspar (any kind) ....156 (I use a potash)
Whiting...30
Zinc oxide...54
Rutile 26
Barium carbonate..60

When small amounts of colourant like cobalt are in the glaze batch, the crystals are usually pink on a blue ground. When 3% copper carbonate is in base glaze, the crystals are black, sometimes greyish, on a green ground.

Barnacle Surface (or Lava Glaze Treatment) Cone 10 Reduction
Possibilities:
A   Silicon carbide, 2% to 10% dry weight to porcelain clay
B   Silicon carbide, coarse or fine mesh, unmeasured, added to porcelain slip. Brushed or sprayed on bone dry piece; bisque fired. Glazed with all kinds of glazes for a bubbly to frothy surface, depending on shiny glaze or matt glaze. I liken this to a coral covering on a piece.

C Silicon carbide slip brushed onto bisque surface and then glaze sprayed over this.

The potter must be careful that silicon carbide does not get mixed with other clays and glazes, for it can make unwanted pinholes in 'straight' forms or glazes.

I have advised that this process can be used with stoneware clays and red firing clays – possibly lower-firing clays. But I think the kiln atmosphere has to be reduction for the silicon carbide to release the bubbles through the glaze. My colleague used this very successfully with stoneware recently.

Lucie Rie CR 150

Reactive Slips

Blue-grey
Dark-red clay 10
Whiting 5
Iron 4.5
Cobalt 1.5
Silicon carbide 1.5

    Applied under 15 Soda glaze.

Blue-grey 2
Porcelain (soda) 10
Whiting 5
Red iron oxide 3%
Cobalt 1%
Silicon carbide 3%

    Applied under glaze 15 Soda plus tin oxide 8%.

Robert Schmitz

Crystalline Glazes
No.1
Ferro frit 3819 .... 44.7
Zinc oxide 24.9
Flint 30.4

No.2
Ferro frit 3134 .... 20.3
Pemco frit 283 39
Zinc oxide 23.7
Flint 17

No.3
Ferro frit 3110 65
Zinc oxide 23
Flint 12

No.4
Ferro frit 3124 51
Zinc oxide 22

Flint 27

All of these glazes are fired to glazes to 2380°F (1305°C) or Orton cone 10. However the exact temperature will vary for each glaze. Some of these glazes are variations of glazes from H. Sanders.

Hildegard Storr-Britz

Matt Brown Glaze with Red Crystals 1150°C
Potash feldspar 66.96
Barium carbonate 82.74
Zinc oxide..32.56
Lithium carbonate 4.44
Quartz...28.8
Nickel carbonate 8.62 (9%)

For a 1250°C firing add potash feldspar 53.88 (25%).

Matt Bluish Glaze with Blue Crystals 1150°C
Potash feldspar 66.96
Barium carbonate 43.34
Zinc oxide..48.84
Lithium carbonate 4.44
Quartz...28.8
Nickel carbonate 7.69 (8%)

For a 1250°C firing add potash feldspar 47.25 (24%).

Beige Glaze with Blue and Red Crystals 1150°C
Potash feldspar 55.8
Zinc oxide..40.7
Barium carbonate 59.1
Lithium carbonate 7.39
China clay..5.78
Quartz...33.76
Nickel carbonate 8

For a 1250°C firing add potash feldspar 20 (12%).

Matt White Glaze 1250°C
Potash feldspar 139.5
Zinc oxide..16.28
Barium carbonate 49.25
Whiting..30

If 5% red iron oxide is added to the above compound a warm yellow glaze with little white-yellow crystals is obtained.

If 5% nickel is added to the above compound a grey glaze with brownish crystals results. The firing should not be conducted too fast, and during the cooling down period the temperature should be kept at 900°C for one hour for glazes fired at 1150°C and at 1000°C for glazes fired at 1250°C. During this hour the crystal effects are formed. Additions of 0.5%-8% of nickel carbonate in the glazes will give lilac to pink crystals in high barium glazes, and blues in zinc oxide glazes.

Ian Wheeler CR 129

Base Glazes 920°C
Lead oxide (red lead) 65
Potash feldspar 25
Barium carbonate 10
Ball clay 5
Bentonite 3

Mix glaze until the consistency of double cream.

Colours
Bright red/orange:
Potassium dichromate 2-8%
Medium to bright yellow:
Chrome oxide 1-5%
Dark mottled green/yellow:
Borax...1-2%
+ Chrome oxide..3%

This base will also take black stain or mixed oxides for black. Try adding red iron oxide for browns; the higher the proportion of lead used the greater the tendency for the glaze to turn red. The use of tin oxide as an opacifier enhances the texture and depth of colour. I apply glaze with a large brush and/or sponge, giving work two or three coatings.

The bisque firing is high, to 1160°C, as the gloss firings are sometimes repeated as many as six times until the desired effects are achieved.

I use a gas kiln as I fast fire, usually for about 3 hours or when the cones are down, Orton 05-06-07. First hour with door open, second hour with door cracked, third hour fully closed. Turn gas off at required temperature, no higher than 920°C and no soaking needed. Keep kiln closed for slow cool down, usually overnight.

WARNING

It is important to note that because these glazes use raw lead they need to be handled with great care. Strict cleanliness with mixing the glazes, including the use of gloves, overalls, good quality mask and thorough washing of hands is of the upmost importance. The disposal, spraying, storage and firing of these glazes should be undertaken with equal care. These glazes are for decorative pieces only and should not be used for any containers with the use of foodstuffs.

Temperature Conversion Tables

N.B. Large cones: Squatting temperature depends on rate of firing

°C	°F	Staffordshire Cones	Seger Cones	Orton Cones
710	1310	018	018	–
720	1328	–	–	018
770	1418	–	–	017
790	1454	015	015a	–
815	1499	014	014a	–
830	1526	–	–	014
855	1571	012	–	–
860	1580	–	012a	013
900	1652	010	011a	–
905	1661	–	–	011
940	1724	08	09a	–
950	1742	–	–	08
970	1778	–	07a	07
980	1796	06	06a	–
1000	1832	05	05a	–
1015	1859	–	–	06
1020	1868	04	04a	–
1040	1904	03	–	05
1060	1940	02	03a	04
1080	1976	01	02a	–
1100	2012	1	01a	–
1115	2039	–	–	03
1120	2048	2	–	–
1125	2057	–	1a	02
1140	2084	3	–	–
1145	2093	–	2a	01
1200	2192	6	4a	–
1205	2201	–	–	6
1230	2246	7	–	7
1250	2282	8	–	8
1260	2300	8a	7	9
1280	2336	9	8	–
1285	2345	–	–	10
1300	2372	10	9	–
1305	2381	–	–	11
1320	2408	11	10	–
1325	2417	–	–	12
1335	2435	–	11	13

Notes

List of Suppliers

A wide range of clays, raw materials, prepared bodies, frits and glazes is obtainable from the following:
Potterycrafts Ltd, Campbell Road, Stoke-on-Trent, ST4 4ET 01782 745000 www.potterycrafts.co.uk
Potterycrafts Ltd, Kings Yard Pottery, Talbot Road, Rickmansworth, Herts, WD3 1HW 01923 770127
Potterycrafts Ltd, 8-10 Ingate Place, Battersea, London, SW8 3NS 020 7720 0050
Hobby Ceramicraft, Odiham Road, Heckfield, Hampshire, RG27 9BG 0118 932 6153 www.hobbyceramicraft.co.uk/now
Ceramatech Ltd, Units 16 & 17 Frontier Works, 33 Queen Street, London, N17 8JA 020 8885 4492
Clayman, Morells Barn, Park Lane, Lagness, Chichester, West Sussex, PO20 6LR 01243 265845 www.the-clayman.co.uk
Bath Potters' Supplies, 2 Dorset Close, Bath, BA2 3RF 01225 337046 www.bathpotters.demon.co.uk
The Potters Connection Ltd, Chadwick Street, Longton, Stoke on Trent, ST3 1PJ 01782 598729 www.pottersconnection.com
Scarva Pottery Supplies, Unit 20, Scarva Road Industrial Estate, Banbridge, Co. Down, BT32 3QD 028 406 69699 www.scarvapottery.com
W G Ball Limited, Longton Mill, Anchor Road, Longton, Stoke on Trent, ST3 1JW 01782 313956
Charles Lamb Geotechnics, 39 Farleigh Fields, Orton Wistow, Peterborough, PE2 6YB 01733 234096
Brick House Ceramic Supplies, The Barns, Sheepcote Farm, Sheepcote Lane, Silverend, Witham, CM8 3PJ 01376 585655 www.brickhouseceramics.co.uk
Celtic Kilncare Limited, Celtic House, Reevesland Industrial Estate, Newport, South Wales, NP19 4PT 01633 271455
Briar Wheels & Supplies Ltd, Whitsbury Road, Fordingbridge, Hants, SP6 1NQ 01425 652991 www.briarwheels.co.uk
Arterial Engineering Works Ltd, Morston Road, Blakeney, Holt, Norfolk, NR25 7BE 01263 740444 www.pottersequipment.co.uk

Materials previously supplied by Podmore & Sons Limited, Podmore Ceramics Limited and Wengers Limited can now be obtained from Potterycrafts Limited

Clays

Spencroft Ceramics Limited, Spencroft Road, Holditch Industrial Estate, Newcastle, Staffs, ST5 9JB 01782 627004
C H Brannam Limited, Roundswell Industrial Estate, Barnstaple, Devon, EX31 3NJ 01271 376853
(Fremington Clay)
English China Clays (ECC International), John Keay House, St. Austell, Cornwall, PL25 4DJ 01726 818103 www.imerys.com
(HYPLAS and other Ball Clays, Molochite)
Morgan Refractories Limited, Liverpool Road, Neston, South Wirral, Cheshire, L64 3RE
(T-material)
Watts, Blake, Bearne & Co. (WBB) Park House, Courtenay Park, Newton Abbot, Devon, TQ12 4PS 01626 332345
(Ball Clays)

Fireclays

Materials previously supplied by Acme Marls Limited are now sold by Dyson Ceramic Systems, Shelton New Road, Hartshill, Stoke-on-Trent, ST4 6EP   01782 577757   www.dyson-ceramic-systems.com

W J Doble Pottery Clays, Newdowns Sand & Clay Pits, St. Agnes, Cornwall, TR5 0ST   01872 552979

(also prepared clay bodies)

UK/USA Substitute Materials

UK	USA
Alkaline leadless frit	Ferro 3110
	Pemco P-991
Ball clay (Hymod SMD)	Kentucky ball clay
	Tennessee ball clay
Standard borax frit	Ferro 3134
	Pemco P-996
Calcium borate frit (Potterycrafts Ltd)	Colemanite; Gerstley borate
China clay	EPK Florida; Georgia china clay; Kaolin
Cornish stone, China stone	Cornwall stone; Caroline stone Kona A-3; Pyrophyllite
Feldspar (Potash)	Bell, Buckingham G-200; Kingman K-200; Custer; Clinchfield 202
Feldspar (Soda)	Spruce Pine 4; Kona F-4
Fremington clay	Albany slip clay
Lead bisilicate	Ferro 3498
	O Hommel 14
	Pemco P6-700
Ziconium silicate (Zircon) (Disperzon)	Opax; Superpax; Zircopax

Notes